Nicholas Chare is Associate Professor of Art History in the Department of Art History and Film Studies at the Université de Montréal. His books include *Auschwitz and Afterimages* and *After Francis Bacon*. He is currently co-authoring, with Dominic Williams, a book about the Scrolls of Auschwitz entitled *Matters of Testimony*.

Sportswomen In Cinema
Film and the Frailty Myth

Nicholas Chare

BLOOMSBURY ACADEMIC
LONDON • NEW YORK • OXFORD • NEW DELHI • SYDNEY

BLOOMSBURY ACADEMIC
Bloomsbury Publishing Plc
50 Bedford Square, London, WC1B 3DP, UK
1385 Broadway, New York, NY 10018, USA
29 Earlsfort Terrace, Dublin 2, Ireland

BLOOMSBURY, BLOOMSBURY ACADEMIC and the Diana logo
are trademarks of Bloomsbury Publishing Plc

First published by I.B. TAURIS 2015
Reprinted by Bloomsbury Academic 2023
This paperback edition printed 2023

Copyright © Nicholas Chare 2015

Nicholas Chare has asserted his right under the Copyright,
Designs and Patents Act, 1988, to be identified as Author of this work.

For legal purposes the Acknowledgements on p.xi constitute
an extension of this copyright page.

All rights reserved. No part of this publication may be reproduced or
transmitted in any form or by any means, electronic or mechanical,
including photocopying, recording, or any information storage or retrieval
system, without prior permission in writing from the publishers.

Bloomsbury Publishing Plc does not have any control over, or responsibility for,
any third-party websites referred to or in this book. All internet addresses given
in this book were correct at the time of going to press. The author and publisher
regret any inconvenience caused if addresses have changed or sites have
ceased to exist, but can accept no responsibility for any such changes.

A catalogue record for this book is available from the British Library.
A catalog record for this book is available from the Library of Congress.

ISBN: HB: 978-1-7853-3012-9
PB: 978-1-3504-1899-8
ePDF: 978-0-8577-2847-0
eBook: 978-0-8577-3845-5

Typeset by Aptara

To find out more about our authors and books visit
www.bloomsbury.com and sign up for our newsletters.

To Adrian, Fred and Griselda

Contents

List of Illustrations   ix
Acknowledgments   xi

   Introduction   1
1   The Ascent of Woman: Climbing Films   15
2   Sexing the Canvas: Boxing Films   41
3   Athletic Gestures: Women's Team Sports Films   67
4   Venus in Spikes: Track and Field Films   85
5   Muscle Pictures: Bodybuilding Films   109
6   Shaping the Self: Martina Navratilova and the Tennis Film   131
7   Surfing Aesthetics: Towards a Matrixial Reading of Sports Films   157
8   Conclusion: Raging Whippet   183

Notes   197
Bibliography   223
Filmography   235
Index   239

List of Illustrations

1.1 *Vertical Limit* (Martin Campbell, Columbia Pictures, 2000): Annie's lack of reach   16
1.2 *Au-delà des cimes* (Rémy Tezier, Tec Tec Productions, 2009): A feel for rock   27
1.3 *Hard Grit* (Richard Heap, Slackjaw Film, 1998): The Braille Trail   32
1.4 *Cliffhanger* (Renny Harlin, Carolco Pictures, 1993): Gabe's big bolt gun   33
1.5 *Au-delà des cimes* (Rémy Tezier, Tec Tec Productions, 2009): Catherine, a mother in nature   37
1.6 *Hard Grit* (Richard Heap, Slackjaw Film, 1998): Moving beyond words   39
2.1 *Girlfight* (Karyn Kusama, Green/Renzi, 2000): Aggressing the lens   62
2.2 *Girlfight* (Karyn Kusama, Green/Renzi, 2000): Confronting the camera   64
3.1 *Bend it Like Beckham* (Gurinder Chadha, Fox Pictures, 2002): Jules's masturbatory gesture   68
3.2 *When Billie Beat Bobby* (Jane Anderson, ABC, 2001): Bobby's tentative touch   77
4.1 *Olympia* (Leni Riefenstahl, Olympia Film, 1938): Gleaming buttocks   95
4.2 *Fast Girls* (Regan Hall, British Film Institute, 2012): Carl manipulating Shania   99
5.1 *Pumping Iron II* (George Butler, Bar Belle, 1985): Working out in tandem   110

5.2 *Pumping Iron II* (George Butler, Bar Belle, 1985): Lips as sex 120
5.3 *Pumping Iron II* (George Butler, Bar Belle, 1985): Bicep 126
5.4 *Pumping Iron II* (George Butler, Bar Belle, 1985): Bev Francis as the monolith 128
5.5 *Pumping Iron II* (George Butler, Bar Belle, 1985): Lori Bowen as muscle temptress 129
6.1 *Pat and Mike* (George Cukor, MGM, 1952): Patricia's shrinking racquet 135
6.2 *Wimbledon* (Richard Loncraine, Universal Pictures, 2004): Lizzie's sexualised grip 138
6.3 *Hard, Fast and Beautiful* (Ida Lupino, RKO, 1951): Millie's beautiful nails 149
6.4 *Bend it Like Beckham* (Gurinder Chadha, Fox Pictures, 2002): Paula's polished superficiality 150
7.1 *Point Break* (Kathryn Bigelow, JVC Entertainment, 1991): The sea as cast member 158
7.2 *Charlie's Angels 2* (McG, Columbia Pictures, 2003): Madison, Natalie and the sea 162
7.3 *Charlie's Angels 2* (McG, Columbia Pictures, 2003): Madison is sent to hell 163
7.4 *Soul Surfer* (Sean McNamara, Enticing Entertainment, 2011): Bethany in touch with the sea 166
7.5 *Point Break* (Kathryn Bigelow, JVC Entertainment, 1991): Bodhi's big gun 174
7.6 *Point Break* (Kathryn Bigelow, JVC Entertainment, 1991): Tyler the garconne 175
7.7 *Point Break* (Kathryn Bigelow, JVC Entertainment, 1991): The force of the sea 181
8.1 *Whip It* (Drew Barrymore, Mandate Pictures, 2009): Barbies in bondage 187
8.2 *Whip It* (Drew Barrymore, Mandate Pictures, 2009): Pigs might fly 194

Acknowledgments

Many intellectually generous, open-minded colleagues, past and present, have contributed valuable ideas during the ten years it has taken to bring this project to completion. I am particularly grateful to the Faculty of Arts at the University of Melbourne for awarding me a grant that allowed me to engage in the research that was needed to write the chapters on boxing and surfing, enabling me to finish the book. I would also like to acknowledge the administrative and curatorial staff of the Australian National Maritime Museum, the Powerhouse Museum and the World Rugby Museum, for their help and assistance.

I am especially thankful to my colleagues in the Gender Studies programme at the University of Melbourne, Jeanette Hoorn, Maree Pardy and Kalissa Alexeyeff, for their friendship and encouragement and also to Barbara Creed, Wendy Haslem, Angela Ndalianis and Mark Nicholls in Screen and Cultural Studies for their support. In addition, I am also grateful to my students on the courses *Behind Visual Pleasure*, *Introducing Gender: Sex, Sport and Film* and *Subjectivity and Sexuality in Art since 1960* for sharing their insights. For *Subjectivity and Sexuality in Art since 1960*, which I taught at the University of York, sports journalist Marina Hyde gave generously of her time and insights. She merits special thanks for inspiring both me and my students with her genuine passion for sporting equality. I am also grateful to my tutors on *Introducing Gender*, Lauren Bliss, Katharina Bonzel, Felicity Ford, Jemma Hefter and Caroline Wallace, for perceptive comments in relation to several of the films that feature in the book.

Specific debts of intellectual gratitude go to Chenez Dyer-Bray for encouraging my thinking in relation to sound and feminine comportment, Muyun Liu for imparting her knowledge of Chinese cinema, and Rachel Macreadie for sharing her insights into self-defence scripts as cathartic narratives. For direct or indirect assistance with particular sports related questions, I am obliged to the bodybuilder Niall Richardson, the boxer Mischa Merz, the climbers Richard Heap and Justin Ions, the runner Betsy North, the surfers Adam Bartlett and Michael Price, and the tennis player Alexander Fitzgerald. I am also thankful for the intellectual friendship of Rina Arya, James Boaden, Justin Clemens, Paul Davies, Michelle Gewurtz, Mark Hallett, Anne Karpf, Peter Kilroy, David Lomas, Silvestra Mariniello, Laura U. Marks, David McInnis, Jeremy Melius, Eddie Paterson, Nathanael Price, Adrian Rifkin, Patricia Rubin, Lesley Stirling, Dan Stone, Marcel Swiboda, Sharon Lin Tay, Francesco Ventrella, Liz Watkins, Anthony White, Emma Wilson and Dominic Williams.

Special thanks must go to my commissioning editors at I.B.Tauris, Philippa Brewster, Anna Coatman and, particularly, my production editor, Lisa Goodrum. They have been a pleasure to work with from start to finish. The book would also not have been possible without the love and kindness of Julie, Peter and Sara Chare and Angela Mortimer and Esther Chare. My deepest debt, however, is to Griselda Pollock, a continuing source of intellectual inspiration and a model of academic generosity.

Introduction

Limbering Up

Stick It (Dir. Jessica Bendinger, USA, 2006), a film about a teenage delinquent with a love of gymnastics who finds redemption through the sport, begins with a sequence of three freestyle BMX riders performing air tricks in the grounds of a house that is under construction. The cyclists are interrupted by some skateboarders who challenge them to a competition. One of the boarders performs an elaborate set of tricks before slamming into a wall. A hooded rider then executes an even more daring routine before smashing through the windows of the house, jamming their front wheel between some balusters, and setting off an alarm. The two groups then scatter to evade police. The daredevil rider, who removes their hooded sweat top whilst running away in a bid to look less of a suspect, is revealed to be a woman, the star of the film, Haley Graham.

The opening to *Stick It* plays with audience assumptions based on stereotypes of gendered behaviour. BMX is typically viewed as a male pursuit. The film therefore indicates early on that it will challenge preconceptions. It forms one of a steadily increasing number of films that centre on female athletes. Until recently, the genre of the sports film was predominantly a male preserve. Aaron Baker, recognising this, suggests that 'the competitive opportunities offered to male athletes in most sports films justify patriarchal authority by naturalising the idea of men as more assertive and determining, while women generally appear in the secondary role of fan and dependent supporter'.[1] Dayna Daniels has also traced how the genre has reinforced the 'second class status of girls and women as athletes'.[2] This situation is now changing. Films featuring female athletes as central characters are being released with increasing regularity.³ These films form the subject of this book.

There have, as Jayne Caudwell has recognised, been 'few scholarly critiques of sports films that focus on women'⁴. Sports films as a whole, however, have been subject to growing scholarly interest since the publication of Deborah Tudor's pioneering work *Hollywood's Vision of Team Sports: Heroes, Race, and Gender* in 1997.⁵ Aaron Baker's *Contesting Identities: Sports in American Film* and Seán Crosson's *Sport and Film* form the most notable publications of the past decade although a number of important edited volumes have also emerged, including *Out of Bounds: Sports, Media, and the Politics of Identity*, *Visual Economies of/in Motion: Sport and Film*, *All-Stars and Movie Stars: Sports in Film and History*, *Sports in Films*, and, most notably in the context of gender, *Gender and Genre in Sports Documentaries*.⁶ Baker, Crosson and Tudor all devote a chapter of their respective books to gender issues. *Sportswomen in Cinema* is, however, the first study to focus exclusively on films about female athletes.

The book considers both documentary and fiction films and, although not comprehensive, strives to provide a sense of the history and geographical diversity of films featuring sportswomen. Each chapter is centred upon a particular form of sport, including bodybuilding, boxing, climbing, surfing, tennis and track and field. Cheerleading, which might seem an obvious choice for inclusion given the success of *Bring it On* (Dirs. Peyton Reed & Jim Rowley, USA, 2000), is not addressed. The cheerleader is, as Tudor recognises, usually in a marginal, supportive position to sportsmen.⁷ Even a film such as *Bring it On*, in which the central characters are female athletes, reinforces patriarchal ideology. Crosson, appreciating this, describes it as ultimately reaffirming the hegemonic order by restating 'familiar and regressive depictions of women'.⁸ The sportswomen in the film, for example, are sexually objectified at times, shown dressed in bikinis. The films of interest here, however, predominantly introduce some kind of challenge to phallocentrism as it is embodied in sport and sports cinema.

Team sports, including basketball, football, handball and hockey, are largely dealt with together in Chapter 3. It is noteworthy that Tudor's discussion of gender issues in relation to depictions of team sports in cinema does not feature any analyses of women's team sports as she states that there are few films about them. As Chapter 3 demonstrates, this is no longer the case with a number of important films released in the last

15 years including, most notably, the football related *Bend it Like Beckham* (Dir. Gurinder Chadha, UK, 2002). The chapter focuses, in particular, on the growing number of films about sportswomen, including *Chak De! India* (Dir. Shimit Amin, India, 2007) and *Forever the Moment* (Dir. Im Soon-rye, South Korea, 2008), that are produced outside of an American and European cinematic context.

This book differs significantly from earlier works in its approach. Baker and Crosson, for example, draw on Marxist thinking, particularly Antonio Gramsci's idea of hegemony, to address how sports films usually function to maintain dominant ideas about masculinity.[9] Masculinity is addressed in the chapters that follow yet as part of a broader analysis which also attends to the issues of sexuality and femininity. For example, Chapter 4, which analyses films about track and field, looks at how sport and sports technology have contributed to the emergence and expansion of sexual fetishes such as salophilia (love of sweat) and spandex fetishism. Chapter 5 examines how films about women bodybuilders that explore the phenomenon of muscle worship provide a means by which to think beyond the penis-vagina coital model of sex.

Sports films now often exploit these fetishes as part of their continuing sexual objectification of female athletes. *Flying* (Dir. Paul Lynch, Canada, 1986), for instance, which charts the journey back from bereavement and physical injury to competitive success of teenage gymnast Robin Crew, includes a sequence that explores positive and negative aspects to sweat. A group of teenage gymnasts discuss which classes they have that day. One of their teachers is referred to jokingly as Mrs B.O., a girl exclaiming of her 'Gross, huh!' This exchange, however, is followed immediately by a shot of a boy exercising, glistening in sweat. The gymnast Stacy, gazing longingly, exclaims 'He is beautiful!' She is reprimanded by the gymnastics teacher, Miss. Stoller, who cautions: 'You're here to train Stacy, not to exercise your glance.' This last word sounds similar to glans, drawing attention to the sexual nature of this act of looking. Stacy is reprimanded for actively desiring the sporting male body, for sexually objectifying it. In this scene the conventional dynamics of looking within patriarchy are briefly contested as a woman's desire for a man is pictured. Stacy is, however, chastised for assuming an actively desiring position.

Griselda Pollock has drawn attention to the restrictions placed on women's gazes in patriarchal culture. Commonly, women are forced to 'assume a masculine position or masochistically enjoy the sight of women's humiliation'.¹⁰ In *Flying*, an alternative to this situation is briefly proffered to the female spectator and then withdrawn. The film is, for the most part, conventional in its depiction of women. Later, for example, Robin and her friend Leah Kilbourne are shown proclaiming 'C'mon let's sweat!' They then embark on an intense workout in Leah's personal gym. The camerawork in this scene functions to produce a highly eroticised scene, focussing extensively on the buttocks and cleavage of the women as they use the gym equipment. The bodies of the two athletes are fragmented, reduced to parts, by way of the fetishistic cinematography. The workout ends with both women panting, an acoustic effect that could be mistaken as post-coital. The exercise scene as a pretext for erotic fantasy is common in films about sportswomen and demonstrates how subject-matter that might ostensibly be thought of as emancipatory, such as a story of female sporting success, is often recuperated by patriarchy. Instances of comparable patriarchal reclamation are examined frequently in the chapters that follow. The workout in *Flying* also reiterates how the sexual appeal of sweat is exploited in sports films.

This book, like Baker's and Crosson's, is also indebted to Marxist philosophy. It draws on ideology, understood as 'a systematic ordering of a hierarchy of meanings and a setting in place of positions for the assimilation of those meanings', to investigate how films about sportswomen form sites of contestation and/or complicity with patriarchy.¹¹ Chapter 2, for instance, which focusses on boxing, considers how the acoustic, the field of sound, forms a site of struggle for gender equality in sport and its cinematic representation. The films *Girlfight* (Dir. Karyn Kusama, USA, 2000) and *The Opponent* (Dir. Eugene Jarecki, USA, 2000), in particular, are attended to as challenges to the patriarchal dictum that women should be seen and not heard. Chapter 3 concentrates on how gesture in film can become a locus of resistance to patriarchal ideology.

The attention to sound and gesture as important features of film signals another crucial way in which this book differs from much of the existing literature on sportswomen in cinema. Previous approaches have mainly provided narrative summaries and analyses. Story has been privileged over the sights and sounds that form the fabric of film. Baker does occasionally assess the importance of cinematography in *Contesting Identities*, focussing, for instance, on the symbolism of lighting as it is employed in *Love and Basketball* (Dir. Gina Prince-Bythewood, USA, 2000), yet his predominant concern is with story.¹² Tudor's attention to cinematography is more sustained. She provides, for example, a beautiful analysis of the sexual politics underpinning camera angles in media coverage of cheerleaders.[13] Her main focus, however, is also narratological. This book does not ignore narrative. It is also, however, closely concerned with the sub-narrative dimensions that are present in many of the films. In order to draw out the significance of these frequently neglected aspects of film experience, it builds on ideas from phenomenology and psychoanalysis, particularly the work of Iris Marion Young and Bracha Ettinger respectively.

Chapter 1, for instance, which addresses climbing films, summarises Young's ideas before drawing on the work of Dianne Chisholm and Michel Serres to critique them whilst simultaneously exploring how some films about climbing such as the documentary *Au-delà des cimes* (Dir. Rémy Tezier, France, 2008), about alpinist Catherine Destivelle, and *Hard Grit* (Dir. Richard Heap, UK, 1998), about the English gritstone climbing scene, provide a way to move beyond traditional ideas about gender difference. *Hard Grit* ostensibly celebrates hypermasculinity yet there are instances in the film that demonstrate how the sport provides men with the means to transcend masculinity. *Au-delà des cimes* similarly documents Destivelle transcending femininity. Despite the criticisms of Young raised in the context of this chapter, her continuing relevance for the study of sport and gender is demonstrated in Chapter 2 which links her ideas about spatiality to boxing and to film narratives more generally.

Chapter 7, which examines the sub-genre of the surf film, engages with Ettinger's psychoanalytic theories as a means by which to produce a feminist analysis of films which is not indebted to the Metzian inspired approach pioneered by Laura Mulvey and subsequently much emulated. For the last 40 years, as Lucy Bolton summarises in *Film and Female Consciousness*, the mainstay of feminist film theory has been psychoanalysis described as 'an examination of the operation and effects of [...] apparatus theory, with its rigid allocation of gender to the constituent aspects of the cinematic apparatus, such as the male spectator, camera, and the director, and the spectacularized female image'.[14] The cornerstones of this approach are central themes from psychoanalysis, 'Freudian and Lacanian concepts of the constitution of the subject, the entry into language, and sexual difference.'[15] Recently, however, psychoanalytically informed analyses of this kind have declined, replaced by readings that endeavour to move beyond scopic models of interpretation and refuse to treat film purely as a signifying system. These alternative approaches to the study of cinema have been predominantly informed by the ideas of Gilles Deleuze or, alternatively, Luce Irigaray.[16]

Feminist film scholars such as Caroline Bainbridge, Lucy Bolton, Catherine Constable and Liz Watkins have all recently sought to foster new feminist discourses on sexual difference and film.[17] Bainbridge's and Bolton's projects are both comparable in aim. Bolton describes her intention as to draw upon Irigaray's ideas in order to identify and describe instances in filmic texts 'that mimic, subvert and rewrite generic conventions in order to demonstrate how the female voice can be heard'.[18] In this approach, an existing template is remodelled, a prevailing language re-employed but articulated differently. Bainbridge expresses a similar desire, setting out to understand how 'women's cinema works to open up space' for the evocation of a feminine imaginary.[19] The modes of analysis of Bainbridge and Bolton both focus heavily on character, dialogue and narrative.

It is striking that Bainbridge fails to acknowledge Watkins's work when she lists contemporary film theorists working with Irigaray's ideas.[20] Watkins differs substantially in that she dedicates far greater attention to sub-narrative elements within film, paying more consideration to cinematography and effects of colour and light.[21] It is this reading in detail that allows her, in her own words, to discern 'not the vision of feminine subjectivity in the cinematic medium, but a femininity which moves against, but is irreducible to the symbolic ordering of it.'[22] Watkins's innovative approach echoes the methodology adopted here in that it recognises that phallocentrism is only fundamentally questioned when aspects of the film that operate beyond signification are allowed to attain prominence and resonate within a given analysis. The cinematic effects described by Watkins, particularly through her remarkable analyses of colour in film, are inscribed within narratives yet cannot be equated to them. They are too often overlooked, mentioned, if at all, in passing.

While placing these kinds of effects at the centre of film analysis, Chapter 7, which considers surf films, is not beholden to Irigaray's ideas, drawing instead upon the writings of Ettinger. This is, in part, because of the significant problems that arise in relation to Irigaray's terms of reference which are seemingly relational (such as fluid to solid, touch to vision, proximity to distance, excess to customary) and therefore bound to a phallic oppositional logic of difference. Additionally, Irigaray's notion of excess is questionable as it requires relationality to the phallic and cannot therefore account for phenomena, such as what Ettinger refers to as the matrixial paradigm to subjectivity, which exist subjacent to it. The chapter therefore exposes the limits of Irigaray's excessive and oppositional logic and shows how Ettinger's ideas, which invite reconciliation between phenomenology and psychoanalysis, provide a way to account for, rather than violently disavow, the maternal, and, by extension, all those others marked as different from the self. Irigaray is, however, still an important interlocutor in Chapter 3 where her work on gesture in psychoanalysis is considered at length.

Much sport is conceived of as antagonistic. Chapter 7 reads surfing differently. It suggests that the artistry in surfing, its aesthetic dimension, is what Ettinger calls co-poietic. This means its aesthetic effects reveal 'traces of the other in me, the non-I and I'.[23] The sport, and particular filmic representations of it, specifically the representation of surfing in Kathryn Bigelow's *Point Break* (Dir. Kathryn Bigelow, USA, 1991), creates 'a vibration or a link reaching toward the material trace of the other'.[24] The film's ability to enable echoes of the other to return in aesthetic experience, its capacity to permit an affective memory of the trauma that accompanies a child's entry into language to emerge, has crucial ethical ramifications. *Point Break*, along with vampire flick *Near Dark* (Dir. Kathryn Bigelow, USA, 1987) and crime thriller *Blue Steel* (Dir. Kathryn Bigelow, USA, 1989), form a distinct set of films within Bigelow's oeuvre. Their titles, which reference luminosity, chromatics, and fracture, point towards the cinematographic strategies they embody, strategies which provide an aesthetic point of access to what Pollock refers to as 'an open holding space for, in Freudian terms, the binding of the shapelessness of the anxiety which is the trace of *das Ding* (the thing) in us'.[25] The aesthetic in film and sport therefore possesses a potential to bring about catharsis, to assuage anxieties stemming from traumas of early psychic life.

Thinking about the importance of sport's aesthetic dimensions in a variety of contexts, including ones not related to dealing with trauma, is another important feature of the book. Chapter 1 also examines pleasure in the practice of a sport. In relation to climbing, however, this pleasure provides a possible means to escape hegemonic ideas about gender rather than a means through which to access traces of trauma. The aesthetic also recurs as a theme in Chapter 5 in which it is argued that Leni Riefenstahl's enjoyment in sport's sensual aspects undercuts her totalitarian sympathy in her documentary of the 1936 Summer Olympics in Berlin, *Olympia* (Dir. Leni Riefenstahl, Germany, 1938). Her film is rendered too pretty to function successfully as fascist propaganda. Rosalind Galt has recently traced the negative connotations prettiness has held in film criticism and Western aesthetics more generally. She draws attention to how glitter is associated with 'working classes, women [and] natives – those who would be distracted by shiny stuff'.[26] Riefenstahl's fetishising of gleam produces a comparable prettiness, lending her work an aesthetic appeal that forms a counterpoint to its celebration of stiff, regimented masses.

This book uses insights from the films that are analysed, including those related to the aesthetic, to enhance understanding of the nature of sport itself, particularly as it relates to gender. The impetus for this approach is T.J. Clark's observation concerning the relationship of visual representations to ideology in *Image of the People*. Clark writes that 'a work of art may have ideology (in other words, those ideas, images, and values which are generally accepted, dominant) as its material, but it *works* that material; it gives it a new form and at certain moments that new form is itself a subversion of ideology'.[27] Film can similarly work with and upon ideology. The films discussed here do not simply reflect dominant ideas about sport and gender, they also frequently form a site of negotiation through which new perspectives are developed and communicated. Sports films can potentially alter how actual sports and their participants are conceived of. This goes for documentary as well as fiction. A documentary film on the surface often simply appears to record reality, yet, like its fictional counterparts, it forms a representation of the world. The documentary interprets rather than naively describes. Documentary and fiction films therefore both possess a capacity to work their material in the way Clark describes. They can therefore impact on the everyday including, as Amy Campbell has recognised specifically of the women's sport film, on our perceptions and biases.[28]

The sporting body, like the sports film, forms another medium, another art form, which has ideology and manipulates it. Theodor Adorno appreciated the ideological character of sport. He famously remarked in *The Culture Industry* that 'sport itself is not play but ritual in which the subjected celebrate their subjection'.[29] For Adorno, the punishing workouts the sportsperson puts their body through mirror the gruelling labours capitalist society imposes on the workers. There is no authentic pleasure to be found in sport and leisure, which are simply theatres where further subjection is unwittingly staged. It is noteworthy that film is also on Adorno's mind during his damning critique of the athlete. He writes 'one is allowed to inflict pain according to the rules, one is maltreated according to the rules and the rule checks strength in order to vindicate weakness as strength: the screen heroes enjoy being tortured on film'.[30] Here Adorno segues from sport to cinema in a single sentence, seeing an encompassing similarity at the level of displays of suffering between the two forms of entertainment. For Adorno, sport, like film, is spectacle.

Ultimately, however, Adorno's criticism of sport is directed more at its audience than its participants. He acknowledges that athletes may be 'able to develop certain virtues like solidarity, readiness to help others or even enthusiasm which could prove valuable in critical political moments'.[31] In this, he appears to subscribe to the communist belief that group sports provide a means by which the individual becomes subordinated to the needs of the collective. This vision of sport is present, for instance, in the documentary *A State of Mind* (Dir. Daniel Gordon, UK, 2005) that follows the experiences of two young North Korean gymnasts, Hyon Sun Pak and Song Yun Kim, who are striving to participate in the Mass Games, a socialist realist spectacle involving gymnastics and other forms of performance. The Mass Games celebrate team work, involving huge numbers of participants operating in near perfect synchrony. They are events in which thousands become a part of spectacle rather than viewing it from afar.

In *A State of Mind*, the two gymnasts are shown engaging in arduous, elaborate and lengthy preparations for the Mass Games as they perfect the moves required for the rhythmic routine they will take part in. Their set piece involves performing with gymnastics balls, which they expertly throw, catch and roll. The intense training shown in the documentary can either be interpreted as providing the groundwork for the togetherness, communalism, which the group of girls will display at the Mass Games or as a steady process of physical indoctrination. The solidarity Adorno feels sport can foster is associated with the former. The documentary, however, hints at the latter. There is, for example, a notable edit in which the film cuts from the repeated thud of a gymnastics ball bouncing to the sound of the worker's siren. This noise, which occurs at 07:00 each morning, summons workers to their jobs. It represents a form of acoustic and temporal control, signalling the docile bodies of the North Korean workers. Michel Foucault refers to how sound contributes to the regulating of bodies in *Discipline and Punish*.[32]

The cut from the bouncing ball to the siren links the two acoustic events, invites comparison between them. It makes it possible to interpret the bouncing of the ball as an expression of disciplinary processes akin to the call to work. The gymnasts, like the labourers, are therefore represented as docile bodies. This message is not, however, contained in the dialogue of the documentary or part of its obvious narrative, which is a conventional one climaxing with the performance at the Mass Games. The editing serves to undercut the seemingly neutral reportage of *A State of Mind*. Camerawork performs a similar role. Hyon Sun, in particular, is frequently picked out by the camera in training and during the performance. This visual emphasis on a specific person works against the communist ethos of the Mass Games and reveals the individualist culture from which the filmmakers derive. Hyon Sun is made the star of the film when there should be none. Analysing the significance of the soundtrack and cinematography is vital to understanding the complex negotiation between belief systems at work in *A State of Mind*. In the documentary, editing and camerawork provide a counter-narrative, a different idea or mind-set, to the version of North Korea embodied in the two gymnasts.

A State of Mind powerfully demonstrates how bodies as representations function as tools of ideology. The flesh of an athlete does not exist outside of ideas, is not unthinking. Muscle is mindful of politics and culture. Louis Althusser draws attention to this through one of his examples of interpellation or hailing, the way ideology recruits its adherents. His famed illustration of this process comprises of 'the most commonplace, everyday police (or other) hailing: "Hey, you there!"'.[33] Althusser continues:

> Assuming that the theoretical scene I have imagined takes place in the street, the hailed individual will turn around. By this mere one-hundred-and-eighty-degree physical conversion, he becomes a subject.[34]

The usually neglected importance of the acoustic to Althusser's imagined scenario has been discussed by John Mowitt in *Percussion*.[35] Equally noteworthy, however, is the role of the moving body in this process. Interpellation is physical as much as mental. Recognition is registered in the muscles and sinews as much as the mind or, rather, the mindfulness of these features of the body is foregrounded. Skeletal muscles are employed to bring the body around to face the hailer, they subject the body to the locomotion that signals, embodies, subjection to the vocal force of the law. If the flesh contributes to becoming a subject-in-language, to assuming the position of the 'you', the 'I', addressed by the law, then it potentially also has a vital role to perform in resisting the commanding voice.

Judith Butler explores Althusser's neglect of the potential for disobedience connected to hailing in *Bodies that Matter*. She suggests that 'the law might not only be refused, but it might also be ruptured, forced into a rearticulation that calls into question the monotheistic force of its own unilateral operation'.[36] For Butler, this rearticulation might assume the status of parody, hyperbole. In *Bodies that Matter*, however, she does not address how the matter of the body, its fibres and tendons, might contribute to such a parodic politics. Butler's fullest elaboration of how physical resistance to interpellation occurs is provided in her essay 'Athletic Genders'.[37] In Chapter 6, the ideas from this essay are taken up as part of an extended consideration of the career of Martina Navratilova. The chapter argues that Navratilova practises a fleshly politics that is resistant to interpellation, her sinews standing firm against subjection to hegemonic somatotypes. Through her physical actions, Navratilova rewrites the laws of female appearance and body comportment. This chapter is unlike the others in that it centres on the career of an individual. Films about tennis are, however, employed throughout to demonstrate the kinds of issues that have shaped Navratilova's experiences as a sportswoman and as a champion of sexual rights.

Navratilova's later on-court achievements enabled her to become a powerful role-model for women over the age of 40. Media appearances on shows such as *Beat the Star* (2008), in which a 51 year old Navratilova competed against 30 year old ultra-runner Rachael Hornigold, further cemented her reputation as a paragon for middle-aged women combating the stereotype of being past their prime. The relationship between ageing and female athleticism has been explored in several documentaries recently including *Racing Against the Clock* (Dir. Bill Haney, USA, 2004), about the competitive efforts of five female track and field athletes aged between 50 and 82, *Champion Bodybuilder Valentina Chepiga: Still Climbing the Hill Over-40, Not Over It* (Dir, Elliott Haimoff, USA, 2010) about a then 48 year-old bodybuilder still participating in contests, and *50 Year Old Freshman* (Dir. Deborah J. McDonald, USA, 2012) about the exploits of open water swimmer Suzanne Heim-Bowen. Fiction films that feature middle-aged sportswomen are, however, rare. A notable exception is *The Gymnast* (Dir. Ned Farr, USA, 2006).

The Gymnast centres on the life of a masseuse, Jane Hawkins. She is a former gymnast who becomes an aerialist, an acrobat who performs routines suspended in the air. Jane, who is 42, is trying to have a baby with her reluctant husband, David. The theme of ageing, the perceived restrictions that accompany it and ways that these can be challenged, runs throughout the film. The opening credits, for example, begin with footage of a young woman on a balance beam at a gymnastics competition, then cut to a domestic interior where a middle-aged woman is shown doing a handstand. The woman in both scenes is supposed to be Jane. In the second scene, however, the motive for her athleticism is not artistic. It is, instead, aimed at enhancing her chances of conceiving. There is, nonetheless, continuity between the different ages and spaces. Hawkins has evidently stayed in shape.

The focus on Jane's hands throughout the film is noteworthy. Hands are often one of the first parts of the body to display signs of ageing such as wrinkles. In *The Gymnast*, however, Jane's hands also provide her with the means to transcend stereotypes about the ageing body. Their strong grip helps her to succeed as an aerialist, performing acrobatics whilst hanging suspended from aerial silks. Aerial acrobatics provides Jane with a way to regain the pleasure in sport that gymnastics provided her with before she suffered a career-ending injury at the age of 22. She forms an artistic partnership with another aerialist, 28 year old Serena, who subsequently becomes her lover. They devise an artistic routine that showcases both their acrobatic skills and physical passion for each other. An entertainer from Las Vegas is highly impressed by it. He baulks, however, at hiring Jane when he learns her age. Only Serena is hired. Months later, Jane receives a birthday card from Serena and, leaving her husband, sets off to find her.

During the end credits of *The Gymnast* which show Jane driving to Las Vegas, she is pulled over by a traffic cop who attempts to breathalyse her. His kit is not working so he asks her to perform a walk-the-line test instead. This field test traditionally involves walking the length of a real or imagined line, pivoting and returning.[38] If the driver is able to keep walking heel-to-toe in a straight line in both directions then they have proved their sobriety. The police officer in this instance directs

Jane to a real road marking which she approaches as if it were a balance beam, performing a gymnastics routine instead of simply walking. In this scene, Jane has recognised her subjection to the law by pulling over after being hailed by the police car's flashing lights. Her hyperbolic walk, however, can be read as embodying something other than strict obedience. Jane simultaneously conforms to and sends up the law. Her ambivalent behaviour, her parody, does not toe the line. She uses athletic agency to draw attention to the performative dimension to interpellation. The routine does more than test the law. It also mirrors the opening of the film. Jane is once more astride the balance beam. Her ability to continue to perform upon it demonstrates her body's refusal to conform to hegemonic ideas about the athletic abilities of the ageing female body. She, like Navratilova in real life, practises a fleshly politics that contests stereotypes.

In the concluding chapter, *Whip It* (Dir. Drew Barrymore, USA, 2009), a coming of age film about roller derby, is analysed for the ways it simultaneously critiques and affirms patriarchal values. *Whip It* touches on many of the themes examined in previous chapters. The sport of roller derby is associated with an ethos of female empowerment.[39] The way it is represented in *Whip It*, however, undercuts its emancipatory message demonstrating many of the difficulties that accompany claiming films about sportswomen for feminism. This reactionary dimension is articulated through costume, dialogue and *mise-en-scène*. The film's cinematography, however, offers a countervailing idea of femininity that is liberating. *Whip It* therefore displays many of the complexities and contradictions that characterise cinematic depictions of female athleticism.

1
The Ascent of Woman: Climbing Films

In *Vertical Limit* (Dir. Martin Campbell, USA, 2000), an action film about alpine climbing, a failed attempt to climb the Himalayan Mountain K2 forms the film's central story. An expedition led by experienced alpinist Tom McLaren and funded by entrepreneur Elliot Vaughn, who is a participant in the climb, becomes stranded on the peak in a storm. Before disaster strikes in the form of an avalanche, Vaughn berates McLaren for wanting to turn back because of an adverse weather warning. He says to his lead climber: 'What did you think? That she was just going to lift up her skirt and pull her panties down for us?' K2 is here figured as a woman, a potential sexual conquest. This choice of metaphor, this gendering, is not uncommon in climbing as will become clear. Mountains are part of 'our natural Mother, the Earth'.[1] Climbing is described by Sally Ann Ness in terms of 'a competitive interest in conquering nature'.[2] Climbing comprises 'of masterful relation to natural environments as an expression of Western masculinity'.[3] Peaks are therefore culturally coded as feminine. In *Vertical Limit*, however, whilst the mountain may be figured as female it is gendered as a masculine space. K2 is associated with the death of a woman climber, the character Montgomery Wick's wife. It is not a space depicted as suited to the female sex. This reflects the reality that climbing of all types is still popularly conceived of as a masculine pursuit. In free climbing, routes are characterised by Dianne Chisholm, drawing on earlier work by Susan Frohlick, as 'hypermasculine spaces'.[4] The remarkable feats of contemporary women climbers such as Josune Bereziartu and Monique Forestier have not yet altered common perceptions about the activity.

1.1 *Vertical Limit* (2000): Annie's lack of reach

Vertical Limit features two female characters portrayed as climbers. One, Annie Garrett, is described by Vaughn as his 'leading lady' on the K2 expedition. He therefore casts her as a secondary lead. Annie ends up trapped in a crevasse along with McLaren and Vaughn, awaiting rescue. She is rapidly pacified as far as the main action goes. At the start of the film her low status is already signalled when her lack of reach during a climb is framed as a contributing factor in her father's death. She is unable to insert a camming device in a nearby rock fissure as her father and brother dangle helplessly, repeating 'I can get it in, I can get it in' yet continually failing to do so (1.1). It is also possible to hear in this phrase a secondary meaning, an admission of her desire, yet inability, to penetrate the cliff face, an acknowledgment of her phallic lack. The other female climber, Monique Aubertine, is a member of the rescue party sent after the initial expedition. She is depicted as a courageous and skilful climber yet only has a supporting role. The main climber in the film is Annie's brother, Peter. He has a combative attitude towards mountains describing them as something to be 'laid siege to'.

Vertical Limit therefore minimises the roles of women as driving forces in the story. Annie's character, for example, is designed to provide a way for her brother to overcome the trauma of the climbing incident in which their father was killed. She facilitates her brother's redemption through requiring him to rescue her. The mother of the bereaved siblings is never mentioned. Climbing is a male universe into which Annie trespasses.

Wick's wife is punished for infringing on male terrain by her death in the mountains. Aubertine is, perhaps, the point of resistance to the negative depiction of women in the film yet her role in the narrative is minimal. The way *Vertical Limit* marginalises, and punishes, female characters is also common to other climbing films.

In *Cliffhanger* (Dir. Renny Harlin, USA, 1993), for instance, the solo-climber Gabe Walker suffers intense guilt because he was unable to save his best friend's lover Sarah in a climbing accident. The role of Walker's girlfriend, Jessie Deighan, is similar to that of Annie in *Vertical Limit*. She is present to encourage Walker to overcome his sense of culpability and provides him with the means to do so when she requires him to save her from falling off a cliff towards the end of the film. Women in climbing films are often given little more than walk on parts. There are, however, exceptions. The film *Snowman's Pass* (Dir. Rex Piano, Canada, 2004) effects a role reversal. The central character is a woman, Diana Pennington, who must overcome the trauma of losing her fiancé in a climbing accident. There are also documentaries, such as *Au-dèla des cimes*, which focus on the achievements of women climbers. These films give women the appearance of greater narrative motility.

This chapter explores freedom of movement in climbing films in relation to gender. It draws on recent scholarship that examines climbing phenomenologically and also on the writings of noted free climber Lynn Hill to examine how some films, particularly the documentary *Hard Grit* (Dir. Richard Heap, UK, 1998), show how the sport provides a means by which to transcend gender categories. This requires approaching climbing with an alternative logic to the one advanced in films such as *Vertical Limit*, constructing mountains as entities to be conquered. Climbing figured as the subjugation of nature forms a reinforcement of patriarchal ideology. The chapter, however, explores a different attitude to the sport. It is one focussed not on conquest but on an alliance between bodies, a physical contract between the animate and inanimate, flesh and rock.

Orienteering

The phenomenological philosophy of Maurice Merleau-Ponty informs how climbing is understood here. At the centre of phenomenology, as conceived of by Merleau-Ponty, is the lived body. For Merleau-Ponty human beings both have a body and are a body. For him the body that is us, and also that which we possess, is bound up with the world. This sounds counter-intuitive. We know there is a clear boundary between our bodies and the world around us. The body appears as a well-defined entity when looked at it in a mirror or, usually, when encountered on screen. This view of the body, however, occurs from a third-person perspective. In such instances, we see the body outside of ourselves. The contours of the body are less apparent when we consider it from a first-person perspective. It is also less easy to see it as an object. Its boundaries are indistinct. The body seen from a first-person perspective is more mobile. It changes location.

Our usual experience is not of the body as a distinct entity but of some aspect of the world that has caught our attention. Our body possesses intentionality. Intentionality is not like intention. Intention indicates a plan that is to be carried out. Intentionality describes a vital aspect of human existence. It is the fact that human beings are fundamentally related to the contexts in which they live. This means that consciousness is always consciousness of an object that is distinct from, but always present to, consciousness. In phenomenology therefore, the sense of self results from a palimpsest of encounters with the world, orientations towards it. Being-in-the-world is a continual process of becoming. If consciousness, our sense of ourselves, emerges from out of encounters with the world then what we notice in that encounter reveals what we are like in terms of what is significant for and to us.

The way we perceive is never separate from our cultural background. If encounters with phenomena are never separable from culture then this has significant implications for the study of gender. There are, however, moments when individuals do not seem to draw on the resources of culture, of language, to make sense of physical experiences. One of the best examples of this way of being in the world is provided by professional sportspeople. Players of ball sports such as water polo, for example, sometimes suggest that when they throw a ball they are aware of nothing. It is just them and the ball. The act of throwing the ball becomes the player's world. The player does all that is necessary to achieve that aim. Body, will and outcome are experienced as a singular and unified event. In this un-thought experience 'throwing the ball' gender seems to cease to be a concern.

Phenomenology, at times, appears to encourage a way of perceiving the world, of being mindful of bodily experience, that looks past gender. It moves beyond the compass of cultural differences. In her highly influential essay 'Throwing Like a Girl', however, Iris Marion Young demonstrates that gender differences inform human lived body experiences.[5] This essay forcefully contends that the lived body is acculturated. Sara Ahmed has suggested that 'phenomenology helps us to explore how bodies are shaped by histories, which they perform in their comportment, their posture, and their gestures'.[6] Young attends to this reality yet her focus is only on how gender as a form of cultural difference informs the body. She fails to address, for example, how ethnicity or geographical context might intersect with sex. Young is interested in a general tendency in feminine physical comportment in a given cultural context, the United States, in 1980. Despite these limitations, however, it is still valuable for its careful elucidation of how patriarchal values insinuate the very sinews of women.

Young combines insights from Simone de Beauvoir and Merleau-Ponty in order to focus on the ways in which the feminine body typically conducts itself in motion. She draws on de Beauvoir's understanding of femininity not as an essence possessed by all women but as a set of conditions that delimit the typical situation of being a woman in a particular society. Young's arguments about feminine existence are grounded in research carried out into the differing ways in which men and women move their bodies. This research shows that in childhood girls do not bring their whole bodies into motion as much as boys do: '[girls] do not reach back, twist, move backward, step, and lean forward. Rather, [...] girls tend to remain relatively immobile except for their arms, and even the arms are not extended as far as they could be'.[7] This corporeal restraint persists into adulthood.

Young argues that in many physical activities, feminine comportment, the ways in which women move their bodies, displays a failure to make use of the body's spatial potential. She suggests that even in simple actions such as sitting, standing, and walking, women differ in their style of using their bodies. In walking and jogging, for example, women are generally not as open with their bodies as men in terms of their bearing and stride. Men often swing their arms in a more expansive way while many women have more up and down rhythm in their step. Women also frequently sit differently to men. Men keep their feet further apart than women do whilst women sit with their legs relatively close together and their arms across their bodies. This tends to be the case whether women are wearing a dress or trousers.

Young also suggests that men and women approach tasks that require force and strength in dissimilar ways. Women often do not *perceive* themselves as capable of lifting and carrying heavy objects or grasping or twisting with force. The perception a woman holds that she cannot accomplish particular tasks will sometimes lead her to fail to summon the full possibilities of her musculature and capacity for movement. Young writes: 'For many women as they move in sport, a space surrounds us in imagination that we are not free to move beyond; the space available to our movement is a constricted space.'[8] The idea that the capacity to move within space is potentially gendered has implications for the study of cinema as will be discussed in the next chapter.

Young states that there are three modalities or manners that characterise feminine movement. These are that women typically exhibit an ambiguous transcendence, an inhibited intentionality and a discontinuous unity with their surroundings. Transcendence refers to that which transcends our own consciousness. It is something objective rather than only a phenomenon of consciousness. The transcendent is usually opposed in phenomenology to the immanent. Immanence relates to our internal world. A person's impressions of an object are immanent. The object, however, cannot be reduced to a series of impressions. There is something of the object that transcends. Merleau-Ponty, however, troubles this distinction between transcendence and immanence. For him, the body is both transcendent and immanent.[9] It forms a hinge between subject and object. This hinge involves transcendence which is different from the transcendent. Transcendence refers to the ways by which we come to know the world and, by extension, ourselves. Transcendence constitutes the subject.

Young writes that 'once we take the locus of subjectivity and transcendence to be the lived body rather than pure consciousness, all transcendence is ambiguous because the body as natural and material is immanence'.[10] The lived-body as transcendence is action. Subjectivity comes into being through encounters with surroundings, through the lived body's orientation towards, and interaction with, the world around it. Subjectivity therefore exists as process, as a becoming rather than a being. Young powerfully argues that if subjectivity is bound up with how we engage with our surroundings then women who are not making full use of their body's potential are going to be restricted in terms of the kind of subject they can become. This is why Young suggests feminine bodily existence represents an ambiguous transcendence.

For Merleau-Ponty, intentionality is linked to motility. Consciousness is bound up with movement. Because women often do not make full use of their corporeal potential feminine bodily existence is, for Young, an *inhibited intentionality*.[11] Feminine bodily existence also displays a *discontinuous unity* in that the part of the body that is transcending towards an aim is in relative disunity from the parts that remain immobile. Women sometimes throw using only their arms not bringing their whole bodies into the motion.

Additionally, Merleau-Ponty argued that for the body to exist as a transcendent entity in the world and practise the immediate enactment of intentions it cannot exist as an object. For women, however, as the three modes of feminine bodily existence demonstrate, the body is frequently both subject and *object* to itself at the same time and in relation to the same act. For Young, women look upon themselves as objects for a number of reasons. A major one is that they do not feel their motions are entirely under their control. Their attention is divided between the task they are performing and the body that must be manipulated into performing it. The central reason, however, is that the feminine subject conceives her motion as the motion that is *looked at*. In her social existence woman is the object of the gaze of another and that is a major source of her bodily self-reference. That sportswomen are figured in film in this way will be discussed in Chapter 4 in relation to the film *Fast Girls* (Dir. Regan Hall, UK, 2012).

Young writes: 'to the extent that a woman lives her body as a thing, she remains rooted in immanence, is inhibited, and retains a distance from her body as transcending movement and from engagement in the world's possibilities'.[12] The reasons behind why women often fail to engage fully in the world's possibilities are located by Young in education, particularly in learning that takes place in early childhood (although we might also consider how women are predominantly represented in, and by, cinema as another probability). There has, however, been a considerable shift in the status of women in Western society since Young wrote her essay in the late 1970s. The kind of physical restriction she regarded as typical of women, if not universal, does not necessarily persist today as is argued forcefully by Dianne Chisholm in her beautiful essay, 'Climbing like a Girl'.

Climbing Like a Girl

Chisholm is critical of Young for instituting masculine motility as an idealised norm. This leads Young to judge women's comportment in relation to a range of activities that are culturally coded as masculine at the expense of alternative activities, and their accompanying motions, that are coded as feminine. It also means that Young fails to engage with 'women's transformative experience'.[13] Chisholm's example of this kind of experience is free climbing, particularly as practised by Lynn Hill. The objective of free climbing is achieving a particular route up a cliff face. The attainment of the summit is of secondary importance to the route used to achieve it. In contrast to the negative modalities for analysis identified by Young, ambiguous transcendence, inhibited intentionality, and discontinuous unity, Chisholm identifies five positive modalities in Hill's way of being-in-the-world, reach, crux-coordination, flow, freedom and synaesthesia.[14]

Hill's reach, her technique of gripping and moving, requires that 'she fit her girl's body to the form of the rock and not to some gender-prescribed body form'.[15] Her crux-coordination, how she manoeuvres through the most difficult part of a climb, involves mobilising free movement in a synthesis of previously used movements and innovations, reached for variations. Flow comprises of privileging style over brute strength in climbing, attaining rapidity and rhythm.[16] Victoria Robinson has examined the 'gendering' of different styles of climbing.[17] In this context, a flowing form of climbing is likely to be coded as feminine. Flow comprises the habitual coupled with the improvisatory. Hill's climbing is routinely creative. Flow is felt by the climber to occur without conscious intervention. The flowing ascent therefore involves thoughtless, yet not unintelligent, flesh.

In such moments actions are in control of the climber. The body asserts its learning, leads the mind. Freedom is freedom of movement, freeing up of movement. It is finding new techniques, new moves, on a climb rather than relying on pre-existing motive models. It is embracing the liberatory potential of the unanticipated. Synaesthesia refers to the recognition in climbers like Hill that they see-touch, that the senses are not discrete. They are imbricated: colour signalling texture, knowledge of how rocks feel informing ways cliff faces are seen, read. Synaesthesia also connotes an intimacy with the physical world, an acquired respect for rock. Hill's embodiment of these five modalities enables her to overthrow, as Chisholm describes it, 'throwing like a girl'.[18] Her movement is not defined or restricted by gender. It is rather what permits her to escape definition by gender as a background to being.

Catherine Destivelle, a free and aid climber who was one of Hill's main rivals during her years as a competitive climber, makes comparable claims about the sport's capacity to slough off gender. During the documentary *Au-delà des cimes* (Dir. Rémy Tezier, France, 2008), which examines her passion for alpinism, Destivelle asserts: 'In the mountains, I don't think boy/girl, I'm practically asexual. It's not because I'm a woman I will not make it or because I'm a woman I must make it.' Her climbing, as she understands it, is not a feminist practice because it leaves the terms that sustain inequality behind. There is no patriarchy in the physical, sensual experiences of ascending a cliff face. The pleasures and pains of the ascent level ideas of difference. Ideation is minimal. The effects of ideology are minimised. This echoes Hill's assertion that 'everyone [is] equal before the rocks'.[19]

Between a Word and a Hard Place

Chisholm, however, does not just appreciate Hill's climbing accomplishments. She also values her powers as a writer. There is something about the style of *Climbing Free* that draws the reader into the world of challenging routes and hard rock. This aspect of Chisholm's analyses, her heavy reliance on the support of Hill's prose for her arguments, merits further attention. There is a tension in the essay between the embodied experience of climbing and its representation after the fact. The framing of the exploits in gendered terms, in both Chisholm's account and Hill's, for instance, betrays language's framing influence. To illustrate the different approaches men and women adopt when climbing, for example, Chisholm contrasts Hill's descriptions of her style with those of Peter Livesey in his text 'I Feel Rock' which describes nine of his climbs.

Chisholm draws attention to Livesey's use of 'sexual synecdoche' in a description of climbing Reed Pinnacle.[20] He refers to the rock face as a 'slash' which Chisholm interprets as slang for the vagina in the spirit of argot such as "slash stash". Later in this account Livesey also refers to the fact that 'you never know with hands in cracks what they're after' which is designed to exploit double-entendre and lends credence to Chisholm's interpretation.[21] The fissure is figured either as anus or, as is more likely in the context of the rest of the prose, a vagina. The ambiguity of this reference to the crack, however, with its potential to allude to an orifice common to both sexes, gestures towards the queer potential of rock climbing. This potential is also hinted at in *Vertical Limit* when the character Royce suggests that 'a smart climber always wears a belt and suspenders'. The practice of grit climbing often involves men becoming intimate with hard crags, feeling their way across ridges, striations, rigid matter, matter often previously touched and fingered by other men. Climbing provides access to a socially mediated 'hom(m)o-sexuality' comparable to that described by Luce Irigaray in *This Sex Which is Not One*.[22] Men touch each other by way of the climb, by way of fingering the literal traces of past passages. Feeling bolts, chalk, and pitons enables relations with other men to be forged. Hom(m)o-sexuality is played out through a touching mnemonic.

Livesey also mentions his 'nut', literally meaning a metal wedge, which Chisholm also reads metaphorically as a reference to the testes. Climbing involves man and his testicular technology finding release in rock as female form. Intercourse is strongly connoted in Livesey's description of climbing what he refers to as El Cap's East Buttress route. This account plays with the double-meaning of Cap. In the narrative it refers both to El Capitan, a rock formation in Yosemite National Park, and to a contraceptive cap. Livesey writes of this route: 'although you know the crack will take good protection, you can't see where to put it once you're arched up in a layback position. There's always a tendency to get going and forget the protection. As the Editor would say: "Just lay back and enjoy it".'[23] Climbing here assumes the position of unsafe sex.

Climbing as it is figured by Livesey is not intimate. Chisholm suggests that 'a rhetoric of masculinity blocks Livesey from exploring the finer phenomena of attending to the feel of the rock'.[24] Rock is reduced to breasts or vagina. The Fairview Dome in the High Sierra, for instance, becomes a 'cuppable tit' and the view from this peak is of 'a pine-chested woman with eleven more tits all around you'.[25] Livesey's descriptions of climbing always resort to sexual metaphor. His understanding of rock is crude. In Livesey's account of scaling Reed Pinnacle, for instance, his body 'is highly masculinized and, at the same time, highly alienated as an instrument of egoistic reason'.[26] Although he describes climbing in terms of sexual intercourse, it is of a disinterested kind. There is no intimacy with rock as body. It never exists in itself. Livesey can never see beyond his gendered language, feel the granite or limestone beneath his fingers. Or, to be more precise, Livesey's descriptions are not able to transcend gender. It is possible, probable, that his physical encounters with rock were not vulgar, that he abandoned his macho façade in the face of a particular cliff, losing his capacity for carnal metaphors as he became focussed on specific movements, efforts.

Hill's approach to describing climbing is more attentive to the thoughtfulness rock demands. She recognises that encountering rock means moving beyond or behind language. Sally Ann Ness has examined this paring of language's mediating effects in relation to the practice of bouldering, a style of climbing that does not involve ropes. Ness draws on what she terms postphenomenological developments in cultural geography as a means to make sense of bouldering as it is practised in Yosemite. Much of Ness's article focusses on the significance, or lack thereof, of three intense vocalisations, screams, made by the climber Alan Moore as he attempted to climb a boulder known as Jacob's Ladder. Echoing Immanuel Kant, Ness describes these exhalations as bearing 'a quality of purposiveness' although not done on purpose.[27] The screams do not doing anything graspable in terms of climbing the boulder, they lack instrumental purpose. They do, however, have expressive force. They are not insignificant.

Ness states of Moore's second scream, 'the rage that was its raw material – or some singular, as-yet-unnamed feeling whose character was on the order of rage – had an assertional quality'.[28] She goes on to suggest that it was 'composed entirely of affect'.[29] His expressivity is reduced to a cry. There are no morphemes. This is no utterance. Moore violently expels unformed sound. Climbing can, Moore demonstrates, foster a letting go of language. It can carry the climber close to raw experience. This experience, at the limits of language, carries an individual beyond gender. Ness writes of Moore's vocalisations as a kind of emerging signification. They are on the way to sense. The screams are non-representational, not yet representational. They do not stand for an experience. They constitute 'an affective field in which human and nonhuman elements of experience [are] ontologically "interlaced" – not yet sorted out via the intellectual symbolic processes of a contemplative subject'.[30] The screams are not intended communications. The interaction between individual and boulder, a between that blurs towards togetherness, causes Moore to surrender authority over voice. It is not his voice that screams. At the moment of his ululating, he has 'entered a state of being in which his life form [is] situated between the multiple human and non-human elements now integrally connected by the attempt'.[31]

Crucially, Moore's scream impacts on all who hear it. Ness writes that 'it also enfolded in its manifesting character all who were present to it [and] temporarily displaced subject-object conceptions and interrupted representational faculties and processes for the entire group'.[32] Ness's assertion that the scream has the capacity to displace the representational framework by which the world is usually encountered suggests how through sharing in the experiences of a climber, be they woman or man, it might be possible to feel a way beyond gender. Representation, as is evident from Chisholm's and Hill's accounts, is haunted by gender binaries. Gender, either explicitly or implicitly, frequently informs processes of sense making. The scream, however, 'propels experience into a realm of possibility where no prior forms of understanding have any conceivable purchase on the likelihood of what might happen next'.[33] The scream voids sense. It therefore opens up uncharted futures, moving beyond prefabricated significations, the recyclable readymade meanings that structure perception in everyday life. Gender, in such a moment, loses its grip on the climber's body.

It is, however, not just through explosive instances of the kind analysed by Ness that this space beyond the reach of gender opens up. The cleft in sense generated by the scream also occurs in other ways by way of the climber's relation to the rock face. The climber enjoying their search for a route is also, unknowingly, feeling their way towards 'a peephole, crack, fissure, hole, window in the densely-packed wall of language'.[34] Michel Serres describes aesthetics, sensual pleasures, as antithetical to language.[35] The latter acts as an anaesthetic dulling experience of the physical world. Aesthetic encounters provide a form of feeling beyond semantic soporifics. The sensuous potential in climbing is strongly indicated in *Au-delà des cimes* (1.2). At one point, Destivelle is filmed from above climbing the Grand Capucin in the Alps. She grips rock, pulling upwards, feeling her way, hand cupping a knob of stone, fingers clasping a sliver of a ridge. This footage is accompanied by a voiceover by Destivelle which describes the tactile pleasures of climbing. She states when she sees 'a bump of granite shining in the sun, I want to go and touch it' and adds 'I think all climbers will attest to the pleasure of touching rock'. The aesthetic dimension

1.2 *Au-delà des cimes* (2009): A feel for rock

alluded to here, Destivelle's refulgent and tactile enjoyments, are akin to the palpable and chromatic pleasures described by Hill when she writes of climbing at New Paltz: 'Oxides and lichens had painted the cliffs with a riot of reds, greens and yellows; sharp edges perfectly shaped for the fingers peppered the walls; and tiers of roofs jutted over our heads.'[36] In Hill's account, the cliffs are figured as a canvas. This also occurs in the documentary *Hard Grit*, which will be discussed shortly, when the narrator speaks of translating bouldering obsessions to 'grit's larger canvas'.

When rock is described as canvas, by extension, the climber becomes an artist. The creative dimension to climbing is therefore reinforced. The metaphor also draws attention to climbing's aesthetic aspects, the judgments that can be made about the quality of a particular climb and also, more importantly here, the pleasures climbers potentially take in the physical world, in stone's appearances and grains. This pleasure is seldom signalled in depictions of climbing in mainstream narrative cinema. A notable exception is *Snowman's Pass*, an action adventure centring upon efforts to retrieve a crashed spy satellite in the mountains of British Columbia. The central character, Pennington, is a mountain guide who enjoys free climbing. Diana describes free soloing as 'the ultimate – just you and nature'. This resonates with Hill's appreciation of people who 'maintain a close connection to the earth'.[37]

There is a scene in the film in which Diana wishes to assess the skills of another climber, Tyler. She therefore sets off up a route alongside him, watched by two belayers. There is a strong sense of the search for grip, of arms stretching, hands feeling, finding, grasping, and hauling, of the process of discovering a route, in the sequence.

The mountain as a potential character in the film is also briefly indicated in a shot towards the end of this sequence. Tyler falls and has to be helped back to the rock face by Diana. The two climb down out of shot and the camera remains fixed on a crack in the rock face. In this brief moment, the mountain as personality is established, a source of potential threat, of menace. Although framed as a 'bad guy', rock here is allowed to assert an identity independent of the climbers. It comes close to escaping the role of extra. The rest of the film, however, comprises of low budget banality and the cliff fades from view. *Snowman's Pass* proffers, before ultimately withholding, one specific example of what Serres refers to as the 'given', actual things in the world as opposed to representations of them.

Snowman's Pass demonstrates the difficulty of moving beyond language to access the given, the aesthetic realm, including the sensual experience that is climbing. Language, however, as Steven Connor has noted, is conceived of by Serres as a space of promise as well as of betrayal.[38] Serres claims that words give up on the given, blunt our experience of the world. The poetic prose of his work *The Five Senses*, however, is rich and luxuriant and appears to offer a possible way beyond the stultifying effects of language. It seems Chisholm identifies a similar liberating capacity, an ability to bear upon the given, in Hill's prose. Merleau-Ponty contended that language 'cuts the continuous tissue that joins us vitally to things'.[39] He saw it as screening the world from the subject. It appears, however, that occasionally language can also re-inscribe relations to things as occurs in writings such as those of Serres. Is such a re-inscription possible, however, through the specific language used in filmmaking? Serres writes that once within language, 'nothing is more difficult than climbing back up in the opposite direction, the vertical path towards life, creation, or incarnation'.[40] He chastises Merleau-Ponty for surrendering sensation to signification through his descriptions of phenomena yet his own writings demonstrate a desire to employ language as a climbing guide to the material world.[41] The documentary *Hard Grit* provides insights into how such an ascent through and beyond filmic language might be possible.

Friction Film

Hard Grit features elite climbers tackling technically difficult routes on the gritstone of the Pennines in northern England. Gritstone is hard sandstone with a rough surface that provides a high degree of friction and is therefore ideally suited to climbing. The opening sequence to the film features Jean-Minh Trin-Thieu climbing a route known as Gaia in the Black Rocks in Derbyshire. The footage is artfully edited. There are shots of different parts of Trin-Thieu's body – his feet, his hands – which capture how the climb brings different parts of the physique into focus as it progresses. This fragmentation is not a form of fetishisation. It is a means by which to suggest the shifting zones of attention and exertion as the climb proceeds. Shots are also superimposed so that, for example, a distance shot of Trin-Thieu's body combines with a close-up of his hand. This produces a disturbance in the field of vision which can be seen to figure the importance of senses other than sight at such moments. Finally, some shots are from far off, to show the size of Trin-Thieu's endeavour and the height he could potentially fall from, and also from below, looking up at the climber, which again serve to emphasise how high up the cliff face he is.

The sequence is accompanied by a heartbeat like sound which quickens in pace as the climb continues, signalling anxiety and also corporeal effort. Trin-Thieu ultimately falls and although his descent is arrested the rope he is attached to spins precipitously and wildly, causing him to badly cut his leg. The climb therefore ends in physical injury, pain. This pain, like the pleasure described earlier in relation to Destivelle's and Hill's experiences of climbing, potentially provides a point of access to the given, to a world unencumbered by sexual difference. Serres describes one form of the given as lacerating and as 'waking us with a slap in the face'.[42] Here rock has violently made itself felt. The cinematography, which visually disorients, also seeks to liberate the spectator of Trin-Thieu's climb from the mastery of language and, by extension, of gender. In the sequence, however, it is not pleasurable aesthetic experience that facilitates this but moments of visual un-pleasure.

Hard Grit embodies the same grappling with language's deleterious effects by way of the linguistic that exists in *The Five Senses*. The ways in which language genders experiences of the physical world are gestured towards in some of the names given to gritstone routes. One referred to in the documentary, for example, is known as Fat Slapper, rendering explicit the feminisation of rock that accompanies its being labelled a phenomenon of the natural world, a progeny of Mother Nature. A route in Derbyshire that is not mentioned in *Hard Grit* is known as Brass Monkeys, the name, a metonym for the testes, presumably deriving from the fact that it requires balls to make the climb. Other routes, however, have gender neutral names that basically foreground the physicality of climbing. A route at Higgar Tor featured in the documentary is known simply as Shit. The route is presumably not called this because it is worthless but rather because it is annoying, a challenge. There is another route nearby, not mentioned in the documentary, called Piss. The references to bodily functions, like the climbs named after kinds of bodies and body parts, reinforce climbing's corporeal character. The body is often used in biologically essentialist arguments as evidence for the existence of sexual difference. In climbing, however, the body as given, in its intimacy with rock, provides a way to move beyond difference, become indifferent to it. In this vein, Hill writes of the egalitarianism of climbing.[43] Intimacy with rock, however, provides more than equality. It permits access to a world beyond the binaries of Man and Woman.

Finding an opening through which to move beyond the constraining effects of language is phenomenally difficult. *The Five Senses* displays a residual phallocentrism at the level of descriptions of materiality that can also be felt in the way the contemporary gritstone scene is portrayed by *Hard Grit*. In *The Five Senses* two kinds of given are postulated. One, soft and gentle, 'is conveyed by language'.[44] The other, hard, the given that matters, is figured in masculine terms. It is, at one point, explicitly linked to the erection, the hard-on, which is the foundation for a meditation on feeling: 'an erection describes the everyday, local and global phenomenon of sensation'.[45] Serres displays a potentially unsettling, if inconsistent, sexual politics. Women are praised by him for their subtlety and delicacy, their remarkable capacity for colour coding clothing, their sensibility.[46] These qualities align women closely with the soft given, with a superficial, sign-saturated existence. Rope that is soft is contrasted with its hard counterpart and described as having become 'invaginated, absent' linking it with the maternal.[47] The language of sexual difference Serres uses to differentiate the given is, however, precisely that. The given is beyond gender, it is only descriptions of it that remain bound to sex.

There is a similar tension in the documentary between the ways gritstone climbing is framed by the film through its narrative, which is phallocentric, and the act of climbing in itself. The presence of women in *Hard Grit* has gone unremarked in existing scholarship on the film.[48] There are, however, four women climbers listed in the film's credits, Airlie Anderson, Lucy Creamer, Sarah Harrison, and Ruth Jenkins. Lucy Creamer, a prominent climber, acts the part of Veronica Lee in *Hard Grit*. Lee accompanied Peter Harding on a route called Suicide Wall at Cratcliffe Tor in 1946. The film provides a reconstruction of that historic climb. Dave Thomas plays the part of Harding. In the re-enactment, Lee is shown making the ascent first. *Hard Grit* therefore acknowledges that there is a long, albeit often overlooked, history of women climbers tackling difficult routes. Hill remarks on the existence of such hidden histories in *Climbing Free*, even revealing that some of her own successes have been veiled. She was the first to make a free ascent of Ophir Broke in Colorado yet it is credited in guidebooks to John Long.[49]

Hard Grit also, however, simultaneously suppresses the participation of women climbers in the contemporary gritstone scene. Creamer only appears in the guise of the past. She is dated. Lee and Harding are shown in black and white. The footage is additionally artificially aged, given an abraded look, as if the friction between projection apparatus and film reel across multiple screenings has damaged the print. Heywood has described *Hard Grit*'s overall visual appearance as prosaic.[50] As this section of the film demonstrates, however, the documentary is actually carefully crafted and quite varied. Through the artifice of aged, distressed monochrome, Creamer as Lee is safely temporally distanced from colourful male climbers such as Seb Grieve, Leo Houlding and Richard Ekehed who also appear in the film. The sexual politics of the cinematography and editing operates, however, only at the level of the film as language. There are moments when the film's language gestures beyond itself.

The Australian Dave Jones is shown ascending a route known as the Braille Trail (1.3). The name reinforces how rocks form a sign system. The climber reads, interprets rough surfaces, sensing their way upwards. Braille, however, is also a tactile writing system for the blind or visually impaired. The name of the route emphasises how vital touch is to any ascent. Hill refers in *Climbing Free* to her fingers reading a handhold like Braille.[51] In *Hard Grit*, because of the narrow holds on the Braille Trail,

1.3 *Hard Grit* (1998): The Braille Trail

practically invisible when Jones is shot from above, parallel with the rock face, the Australian states of the route: 'It's this thing that only just exists.' The route is represented as at the limits of perception, at the edge of figuration. Jones's description brings to the fore how climbing can expose the limits of language. The text that is Braille Trail is elusive, of such low relief that it hardly registers. It does not seek out a readership. It has to be searched for, coaxed to appear, by sensitive fingers.

The route Jones ascends can only be discovered through time and effort. This process of discovery can, in turn, only be communicated to the film's viewers through camerawork that is patient. The documentary develops a feel for its subject-matter in the same alert, attentive way that a climber discovers and negotiates a route, overcomes a crux. This kind of approach to filming climbing occurs infrequently in mainstream narrative cinema which is fast-paced and involves editing that produces rapid changes of shot. The necessity to move rapidly in mainstream films is made clear in *Cliffhanger* where realism is sacrificed in the interests of Walker achieving a speedy ascent. He is portrayed free soloing with the aid of a massive bolt

1.4 *Cliffhanger* (1993): Gabe's big bolt gun

gun (1.4). Climbers do occasionally use drills to insert bolts on routes but the time taken to do this would obviously impede the narrative so Walker possesses a piece of equipment that smashes bolts into the rock face.

The portrayal of the gun is revealing for two reasons. It demonstrates that the pace of climbing in mainstream narrative cinema cannot keep pace with real climbing. Fiction films, particularly action films, are too fast. Routes that would require a day of effort must be negotiated in two hours, which translates to ten minutes of screen time, if that. It also displays a lack of knowledge of the ways in which climbing supports the performance of masculine identity. The gun smashing bolts (with hangers attached) into rock figures Walker as a manual labourer. It assumes the status of a pneumatic drill. Its penetrative capabilities also invite its coding as phallic. It acts visually to affirm Walker's masculine credentials. The gun provides Walker with the capacity to dictate a route on his terms, to mould the mountain to his needs, to triumph over the natural by way of the technological. To most climbers, however, such an approach would be anathema. Walker unmans himself every time he fires a bolt into the cliff. His actions invite an informed audience to speculate that he lacks the ability to overcome the most difficult part of a climb which is why he must resort to invasive technology such as the gun to assist him. Walker has no feel for rock, no respect for it. His actions are comparable to those of Ray Jardine who committed the 'atrocity', as some label it, of chiselling edges for his fingers and toes in the rock of the Nose at El Capitan. Jardine, however, unlike Walker, recognised how appalling his actions had been because 'the holds he created stood out as being blatantly man-made'.[52]

33

Hill has suggested that Jardine's initial actions demonstrated that 'he failed to recognize that the spirit of free climbing is about adapting one's personal capacities and dimensions to natural features of the rock, not the other way around'.[53]

Style over Summit

There is an ethic to rock climbing, strongly advocated by Hill, which is bound up with its aesthetic potential. This is the case both in relation to the aesthetics of a particular style of climbing and of rock itself. Walker's style of climbing is one of subjugation. The route he takes is bent to his will. He alters the rock features forever. Hill, however, describes herself as 'a climber focused on aesthetics rather than summits'.[54] Climbing with style is more important to her than attaining a given summit. Hill, like contemporary climbers Nancy Feagin and Andrea Hah, has a background in gymnastics, an athletic activity explicitly linked to artistry via its artistic and rhythmic forms. Her preferred analogy for climbing, however, is terpsichorean. She writes of dancing over rock, of using ballet-like free climbing movements, and suggests that 'the beauty of climbing is that each person is free to choreograph his or her own way of adapting to the rock'.[55] Beauty is inscribed in the dance across rock, or rather with rock: the *pas de deux* of climber and cliff.

It is not just making a climb, but how you make a climb, that is crucial. This is what enables climbers to strive for what Hill refers to as their 'masterpiece'.[56] Hill's use of language here is, however, misleading at least in terms of her own practice. Hill's greatest climbs, for example, demonstrate immense skill yet she disavows any mastery over rock. She suggests that free climbing, for example, requires moving without altering the rock, entering into a 'pact' with it.[57] This pact, an agreement between human and natural worlds, resonates with Serres's call for a natural contract. Serres suggests that nature has become tainted with 'the sullied world [revealing] the mark of humanity, the mark of its dominators, the foul stamp of their hold and their appropriation'.[58] The actions of Jardine and Walker form sullying of this kind, they spoil the environments they encounter. The logic that informs their climbing is to rule over rock, rather than respect and work with it.

Serres suggests that humanity has not always acted in this defiling way towards the natural world: 'in bygone days, the individual subject was practically invisible, blended in or distributed on this Earth among the forests or mountains, the deserts and ice floes, lightweight in body and bone'.⁵⁹ In this period of history, prehistory, before the word assumed such weight and import and the world became smothered by language, a more respectful attitude towards the earth, including rock, existed. I have speculated on the possible character of this earlier relationship between human and nature, specifically stone, elsewhere.⁶⁰ That rock climbing might potentially provide a means of returning to this former attitude is suggested by some of the camerawork in *Au-delà des cimes*. The cinematography often involves zooms towards, and out from, climbers on cliffs, a series of shifting scales. This reinforces the enormity of the mountains, their massive dimensions, and also connotes the void so often referenced in the film. The climbers are swallowed by each mountain's immensity. In this precarious situation they reflect the general condition of humanity in past times as it is described by Serres.

The significance of this cinematography is, however, overdetermined. There also appears to be a desire to exercise visual mastery over the climbers. The camera exerts control over the climbers through enabling their appearance and disappearance. The climbing sequences display a rhythm via the variety of focal lengths that are used. Zooming in extends the audience's vision, bringing the bodies of the climbers into view, zooming out contracts the seen, rendering their bodies invisible. From a distance, the cameraperson (in this instance, Thierry Machado) controls the extent of the visible via the use of a varifocal lens. This camerawork simultaneously affirms the courage of the climbers as they ascend the massif, and asserts the power of the director of photography over the visibility of the film's subjects, exhibits control over visual existence. The significance of this demonstration of power via a visual coming and going will be examined in the next chapter.

Climbing's potential to provide a means to access the physical world in ways not usually possible in the present is signalled by Serres's discussion of alpinism in *The Natural Contract*. He suggests that a group of mountaineers roped together on a tough climb 'finds itself bound and submitted not only to itself but to the objective world'.⁶¹ Their social contract joins a natural contract and, in such circumstances, 'the piton is an appeal to the strength of the cliff, which must be tested before any bond can be made to depend on it'.⁶² The free climber, such as Hill, is like these mountaineers in that they also enter into a natural contract with the rock face. They become intimate with nature, climber and cliff intertwine, share of each other. The climber leaves traces of their passage on the rock, chalk, skin, blood. Scuffs of cliff, dirt, dust, lichen, adhere to the climber's body and clothes. To climb is to engage in material exchange. Every contact with the rock leaves a trace. Whether this exchange is principled or unprincipled, however, depends on the climber. Walker in *Cliffhanger* attacks the rock. Hill and Destivelle, and the gritstone climbers, embrace it.

Destivelle states in *Au-delà des cimes* that 'when we climb well, we osmose with the rock'. This suggests that the features of a route are gradually assimilated, incorporated into the climber's body, through a process of becoming together, of imbrication between flesh and stone. Rock is not a passive entity. It speaks, asserts its presence. Destivelle lets her body 'adapt to what the rock is telling [it]'. Her philosophy of climbing is, like Hill's, one that requires working with, rather than ruling, rock. She states 'for me rock is something living, it has a personality'. The climber who approaches their sport like this enters into a natural contract, one in which world and human are accorded equal rights. Destivelle, Hill and the gritstone climbers have a relationship to things in which mastery and possession have been set aside 'in favour of admiring attention, reciprocity, contemplation, and respect'.[63] Respect is what the climber gives to the given: 'it would be an injustice, a disequilibrium for us to receive this given free, without ever rendering anything in return'.[64] A climber such as Walker in *Cliffhanger*, a climber who injures and dominates the surrounds, behaves as a parasite in Serres's terms, condemning to death the world 'he pillages and inhabits'.[65]

Climbing that is not parasitical, that is undertaken in a spirit of reciprocity, permits the climber access to a piece of the world, enables them a hold on the given. The stuff that matters asserts itself beneath their palms, at their fingertips, presses for attention and invites aesthetic appreciation. This pressure the rock gives by its refusal to give, by its solidity, 'beckons' the body beyond language. During the time this beyond is embraced, a space is opened within which the refusal of trapping roles of either man or woman becomes possible. This does not, however, mean that the climbers embody undecidability. The undecidable in gender still operates through the binary of man/woman even as it refuses resolution as either male or female. The climber exists at the limits of language, beyond binaries. Theirs is a wordless world.

1.5 *Au-delà des cimes* (2009): Catherine, a mother in nature

Film is resistant to communicating this world. *Au-delà des cimes*, for example, through its cinematography and editing, consistently strives to think of climbing philosophically, to render it an idea. This goes against the felt philosophising that comprises the act of climbing as Destivelle describes it. The film also refuses to refuse gender despite Destivelle's avowed resistance, in a climbing context, to the terms of sexual difference. The documentary ends with footage not of Destivelle at the cliff face, engaged in her profession, her passion, but with a shot of her and her son. The son compares an insect crawling on his hand to his mother's climbing, commending the creature's superior grip. It is an innocent comment yet its inclusion at the end of the documentary is not innocuous. Destivelle's accomplishments are shown to be limited. Her life as it is framed on screen culminates in motherhood (1.5). Motherhood can here be interpreted as an assertion of her femininity and the culmination of her life, the summit of her achievements. The threat or promise, depending on your perspective, of a world outside gender is here domesticated, made to fit a patriarchal view of the world. The narrative of the film strives to refuse Destivelle's message.

Teresa de Lauretis has argued that feminist theory should not be sought in 'the chinks and cracks of masculinity'.[66] The way *Au-delà des cimes* frames Destivelle's career shows that this is indeed the case. The cinematography, editing and narrative elements of the film each operate to negate Destivelle's insights. Through their gendered language, they function largely on men's terms. Destivelle, however, employs her pleasure in the non-gendered chinks and cracks of the mountains as a means to escape sexual categorisation in her embodied existence. The challenge is to communicate this pleasure, the aesthetic gratification provided by the given, through film. *Au-delà des cimes* is unfaithful to this pleasure. Its presentation of climbing is as an activity somewhere between a practice of existentialist philosophy and a mysterious, religious experience. The choral music composed by Jérôme Lemonnier encourages a soulful response to the documentary, as does the footage of the statue of the Virgin Mary on the Aiguille de Grépon that appears during the second climb featured in the documentary and at its end, and also some of the camerawork such as a shot on the first climb, heavenwards, featuring cliff against a lapis sky. The given is not stuff that provides spiritual sustenance, it bestows carnal pleasures. To get a grip on the given, an insight into a world beyond gender, climbing, in its rawness, requires communicating.

Hard Grit, on occasion, provides a means to briefly access the outside to culture that rock can give. The documentary, by way of its gritty realism, provides the viewer with something affirming, an insight into matters of the world. Material pleasures fall out of the action-adventure climbing film and are also suppressed in *Au-delà des cimes*. The climbs in the latter documentary take place, in large part, in near silence in contrast to the lively electronic score that accompanies the ascents in *Hard Grit*. In *Au-delà des cimes*, the loudest climb is the one at Aiguille Vert, when the sound of axes chunking, of fragments of névé falling and sliding down the cliff can be heard. The other climbs feature only occasional gasps of efforts and the steady clinking and jingling of karabiners, chocks and nuts that are being carried. This soft metal symphony possesses a degree of aesthetic appeal. It provides a substantial acoustic pleasure. The given, as conceived by Serres, does not, however, gently break language's hold on perception. It awakens individuals to the pleasures of their fleshly existence in painful ways. The intelligent techno and post-techno sounds on *Hard Grit*, are more aggressive than the diegetic soundscape or classical compositions of *Au-delà des cimes*, fostering a sonic environment more suited to the appreciation of noise, the underside to language.[67]

The process of conjoining with an environment, as previously mentioned, also takes time, time an action film will not usually allow. It is

1.6 *Hard Grit* (1998): Moving beyond words

therefore necessary to look for cracks in the celluloid, grasp them and haul the viewer towards them. *Hard Grit* with its repeated physical exertions, stretching and grasping, pulling and straining, progresses and arrests progress. Its differently repeated experiences of hard grit work cumulatively to vehicle a feel for rock. Through this, the documentary presses against language, engendering a kind of liberation from gender of the kind celebrated by Chisholm, and described by Hill and Destivelle. The sharp, or simply unyielding, solidity of grit chafes the hands of climbers. The feel of hard rock insinuates its way into the viewer's perception. The recurring shots of chalk being applied, and of chalk residue, impress this material on the viewer. Chalk is usually associated with education, writing practices. Chalk in climbing, however, is actually magnesium carbonate. It soaks up sweat and improves grip. In *Hard Grit*, it educates through the way it exsiccates language. Words lose their grasp on things. Climber and rock are shown in union. Dave Jones's ascent of the Braille Trail simultaneously forms a suppression of language and a rising above a phallic logic of domination. He is shown not mastering the wall but working with it, leaving words behind to feel things (1.6).

The sequence is sensual to behold. The moment of osmosis, as Destivelle calls it, or harmony, as Hill refers to it, between Jones and the grit is accompanied by a climbing free of gender.[68] It also involves an ascent into a space where a new ethics can emerge, a natural contract between two bodies, 'joined in a single aura'.[69] This contract, which must remain unsigned for there is no place for language where it is made, is one that bonds climber and cliff in a relationship that is equitable and non-appropriative.

2
Sexing the Canvas: Boxing Films

The Pugilist in Modern Life

The boxing ring is

> a place of some precision, being no less than sixteen nor more than twenty feet square, not more than four feet above the floor, bounded on all sides by at least four ropes, these not less than one inch in diameter, the lower rope being eighteen inches above the ring floor, the second rope thirty inches, the third rope forty-two and the fourth fifty-four; the floor being padded and the padding covered with canvas, tightly stretched and laced securely in place under the apron.[1]

The canvas, traditionally made from cotton, was usually white in colour for much of the twentieth century, and is now normally blue although other colours including black and red are sometimes used. This canvas forms part of a gendered space: the boxing ring. It sometimes functions as a metonym for the ring in its entirety. The boxing ring, like mountains in the previous chapter, is culturally coded as a masculine. The narrative space of the boxing film was also, for a long time, the exclusive domain of men.[2] In recent years, however, a number of films about boxing have been released with women as central characters, either fighters or, in the case of *Against the Ropes* (Dir. Charles S Dutton, USA, 2004), as a manager.

Griselda Pollock's exploration of the impact of the gendering of specific types of spaces in nineteenth-century Paris in her book *Vision and Difference* provides useful insights in relation to the study of gendered spaces and their representation. Pollock explains that several dimensions often require analysis in the study of such spaces. The first dimension is space as location, in Pollock's chosen context this requires considering what spaces bourgeois women Impressionist painters depicted in their works. In boxing, the space that is gendered male is seemingly self-evident, it is the ring. Films, however, demonstrate that boxing is not a sport that solely takes place there. Any aspiring fighter also requires access to a boxing gym. This is also a gendered space. In *Girlfight* (Dir. Karyn Kusama, USA 2000) and *Million Dollar Baby* (Dir. Clint Eastwood, USA, 2004), for example, women who wish to learn to box must first convince a gym to accept them.

The second dimension Pollock considers is 'that of the spatial order within paintings'.[3] Pollock perceives boundaries that existed between the spaces of masculinity and of femininity as informing the spatial constructions of some works by the Impressionist painters Mary Cassatt and Berthes Morisot. The two artists produce paintings that are characterised by closeness and compression. The compaction of pictorial space in their works is read by Pollock as homologous with 'the social confinement of women within the prescribed limits of bourgeois codes of femininity' at the time.[4] Pollock, however, is disappointed with this aspect of her analysis labelling it as social reflection theory with no explanatory value.[5] The paintings in such a reading are reduced to being illustrative with any performative (and, potentially, transformative) potential they might possess elided.

Pollock therefore argues that a third dimension also requires attention, in addition to the kinds of spaces represented and the ways in which those spaces are themselves spatially represented. This third dimension is 'the social spaces from which the representation is made', spaces 'from which femininity is lived as a positionality in discourse and social practice'.[6] It is space the experience of which is the product of 'social locatedness, mobility and visibility'.[7] Pollock draws on phenomenology to think through this space. There is a growing literature that draws on insights from phenomenology to study film. Phenomenological approaches, however, often fail to address cultural and gender differences of the kind that interest Pollock. Vivian Sobchack's nuanced understanding of the interaction of ontological conditions and epistemological limitations in the lived-body at a given historical moment provides a rare exception to this. She recognises that in phenomenology, 'sexual difference (and orientation) and "racial" difference have been ignored, although each human lived-body is, to at least some degree, a sexed and sexual body, and each has a skin, one of its qualities being colour'.[8] Sobchack acknowledges that 'the essential body is always a qualified body' by which she means that being-in-the-world is always being-in-a-particular-world.[9]

Pollock strives to recuperate one such particularity, bourgeois woman's being-in-the-world in Paris in the 1870s and 1880s. Her aim in doing this, however, is to reveal how the production of cultural forms such as painting potentially generates an opening through which alternative spaces of femininity can be negotiated. The world at a particular moment is always open to re-particularising. For Pollock, it is necessary to seek out other spatial possibilities because 'the spaces of femininity still regulate women's lives – from running the gauntlet of intrusive looks by men on the streets to surviving deadly sexual assaults'.[10]

The approach Pollock adopts, although formulated in relation to painting, is also highly informative when taken up in the context of space and motility in film at the levels of camerawork and narrative. Her work encourages exploration of bodily motility and its limits in the boxing film, not just in terms of women climbing into, or not climbing into the ring, but at the level of cinematography. Her subtle tracking, tracing, of the interface between artist and subject-matter is suggestive, in a cinematic context, of the integration of a dual motility (that of the body being filmed and of the camera doing the filming). This space of encounter will be examined, in particular, in relation to *Girlfight*, a film about a troubled teenager who learns to control her aggression through boxing. In *Girlfight*, the ways in which Patrick Cady's camerawork, under Karyn Kusama's direction, forms a hinge between the lived body and its representation will be examined.

In *Vision and Difference*, Pollock attends to visual rather than audio-visual representational practices. There is, however, an additional spatial dimension to consider in relation to depictions of boxing in film, which is the acoustic. Sound is also a spatial phenomenon. This chapter will therefore also additionally focus on how what Sobchack refers to as 'the epistemological conditions by which embodiment is culturally and historically known' are registered acoustically.[11] It will attend not just to the spaces of masculinity and femininity in boxing but also to how sound is registered in, and travels across, those spaces.

Physical Feminism

In sport, generally a traditionally male preserve, the space of contest, the court, field, or pitch, is often gendered as masculine. Deborah Tudor, for example, considers how a domestic space coded as feminine is contrasted with the masculine space of the baseball field in *The Winning Team* (Dir. Lewis Seiler, USA, 1952), a biopic about the career of Grover Cleveland Alexander.[12] The ostensible gendering of the boxing ring as a masculine space is a common theme in films about the sport in which the central protagonist is a woman. *Against the Ropes*, a film loosely based on the life story of boxing manager Jackie Kallen, is exemplary in this respect. It begins with Kallen as a young girl being told 'You do not belong up here' when she climbs into the ring at the gym where her father teaches. In her psychoanalytic reading of boxing, Shelley MacDonald identifies it as an 'oedipal contest'.[13] Fights form 'an oedipal challenge to the father, an overthrowing of his phallic stronghold'.[14] Boxing in such readings is all about manhood and becoming a man.

The ring cannot, however, be conceived of as ever simply a gendered space. It is, for example, frequently also a classed, ethnicised, and/or nationalised space. It is more like a series of spaces in and through which differing identities and ideologies have been, and are, articulated and embodied. The boxing ring, for instance, holds an important place in Hispanic culture. In the annals of boxing history a number of the great boxers, men such as Marco Antonio Barrera, Hector Camacho, Julio Cesar Chavez, Roberto Durán, Kid Gavilán, Oscar De La Hoya, Carlos Monzon, Erik Morales and Felix Trinidad, have been Hispanic. In the present, however, it is not only Hispanic men who fight regularly in boxing matches but also women.

The rise of the phenomenon of the Hispanic woman boxer has been powerfully attested to by the artist Delilah Montoya as part of a set of photographs titled *Women Boxers: the New Warriors*. A number of the women in these photographs, women such as Mariá Lucy Contreras, Jackie Chávez and Mónica Lovato, are Chicana or Latina. Hispanic women boxers have also received cinematic treatment in the films *Girlfight* and *Knockout* (Dir. Lorenzo Doumani, USA 2003). There are, however, women from a variety of class and ethnic backgrounds who now box professionally just as there are numerous female competitors, including Kyra Gracie, Claire Haigh, Ronda Rousey and Cristiane Santos who now participate in Mixed Martial Arts (MMA). Sportswomen are becoming commonplace in combat sports. Their rising numbers are reflected in the growing amount of films that depict women fighting competitively.

Combat sports can be interpreted as embodying physical feminism. Practitioners of this kind of feminism can provide an alternative way of imaging womanhood which offers a valuable role-model and counterpoint to traditional iconographies of femininity grounded in fear and passivity.[15] Physical feminism is 'feminism in the flesh'.[16] It is a form of feminist activism which is articulated through the body, through changes in bodily comportment that challenge stereotypes about women's corporeal potential. In this sense it provides similar possibilities to the practice of climbing discussed in the last chapter. The values of patriarchy, including the idea that women are passive, physically weak and require male protection, are impressed in the flesh. Male domination is 'an embodied politics'.[17] In *Real Knockouts*, a work which argues for perceiving women's self-defence as a form of physical feminism, Martha McCaughey contends that women can pose a substantial challenge to rape culture through dismantling 'the assumption that women have victim-bodies, that is, weak, small, boundariless, and ineffective bodies'.[18] She suggests that learning how to fight, to defend the self, 'exposes rape culture as an embodied ideology'.[19]

Women who can fight counter the myth of male strength and female weakness, a myth which helps to facilitate rape culture. Their strong bodies comprise a powerful rhetoric, a persuasive argument articulated through the body. Physical feminism as sexual politics is therefore a somatic politics. It is expressed through muscles and sinews, through aggressive and confident physical movement. This corporeal politics demonstrates that 'patterns of movement' are habitual rather than natural.[20] That physical, and mental, strength can be cultivated by women just as successfully as by men. The body of the woman boxer, aggressively confident, forms a physical counterpoint to the patriarchal privileging of male corporeality. She shows that the physical is political, practising a form of consciousness raising through the flesh.

McCaughey refers to boxing only tangentially in her work but the female pugilist appears to provide a comparable expression of corporeal feminism to that of the woman who has become adept at a martial art. Boxing may also have more appeal for many women as a form of physical politics. McCaughey's analysis largely ignores how alienating some kinds of martial arts courses, with their unfamiliar, ritualistic component, would be for women from backgrounds such as the projects in New York or the barrios of Los Angeles, those places against which the dramas of *Girlfight* and *Knockout* respectively unfold. African-American and Hispanic women will often be familiar with boxing because the men in their lives will hold an interest in or even practise the sport. It comprises a familiar activity even if it is associated with masculinity. Martial arts courses and firearms training courses (the latter providing another example of physical feminism for McCaughey) could also risk being beyond the financial means of many women living in relative poverty in countries such as the United States. If physical feminism is restricted to these kinds of courses then it becomes a bourgeois preserve. Boxing therefore offers an important supplement to the examples of physical feminism provided and examined by McCaughey.

Violence in the Home

It is implied that the reason the main character in *Girlfight*, Diana Guzman, a 'teenage Latina', implicitly joins a gym and begins to box is because as a child she witnessed domestic violence.[21] Her father, Sandro Guzman, beat his wife repeatedly until eventually she committed suicide. Diana's discomfort in domestic space, a space still often gendered as feminine, is indicated by the use of a slow zoom at one point when Diana, her father and her brother Tiny are having dinner. The use of the zoom is not obvious to the spectator, the camera almost imperceptibly closing on the characters, but the proximity it gradually generates should be one which brings home the intimacy of this family. Instead, however, through the conversation at the dinner table it records, it functions to foreground the insolvable distance between the father and his children brought about by his brutal behaviour.

The zoom also serves to compress space. It restricts the audience's field of vision and gets in the face of Diana. The framing of shots, especially at mealtimes, also emphasises containment. The cinematography, through such techniques, can be seen to confine Diana. It movement embodies the patriarchal logic identified by Young which works to inhibit women's embodied existence.[22] Zooming in, getting close, reduces the space available for a character to inhabit. It diminishes the distance between audience and character potentially producing intimacy yet also intruding on physical space. The close-up can act as an encouragement to empathy, as Mary Ann Doane suggests in *The Desire to Desire*, or as a form of physical oppression.[23]

The film begins with a scene of a downcast Diana in a school corridor, standing with her back to a row of lockers. The camera advances towards her until it is in close-up. She raises her eyes to address the lens, confronts the camera's invasive presence. The camera will regularly intrude on her personal space throughout the film. She is shown at one point, for example, channel surfing at home, bored and restive. The camera gradually advances on her. It presses up to her. In its refusal to maintain a discreet distance, in its obtrusion, the camera mirrors men's invasion of women's space as identified by Young.[24]

Diana is not just painfully aware of the reality of violence in the home. She also describes the potential for violation as something that haunts her general surroundings. At one point in the film, she speaks to her future boyfriend, Adrian, of the danger of being 'raped in your own fucking stairwell'. In this context, in which violence against women is a common occurrence, boxing offers a way of seeking to avoid potential abuse and disrespect though developing the capacity to defend against physical attack. A key moment in the film occurs when Diana physically overpowers Sandro and 'by being as threatening as he ever was,' holds 'a mirror up to her father where he can see what abuse looks and feels like'.[25]

Diana therefore appears to cultivate equality, or even superiority, in aggression with men. This opens up the important question as to whether Diana is compounding the problem of violence in the home (rather than challenging it) through borrowing of its logic. She now participates in violence rather than being a potential recipient of it. After she takes up boxing, however, Diana's aggression is never directed towards those incapable of being aggressive themselves. The aggression she displays seems to be of a different order to that of, for example, Sandro. It is defensive rather than offensive. It is also important to note that after she confronts Sandro he is 'transformed by the experience'.[26] He no longer queries and mocks her pursuit of pugilism. The cultivation of aggression in women therefore opens itself to being read as an important dimension in the feminist struggle against a culture that fosters male violence.

Girlfight as an exemplar of physical feminism teaches that women must develop the potential to respond to aggression with aggression in order to break a cycle of viciousness that is founded on the belief that women are incapable of reacting to violence with violence. Diana's actions alter Sandro's perception of her. He previously ignored her but now he sees her. She takes up space. Diana says to him: 'All those years you just looked right through me'. She has, however, now become a woman of substance.

That this is the case is confirmed shortly after in a scene with Adrian when Diana, recognising her new found status, says: 'So I'm someone, huh?'

Diana's emulation of her father demonstrates the artificiality of the notion that aggression is a purely masculine trait. She is not, however, a carbon copy. She channels her aggression differently. It is only within the confines of the ring that Diana is actively, rather than reactively, aggressive. Here, however, aggression is invited rather than imposed upon people. It is expected that it will be both received and returned. The boxing ring forms a place in which hostility is both sanctioned and encouraged. Aggression, however, is conventionally coded as a male quality. The boxing ring, as an outlet for aggression, is a space traditionally gendered as masculine. Diana's presence in this space therefore embodies a challenge to gender stereotypes.

Mirroring

The only women traditionally seen in the boxing ring are the so-called 'ring girls' who climb into the ring between rounds to announce the number of each forthcoming round by holding up large numbered cards.[27] The ring girls, frequently tall and slim, 'sexily strut, in very high heels'.[28] Carlo Rotella describes the public 'body work' they perform as akin to sex work.[29] Shelley MacDonald suggests 'she always stands on the periphery, the inner sanctum is for men only'.[30] One of these women is depicted briefly in *Girlfight* in the scene in which Diana accompanies her trainer, Hector, to watch a night of professional boxing matches at the Tropicana in Atlantic City. The blonde woman is shown occupying the ring only in the 'between time' of the fight. She participates in the fight during its suspension. She does not step into the ring when it is a charged space of combat but when the boxers are in their corners and at rest.

The ring girls are present to add 'glamour' to the sport. In *The Opponent*, a film about a woman, Patty, who is trapped in a violent relationship and takes up boxing as a means of escape, Patty's introduction to the sport is as a ring girl with her friend June at a fight night. Their employer, Fred, describes them afterwards as 'the only two knockouts in the ring'. The women who perform roles such as that undertaken by June and Patty are also present to implicitly offset any potential homoerotic anxiety amongst the male spectators generated by the body of each boxer being 'on display'.³¹ Those men and women who are present at a match have paid for the privilege of watching a series of muscled, sweat-glistening physiques engage in fights which occasionally involve almost as much clinching as punching. Boxing requires a significant amount of physical contact beyond the landing of blows on an opponent. The scene showing the audience at Atlantic City opens up important issues around desire and the gaze in relation to boxing as it is represented in *Girlfight*. The camerawork in the scene appears designed to mirror what Diana sees, what holds her attention, the shots and reverse shots establishing our relation to her gaze. She smiles, signalling her visual pleasure in the spectacle, men being the objects of this appraising and appreciative look. Katharina Lindner has drawn attention to how *Girlfight* reverses gender norms at the level of looking.³²

The gaze in films frequently, although not always, functions to reinforce patriarchal values, as Laura Mulvey has famously observed, Women in mainstream cinema are often displayed as sexual objects, present to satisfy and signify male desire.³³ Woman as such a construction is supposed to function as the object of the gaze not to possess it. This is echoed by Young when she writes that an essential aspect of sexist society for women is that 'of living the ever-present possibility that one will be gazed upon as mere body, as shape and flesh that presents itself as the potential object of another subject's intentions and manipulations, rather than as a living manifestation of action and intention'.³⁴ In Atlantic City, Diana owns her desiring look in a way that is still a relative rarity in mainstream cinema.

There is, however, another notable instance of the inscription of a clear female gaze in *The Opponent*. When Patty first meets Tommy, who will become her trainer, they are in a limousine. When not boxing, he moonlights as a chauffeur. Patty is seated in the back of the car and as they talk, Tommy is filmed looking in the rear view mirror in order to see her. The camera provides the audience with Patty's sight of herself being seen. In the exchange both each other as reflection, talk to each other's representation. It is, however, Patty's point of view that is privileged. In *Girlfight*, there is a scene after the visit to Atlantic City in which Diana is shown boxing with another woman, Ricki Stiles, Hector looks at Diana not with desire but with approval and admiration. The two boxing films therefore stage challenges to dominant modes of looking and to the power relations they uphold. They show that there are others ways of seeing women and for women to see than those prescribed by patriarchy and by the culturally dominant forms of representation that perpetuate its values.

The role of vision in the maintenance of sexual difference is established early in *Girlfight* when the viewer sees a schoolgirl, Veronica, putting on make-up in a mirror in the girl's toilets. This offers a view of women as narcissistic and overly concerned with perfecting a beautiful appearance. The shot of Veronica, vain and self-absorbed, authorises 'the spectator's enjoyment of her displayed and shapely form'.[35] Later in the film, however, Diana is shown shadow-boxing in a mirror in her bedroom. The mirror here is not employed as a means to beautify the self but rather as a tool by which to improve pugilistic technique. A third use of mirrors by women is provided in *The Opponent*. Patty is shown in the run-up to working as a ring girl applying concealer to hide the black eye her boyfriend has given her. She checks in a mirror that the bruising has become invisible. Later in the film, however, she looks in a mirror at the gym whilst skipping, observing her footwork. The mirror can therefore function either to reflect oppression or contribute to empowerment.

In another scene, Diana weighs herself at Hector's house and her increase in weight is understood as a thing to be celebrated rather than as something shameful and to be condemned. Self surveillance is exercised in regard to weight but not as a means to conform to oppressive ideals of female slenderness. The traditional concerns with appearance and weight are contested. Diana provides an alternative image of femininity for young women in general and Hispanic women in particular, to see, identify with, and aspire to. Her body and demeanour, her aggression and vigour, is one which resists a patriarchal logic of female corporeal disempowerment. She represents instead 'the ethnic female action heroine with a hard body' who 'is not sexually objectified'.[36]

Sounding Like a Girl

Young's understandings of feminine bodily comportment, and some of the limitations of her analysis, were discussed at length in the previous chapter. For her, the impact of patriarchy manifests itself in women's bodies through a modality characterised by restricted motion. As part of her discussion of this modality, Young draws attention to how the role of vision, the quality of being looked at, impacts on women's self-perception in patriarchy. She also identifies how a woman must live with 'the threat of invasion of her body space'.³⁷ Touch, as will be discussed in more detail in the next chapter, is frequently experienced differently by the sexes. Young, however, does not examine the potential relationships that exist between bodily comportment and the other senses, smell, taste, and hearing. Hearing, in particular, is bound up with spatiality in obvious ways. Sound travels through space. It is projected into space.

Young argues that women's objectified bodily existence, their consciousness of being looked at, means that, on the whole, they are forced to 'take a distance from and exist in discontinuity with [their bodies]'.³⁸ Women, however, are also conscious of being heard or of not being heard. The consciousness of audibility, of being too loud or not loud enough, also impacts on embodied existence. Women often do not 'throw' their voices far enough. The vocal restrictions they sometimes place on themselves restrict their use of space, how far their speech, and other vocalisations, carries. In the desire to sound 'ladylike', some women will monitor, moderate, the volume of their voice. Loud volume is linked to male dominance.³⁹ This was powerfully demonstrated in the last chapter by the way Ness responds to the commanding vocalisation, the fierce scream into surrounding terrain, of the male climber.

The impact of patriarchy on feminine acoustic comportment is not, however, restricted to issues of loudness. Women often do not exploit the range of their vocal palette to the full either. The muscles in the larynx are used to 'colour our voices with affection, bitterness, pleasure, disgust, etc.'.⁴⁰ The formidable range of expression enabled by these muscles has led Anne Karpf to describe the vocal chromatics performed by people in general as rendering them 'Leonardos of the larynx'.⁴¹ The space immediately surrounding a given person provides the canvas they paint with their vocalisations. There are some forms of colouring, aggression, condescension, starkness, that women are less likely to employ.

Karpf also draws attention to how the way some women speak 'with shoulders rounded, chest collapsed, and without taking a full breath' may be bound up with a desire not to take up too much space.⁴² The physical timidity described by Young has a practical impact on vocalisation. Bodies that move freely in, and through, space are more successful at projecting sound into it. Sound, however, is not restricted to the voice. Many of the sounds encountered in everyday existence, including whilst participating in sports, are produced by technologies other than the vocal chords. Here too, motional timidity will translate into a loss of volume. This has implications in terms of the ways in which quieter actions may reinforce women's negative perceptions about their physical abilities.

In *Listening and Voice*, Don Ihde refers to what he calls 'the voices of things'.[43] These voices are sounds made by things, either independently as in birdsong or through human action such as when a boxer strikes an otherwise silent punch-bag. Ihde suggests that 'the voices of things bespeak the multiple dimensions of the thing'.[44] He uses the example of a table to illustrate this, suggesting that 'the solidity of the table is bespoken when it sounds, even in some cases telling us of its kind of materiality'.[45] The noise of knuckles can also be heard. A duet is involved. The boxer who punches a heavy bag similarly sounds it, revealing its relative hardness and solidity. They also, however, sound themselves. They disclose the firmness of the gloved fist and also the force of their blow. Durán was popularly known as '*manos de piedra*', 'hands of stone', the quality of hardness attributed to him could be heard when he took to the ring. The boxer listens to, as well as feels and sees, their strength. The less forceful the boxer's punch is, the quieter the sound of the impact of bag and glove. If a man or a woman punches with inhibition, they will hear their half-heartedness in the sound of the blow. In this way, a woman's lack of belief in her physical capacities will be echoed back to her. Sound, as well as motion, is therefore a vital site of contestation for women's liberation.

This is, however, often not recognised. In *The Opponent*, for example, when training Patty in front of a mirror, Tommy initially asks her to visualise herself as Wonder Woman. Patty will be familiar with this image of female empowerment from comics and television. Gloria Steinem has written of how inspiring the comic book character potentially is as a role model for both adults and children.[46] Wonder Woman, however, is primarily registered as a figure to be looked at by Tommy and (if she follows his instructions) by Patty. Tommy's point of reference is therefore potentially telling. He may choose Wonder Woman as an example rather than a boxer such as Muhammad Ali or Durán because he feels Patty will be unlikely to know what these fighters looked like in action. He may also, however, select the Amazon princess because this is how he wants to visualise Patty. The choice of illustration might signal his desire for her, a desire that is given explicit expression later. What is most noteworthy about the scene in the context of sound, however, is its emphasis on achievement through vision. Tommy does not ask her to imagine the sound of Wonder Woman. Sound, however, is a key way by which achievement and cruelty are shown in the film.

The abusive boyfriend in *The Opponent*, Jack, recognises that his aggression is, in part, acoustic. He apologises to Patty at one point for raising his voice. She responds by asking 'Can I go now?' It is noteworthy that this question is uttered more softly than Jack's apology. Patty is oppressed by, and afraid to make, sound.[47] The vocal violence enacted against women under patriarchy is also demonstrated later at Patty's first fight as an amateur. Her appearance in the ring is greeted by catcalls and shouts of 'Take it off!' prompted by her attractiveness. Some of the audience would prefer to witness a striptease rather than a boxing match. Patty's opponent, a heavyset woman, is greeted by a shout of 'Don't take it off!' Woman's role as spectacle for the male gaze and as sexual object is communicated through sound. Once the fight starts, however, the majority of the audience begin to cheer and clap in recognition of the courage and determination of the two fighters. There is an audible shift in perception, perhaps an acoustic registration of the breaking down of stereotypes. Jack witnesses some of this fight and then confronts Patty afterwards, intent on taking her back to his house. Tommy tries to intervene suggesting that she does not wish to leave with him: 'All I'm saying is . . . ' Jack cuts him off. His asserts his command over acoustic space by silencing others.

Patty, however, gradually learns to make forceful sounds of her own, to intervene energetically in space acoustically. This liberating noisiness can be heard most clearly in the last fight of the film in which Patty confronts the fighter Red Lennox played by actual boxer Andrea Nelson. Patty's punches, and the blows she receives, register with significant acoustic force. The sounds function to assert the impact of the blows the two women are trading. In Ihde's terms, the aggressive duet bespeaks two powerful and resilient bodies. Women listening to this encounter can hear forceful sounds that challenge the usual male dominance of acoustic space.

The journey towards sonic freedom that can be heard in *The Opponent* is acoustically mirrored in *Girlfight*. In an early scene, Diana is shown walking towards the gym taking money for her brother's boxing lesson to his trainer. She strides beneath a subway overpass and the sound of the train's horn and the loud clunking of the bogies along the track can be heard. The urban environment is figured as a site of acoustic oppression. The domestic violence featured in the film is also registered sonically.

Sandro initially endeavours to exert control over his daughter's voice in the scene in which they physically fight. As Diana is berating him for his wife-beating, her father angrily responds shouting 'Shut up with that... I said shut up with that!' Sandro here bellicosely endeavours to exert control over acoustic space and silence his daughter's vocal accusations. In his rage he then smashes a beer bottle. This noise echoes that of an earlier scene in which Diana shatters a plate in anger. Here aggressive similarities between father and daughter are asserted through sound as well as vision.

In the boxing ring, Diana learns to make herself heard. The fight with another woman boxer, Stiles, for example, involves numerous loud thwacks, the sounds of both pugilists punching and being punched. Diana's ability to produce forceful noises of this kind contributes to her growing sense of control over space. The ring becomes a place where she can impose herself acoustically. Diana, of course, also acts as a sounding board for Stiles's strength. The punches from Stiles she withstands whilst practising her sport reaffirming her growing sense of substantiality, her own body's durability. Like Patty against Red Lennox, she hears her way towards freedom from acoustic oppression through the loud sounds of combat. The sounds made by Diana's body offer aggressive acoustics for the female listener to identify with.

Making Space

Girlfight and *The Opponent*, however, do not only challenge the acoustic gendering of space. They also involve liberated uses of zones of existence culturally constructed as masculine. *Girlfight*, as already examined, draws attention to the dangers women face in urban spaces. Violence against women frequently causes trauma. This can lead to physical inhibitions, including a reluctance to venture into specific spaces. Sexual assault victims, for example, can employ what are called avoidance coping strategies to deal with the trauma of their experience. Avoidance coping strategies are negative as they involve averting dealing with stressful or traumatic events. Coping strategies of this kind include the use of alcohol or drugs, withdrawal from others, moving to a new place, and quitting employment or education.[48] Withdrawal from others can involve a reluctance to socialise and participate in group activities. It has a spatial dimension. The withdrawn individual reduces their openness to the world. Diana and Patty do not employ avoidance coping strategies despite their harrowing experiences of violence in the home. Rather, boxing provides them with an approach coping strategy.

Approach coping strategies are active rather than reactive. They involve confronting the source of stress or trauma through activities such as joining a support group, visiting a therapist or undertaking self-defence classes. Self-defence is usually associated with martial arts but boxing forms their equivalent in these films. Studies have suggested that participating in self-defence classes, practising the kind of physical feminism encouraged by McCaughey, potentially improves the wellbeing of women with chronic symptoms of trauma.[49] A project called Taking Charge, a therapeutic self-defence programme designed for 12 female army veterans with Post Traumatic Stress Disorder (PTSD) caused by sexual trauma, produced findings that support this view.[50] Diana and Patty are not portrayed as suffering from sexual trauma yet they are shown to be victims of violence. Boxing proves therapeutic for them in that it enables them to discover a new openness towards the world and experience an altered relationship to space.

The theme of space is referred to openly in the dialogue of *The Opponent*. Jack states to Patty at one point: 'I've been giving you space, right?' Space, however, should not be his to give or take. Boxing as a sport is, in part, about fighting over the control of space. It therefore enables Diana and Patty to learn to resist spatial constraints. Ring craft, the tactics employed in the confined space of the boxing ring, can involve reducing the space available for an opponent to move in. Adversaries can be cornered or pinned against the ropes. Fighters, however, may also need to create space themselves in order to punch with as much force as possible. Boxing is therefore, in part, a ritualised battle over space, access to it or denial of it. It teaches fighters spatial awareness not simply in terms of mindfulness of their immediate surroundings, but also in relation to how space is always bound up with control and mastery. The ring forms a microcosm of society, with its gendered, classed, ethnicised, aged and other spaces. The ring may involve battling over space yet it simultaneously teaches awareness of and respect for it.

The way boxing contributes to broadening the space available to the women is registered in the climactic fights they participate in. These occur in bigger auditoriums than the previous contests. There is literally more space in these scenes. This increased room outside the ring provides a metaphor for the greater spatial freedom boxing has permitted the women in their everyday lives. In this context, *Million Dollar Baby*, in which boxing leads Maggie Fitzgerald to become paralysed and confined to bed, can be read as a film that punishes woman's desire for space. It echoes the story of the female toreador, Lydia González, in *Talk to Her* (Dir. Pedro Almodóvar, Spain, 2002) who has dared to transgress the gendered space of the bullring. Lydia is fatally gored but suffers a lingering death, comatose for a long time in a hospital bed. The desire of these women for greater freedom of movement, more social space, is punished by immobility. There are also boxing films such as *Punch* (Dir. Guy Bennett, Canada, 2003), which features topless boxing at a bar, in which women's spatial freedom simply remains restricted throughout. In *Punch*, all but one contest is in a ring situated in claustrophobic confines. The last fight, a brawl, occurs in a garage.

The growing freedom of Diana and Patty is also communicated through interactions with male characters in the films. There is, for example, a scene in *Girlfight* in which Adrian acknowledges to Diana: 'I don't feel too big right now, as a matter of fact I feel pretty fucking small around you!' Boxing has enabled Diana to increase in stature. She now takes up more space in Adrian's perception. In *The Opponent*, Jack manhandles Patty. In the scene in which he states that he has been giving her space, he subsequently takes hold of her so that she has to insistently state 'Let go of my arm!' Later, however, when Jack confronts Patty in a bar, standing in front of her, she confidently pushes past him. Boxing has given her the assurance to assert her right to space and successfully challenge his efforts to restrict her access to it.

The ends of both films also demonstrate the centrality of space to their narratives. *The Opponent* ends with Patty walking ahead of Tommy into the fire-damaged remains of the gym which had been subject to an arson attack. She disappears inside. Tommy calls after her: 'Patty, Patty, where are you going?' She is shown to be choosing her own path here. Tommy has to decide whether to follow her in whatever direction she takes. The ending is one that depicts a spatially independent woman. It is a conclusion that is echoed in *Girlfight*. In the final scene, Adrian seeks out Diana after losing to her in their gender blind boxing contest. She is in her locker room at the gym and has just removed some chipboard which concealed a cracked window, filling the previously dingy space with light.

Their conversation is mutually respectful. The esteem they hold for each other born of their encounter in the ring. It is a bodily admiration that is known through subsequent bruising, tender flesh: memories of forceful impacts. Adrian and Diana are a class apart from most around them. Adrian says 'I gave you everything I had.' Here, his unreserved aggression, skilfully deployed, marks his high regard for Diana. The two fighters have shared a particular kind of intimacy: violent, artful and measured. The fact that neither held back, that there was no gentlemanly courtesy, no ladylike reserve, there were no spatial checks, meant they produced a fight of intense, immense depth, one determinedly detached from gender. Like the aftermath of Chris Eubank's magnificent first fight with Nigel Benn, in which hatred was replaced by profound appreciation, post-fight Adrian and Diana are reconciled. They had never disliked each other. Adrian, however, struggled with Diana's desire to take to the ring, her right to fight him. Through their equality in violence they demonstrate how aggression, as Maud Lavin suggests, can provide openings, potential forms of empowerment.[51]

Diana's superior ring craft has shown Adrian that his dreams of a career in boxing will never become a reality. Resigned to this, he wistfully states: 'Boxing, going pro, I wanted it to be my ticket out...' The couple are still spatially constrained in terms of class. They continue to be bound to the projects, to New York's public housing. Diana, however, has discovered new spatial freedom. She reaches out, caresses his face. It is a gentle gesture. Notably, she is initiating contact, moving into Adrian's body space. Caudwell has read Diana's initiating of sexual intimacy as disturbing heteronormativity.[52] This moment should not be understood as invasive, as a simple reversal of the patriarchal dynamics of touch. The two lovers have already demonstrated in the ring that they afford each other equal opportunity in terms of physical contact. Diana's affectionate gesture is an extension of that liberated tactility. They embrace each other, holding each other as if in the ring (except that this time there is no need to break apart, no requirement to make room in order to resume fighting). Diana looks over Adrian's shoulder, out of the window, into space. It is a space she has fought hard for and finally attained.

A Role of One's Own

In *Girlfight*, once Diana has demonstrated her dedication to training, she is given the key to her own locker. She cannot, however, change in the men's locker room. Her own 'locker' therefore turns out to be not a locker but a former storage space. Boxing provides her with a room of her own. She is given her own space in the gym. *Girlfight*, however, does more than depict its central character attaining spatial emancipation. The film also grants Diana as a character narrative freedom. Narrative can also be conceived of spatially. The storyline of a given film provides certain characters with room to grow and develop and restricts others to bit part roles involving little or no elaboration of their personality. In the context of the novel, E.M. Forster defined characters as either flat or round. Flatness is associated with a lack of relief or projection. The flat character does not take up much space. In sports films, women characters have traditionally assumed this shallow status. Jessie Deighan, whose minor role in *Cliffhanger* was discussed in the last chapter, provides a good example of this one-dimensionality. In *Girlfight*, Veronica, who never rises above vacuous vanity, provides another.

Forster suggests that, in its purest form, the flat character is 'constructed round a single idea or quality'.[53] They are like 'little luminous discs of a pre-arranged size, pushed hither and thither like counters across the void or between the stars; most satisfactory'.[54] Forster takes pleasure in characters of a set volume that can be pushed around. They do not require much investment from the writer. They also demand little of the reader, who easily recognises them. Flat characters, however, can be a cause of controversy as Forster acknowledges when he recounts an argument about their value conducted between Norman Douglas and D.H. Lawrence, described as 'a doughty pair of combatants, the hardness of whose hitting makes the rest of us feel like a lot of ladies up in the pavilion'.[55] Forceful combat, be it at boxing or, as may be the case here, cricket, is figured as a masculine pursuit, although not one all men can engage in. Douglas and Lawrence trade blows with words rather than bats or fists in Forster's enlightening analogy. It is one that implies that some ways of writing, confrontational, quarrelsome, are unladylike. The literary spat is a man's privilege. Some modes of authoring, forms of narrative, literary or filmic, are gendered spaces.

Forster's first example of a writer who produces round characters is Jane Austen. Round characters are changeable, possessing the capacity to surprise readers. They possess a dimension which enables them to, at least momentarily, resist appearing formulaic. The round character grows. Diana's process of becoming a woman of substance, her development, gives her a rotundity the ever vain Veronica lacks. Forster's choice of

Austen's writing as one of characteristic roundness demonstrates that the novel is not a literary genre that is coded as masculine. Virginia Woolf also recognised the capacity for women to write novels in *A Room of One's Own*. She uses Austen as an example of this achievement and also to explore why, in the early nineteenth century, women were predominantly restricted to that literary form. Woolf believes the novel was favoured as it required less concentration. It could be composed in a general sitting room, by a woman with no room of her own.[56] Woolf imagines Austen in such a room, being 'glad that a hinge creaked, so that she might hide her manuscript before anyone came in'.[57] She describes the author as concealing her compositions, covering them with blotting paper.

Woolf's historically informed vision of Austen is of a woman who must behave timidly in relation to her chosen profession. Her lack of openness about her novel writing, her inhibitions, echoes Young's description of typical feminine movement under patriarchy. In his discussion of Austen, Forster's analysis suggests that this reserve extends to the content of the novels. He states that 'physical violence is quite beyond Miss Austen's powers'.[58] There is no space in her works for pugnacity. Austen is 'feeble and ladylike' and has no stomach for such things.[59] She fulfils one of the many criteria Woolf discovers men have ascribed to women to explain the poverty of their sex: 'weaker muscles'.[60] Because of this frailty, violent events in Austen have to 'take place "off"–'.[61] They occur beyond the space of the page. Here, however, it appears to be Forster who refuses to depict Austen in the round. There are strong characters in her novels that belie the feebleness he attributes to her even if there is no on page violence.

Most notable, in this regard, is Catherine Morland in *Northanger Abbey* who preferred 'cricket, baseball, riding on horseback, and running about the country at the age of fourteen to books'.[62] Morland at 15, however, is pleased 'to look *almost* pretty'.[63] Young states that 'an essential part of the situation of being a woman is that of living the ever-present possibility that one will be gazed upon as a mere body, as shape and flesh that presents itself as the potential object of another subject's intentions and manipulations, rather than as a living manifestation of action and intention'.[64] Austen describes this situation coming into being, the emergence of Morland's awareness that she is there to be looked at. Aspects of Diana and Veronica are present in Morland. The novel makes clear what the young woman has to give up if she wishes to become a 'catch'. She must sacrifice vigorous movement through space. Reserve is not an innate quality. It is cultivated. Through the character of Morland, Austen shows she recognises the limits of her situation and what is lost because of it.

Woolf does not find that Austen's straitened circumstances, her covert literariness, impacted on the quality of her writing. She does, however, detect flaws in other women novelists such as Charlotte Brontë, which she ascribes to constraints placed on her because of her sex. Brontë 'will write of herself where she should write of her characters' because 'she is at war with her lot'.[65] In such circumstances, Woolf asks, 'how could she help but die young, cramped and thwarted?'.[66] The strong character development in *Girlfight*, in Kusama's script, seems to demonstrate that there is less restraint imposed on contemporary women writers. The space of the page is more open to them and, by extension, the characters they delineate are rounder and challenge the flat supporting roles traditionally accorded to women in sports films. Through its script, *Girlfight* illustrates the reduced social confinement of some women screenwriters in the present. Stories can now be written for the boxing genre in which women transcend the background story, are foregrounded as athletes in their own right, rounded. In this context, when Diana is granted a room at the gym it also signals Kusama has a room of her own. The themes of pugilism and of violence in the home also show that aggression can take centre page in Kusama's writing.

Brushes with the Camera

In *A Room of One's Own*, during her investigation of women's status through history, Woolf discovers that wife beating was formerly a recognised right of man.[67] Violence against women is not, however, restricted to the physical. The reduction of woman to an objectified bodily existence, her subjection to the male gaze, as discussed by Young also forms a kind of brutality. Woman's reduction to spectacle flattens her. She is inhibited, rendered superficial. Cinematography can contribute to this process of compression. The close-up, for example, is frequently employed to film female characters. This technique detaches the face of woman, or another body part, from the rest of her body, decapitates or amputates. It is also invasive. The close-up encroaches, closes down distance. It restricts space, reducing seen to surface, to an image rather than 'threshold onto a world'.[68] As Doane explains, this process of approach, of diminution of distance, leads the close-up to use up and exhaust all space.[69]

Space is central to Woolf's polemic. Early in the essay she recounts two instances of the policing of space by men. She is harangued for walking on the lawn at an Oxbridge college, a privilege not accorded to visitors. She is also advised that she cannot enter a college library without a Fellow escorting her or presenting a letter of introduction.[70] She is forced to occupy particular spaces and refused entry to others. In film, space is also frequently policed. This renders the film set like a boxing ring, the screen like canvas. It is a space across which conflict over space is played out. It is itself a space of conflict. Camerawork can involve closing down space, closing in on things. Or it can broaden horizons, provide panoramic views.

Girlfight begins with Diana's back to a wall of lockers. As discussed already, there is a sense of claustrophobia evoked by camerawork, by zooms in, close-ups, and tight framing. Diana's downcast eyes at the start of the film signal a desire to avoid the look of the camera. To avoid can mean to withdraw, to retire, to retreat. It is associated with the surrender of space. Her attitude is, however, ambivalent. In the opening scene she eventually raises eyes, addresses the lens. She has not physically moved forward yet her gaze crosses space. It signals an approach towards the camera. To approach means to draw nearer to. It involves advancing through space. The film ultimately shows that Diana is willing to confront not just her father but the culture he represents as it is embodied at the level of cinematography.

This is made most obvious in Diana's fight with Stiles. The contest incorporates an editing technique which causes brief instances of blindness to form part of the viewing experience. In the fights, the camera is occasionally positioned at the level of where the face of an opponent would be. The lens becomes the face of the opponent (2.1). It alternates between being the face of Diana and of Stiles as it is punched. During the portrayal of the landing of particularly hard punches, the film cuts briefly to a white screen, a blank image, a nothing.[71] On one level, this blankness signifies seeing stars. It is a celluloid attempt to embody the experience of pain (a kind of non-experience), to depict the feel of the impact of a punch. The technique brings a sense of discomfort to the film comparable to the painful sequences in *Hard Grit* discussed in the last chapter. There is an effort to give the 'given', the body in pain. Elaine Scarry has referred to pain as language destroying. It brings the body to the fore.[72] Here the film image is repeatedly briefly wiped out. The spectacle

2.1 *Girlfight* (2000): Aggressing the lens

of the match is recurrently marred. This is done to suggest the shocks of blows. It comprises an assault on film language that also gives emphasis to the corporeal.

The head punch is highly fetishised in boxing. Writing of the drama of the contest as it is captured in still photographs, Lynda Nead sees the essence of portrayals of head punches to be 'the physical juxtaposition of two kinds of body: the puncher and the punched; the ideal and its disfigurement'.[73] This juxtaposition is bound up with masculinity via a series of dualisms: 'victor/vanquished; metal instrument vs. rubber face; hard man vs. soft, feminized man'.[74] Boxing is a binary exposition *par excellence*. Through drawing on the idea of 'pulp' as an aberrant material that is both hard and soft, Nead interprets the head as it is punched, pulped in boxing matches to contribute to the contest as deconstructive event. It is an event in which traces of femininity are found at the centre of a spectacle that should be a bulwark for masculinity. The hard body is given a pasting, bloodied, rendered fluid. Nead does not pursue in what ways this dynamic changes, if at all, when the boxers striving to embody and maintain hardness happen to be women. If boxing also enables access to the given, however, then there is an aspect of fighting that is divorced from the deconstructive dimension Nead identifies. Hardness as the given, as a slur of sensation beyond language, operates in addition to, in excess of, the kind of hardness that stands for masculinity.

In addition to signalling stinging punches, gesturing towards the given, the white flashes also form instances of absence within the sequence. There is a lack of image. The seamless continuity usually perfected by way of smooth editing is here interrupted. In this 'economy of vision', the viewer is made to apprehend lack.[75] Sight, scopic mastery, is interrupted. Mischa Merz has written that 'the technique of evasion gets to the heart of what is artful about boxing'.[76] In these whiteouts the object of the gaze sidesteps the gaze. The viewer is forced to see nothing. They are momentarily isolated from the spectacle, seeing only film, a layer of white, a screen. This way of depicting the fight can be interpreted as striking a 'blow against the monolithic accumulation of traditional film conventions' that frees 'the look of the camera into its materiality in time and space and the look of the audience into dialectics and passionate detachment'.[77]

It is also, however, possible to read this sequence as foregrounding a contest that has been taking place, occupying screen space, since the beginning of *Girlfight*. This bout is between the body being filmed and the body of the camera. The sequence with the whiteouts shows the camera under attack. The lens does not simply figure an opponent's face. It is not only a stunt-double for the fighters. The lens also receives punches as a lens. There is a dual motility at work here. In the ring, the camera, a motile body throughout the film, is shown stilled, stunned, unsighted. Diana and Stiles both repel the lens's invasive gaze. It is constantly knocked out of visual and spatial circulation. This inhibiting of the camera, a technology for controlling screen space, an appendage of patriarchy, fosters instability in relation to gender roles.

The two fighters keep the camera at arm's length through flurries of punches. These blows, blurs of motion, make space for them. They enable the women to keep out of the camera's grasp. The fighters refuse to be clinched by the lens. When it is announced that Diana has won the fight, the camera provides a bird's eye view of her. There is a seeming return to visual mastery. Diana, however, leaps up and down to celebrate her triumph, her upraised fists closing on the camera. She then walks out of shot. This fight signals a new relationship between the technological body and the body of the character. That a change has occurred is reinforced when a close-up of Adrian seated at ringside occurs post-match. His space is impinged here. In this instant, the camera as tool of patriarchy is confronting itself. The shot signals Adrian's recognition of Diana's

2.2 *Girlfight* (2000): Confronting the camera

immense ability, her rightful claim to move as an equal in the space of the ring.

It becomes obvious in the subsequent fight against Adrian that the entire film has, on one level, been a fight against the camera. Just before the start of the third round in this bout, Diana looks up in an echo of the scene of her standing against the lockers. This act of repetition links the two scenes. It foregrounds that the entire film has been about the relationship between woman and camera (2.2). Diana confronts the lens rather than panders to it. In this fight, which also involves whiteouts, Adrian's loss symbolises the defeat of a particular mode of film making. It is one in which the camera moves through space, owns its surroundings, with the same air of entitlement as men in patriarchal society. The camera in *Girlfight* is made, instead, to keep a respectful distance.

There is, as mentioned already, a noticeably restricted depth of field in *Girlfight*. The depth of field has, however, increased in the arena where Adrian and Diana fight. This growth echoes that of Diana's character who also now has expanded prospects.[78] Boxing has given her more existential room for manoeuvre and has also enabled her to put the camera on the back foot. During the narrative arc of *Girlfight*, the lens is gradually pressed back. Its ability to own space is restricted. This situation reaches its apex in the fights with Adrian and Stiles when the camera is stopped in its tracks. In these moments, the camera as body is made to assume the position Diana has occupied for much of the film, it is deprived of motility. There is, however, no simple reversal of power relations at work here. Instead, *Girlfight* shows that norms of bodily comportment are changeable and that gendered spaces, those of ring and screen, are open to renegotiation.

Afterimages

Boxing films such as *Girlfight* and *The Opponent* paint a different picture of women's sporting prowess from the frailty myth frequently propounded under patriarchy. The ring becomes a space within which battles over sexual equality are also fought. In *The Art and Aesthetics of Boxing*, David Scott detects an 'expressive relation between the canvas and ropes of the ring and the canvas and frame of a painting'.[79] Merz also uses an analogy with the visual arts to describe her move from boxercise to learning boxing proper, suggesting it was 'like moving from finger painting to figure drawing'.[80] This emphasises boxing's aesthetic aspect. In film, the screen is also occasionally referred to as a canvas. Galt provides an example from early film of the director, in this instance Abel Gance, conceived of as a painter.[81]

I have explored the psychic anxieties surrounding the blank canvas, which is figured as feminine lack, in painting.[82] The boxing ring has also been analysed in psychoanalytic terms by Shelley Macdonald who identifies it as 'a maternal structure'.[83] MacDonald draws on Kleinian and Lacanian psychoanalysis to produce her reading of the psychic significances of boxing. She does not, however, consider the canvas in relation to lack, to symbolic castration. The actions of fighters within the confines of the ring can be compared to those of painters anxiously responding to their cotton canvas as lack. Pollock has argued that the artist's unprimed canvas preserves 'the lingering trace of the necessary feminine other projected now, as one of many dimensions and associations, onto the space of inscription'.[84] The action of painting is therefore sometimes motivated by a desire to master what this lack evokes, the (m)Other. Viewing a finished painting by an artist such as Jackson Pollock is to confront 'the relentless pacing, covering, knotting a surface of his own making and a sealing over of the threatening surface of the once blank canvas'.[85]

The motions of two boxers, their efforts to control ring space, their ducking, weaving, advancing, retreating, is comparable to Pollock's painterly exertions. Their fight is both against each other and against the canvas which they also seek to fill with fury and with sound. The boxing ring also forms an acoustic canvas of the kind envisaged by Karpf. Canvasses of this kind can also signal lack by way of silence. The aggression during a fight is direct towards two opponents, the other fighter and the troubling absence framed by the ropes, the canvas and its psychic significance. In this context, the actions of boxers such as Diana and Patty taken on added significance.

In painting, some artists such as Helen Frankenthaler have provided alternative ways of relating to the canvas as lack, different ways of relating to absence.[86] Diana and Patty, however, do not innovate in this way. They practise the same aggressive response to the canvas as their male counterparts. *Girlfight* and *The Opponent* show women liberating acoustic and physical spaces previously excluded to them. In both films, however, psychic space remains patriarchal territory and the figure of the (m)Other persists as opponent, as a presence to be denied and obscured. The technique of the whiteout employed in the fights in *Girlfight*, however, demonstrates cinematography and editing operating to undermine the narrative of mastery played out through each contest. The whiteout re-inscribes the blank canvas within the ring. It shows the screen as surface, dealing an annihilating blow to any sense of depth.[87] The trace of the Mother as psychic figure refuses to be knocked out of screen space. This leads *Girlfight* to gesture towards another way of relating to the maternal, one that accommodates rather than excludes, and a different conception of subjectivity.

3

Athletic Gestures: Women's Team Sports Films

Gestural Politics

In *Personal Best* (Dir. Robert Towne, USA, 1982), a film about a group of American women striving to qualify for the 1980 Summer Olympic Games in Moscow, there is a scene in which gender subversion is signalled through a visible action by a sportswoman, Tory, who makes a wanking gesture at her coach early in the film to signal he is a jerk. Later another female athlete makes the same gesture whilst telling a racist joke. The women adopt a masculine mannerism for their insult and witticism. Their miming of masturbation involves appropriating a gesture coded as male, a grip and motion tied to men's anatomy. The behaviour is 'unladylike'. It is a gesture Jules, a footballer, also uses in *Bend it Like Beckham* (Dir. Gurinder Chadha, UK, 2002). This film centres on the exploits of another player, Jesminder 'Jess' Bhamra, a young Punjabi Sikh. Jules's gesture is in response to some boys, who are friends of Jess, asking her if women players swap shirts at the end of every match (3.1). The cross-gender gesturing engaged in by Jules and Tory is potentially present in all athletic activity performed by women given sport's traditional association with masculinity. That participation in sport might be conceived of as gender bending is indicated by the sequence in which the women athletes in *Personal Best* play American football. During the game, two male athletes adopt the role of cheerleaders, shaking pom-poms. Their actions, their gestures, imply that they are mirroring the atypical gender behaviour of the women.

3.1 *Bend it Like Beckham* (2002): Jules's masturbatory gesture

Gesture is defined by Adam Kendon as 'a name for visible action when it is used as an utterance or as a part of an utterance'.[1] Gesture is an energetic operation, athletic, that either alone, or accompanied by other means, forms an utterance. It describes physical expressions or statements. These expressions, Kendon is at pains to point out, are manifestly deliberate.[2] Gestures are intentional not accidental. They are subject to voluntary control.[3] The agency of the unconscious, its potential contribution to the production of visible utterances, is not acknowledged by him. The kinds of information intentional visible utterances can convey varies from giving instructions, look there, sit down, go away or fuck off, to communicating emotions such as elation, unhappiness, anger, or disgust.

Gestures can be made using various areas of the body, most commonly the hands and face, but also the shoulders, knees, posterior and other features. They frequently involve extending the body into space, such as giving the thumbs up or pointing with the index finger. The Renaissance scholar Giovanni Bonifacio believed that humankind has gradually reduced the number of gestures they use in communication, devising instead 'an almost infinite number of words'.[4] The turn to spoken utterances therefore caused physical exertions, and spatial exploration, to decrease. Word of mouth encourages a sedentary lifestyle. There are, however, conditions in which audible speech becomes difficult, if not impossible. Sporting competitions form one of these. The water polo player surrounded by the sounds of a cheering audience, of teammates and opponents pounding through the water, splashing and surging, is not drowning but waving, seeking to secure the attention of a teammate and signal her availability to receive a pass.

Gestures form a regular feature in sports films, used by coaches, athletes and spectators to communicate a variety of information. Tudor explores the significance of the gestures of a spectator, Myra Fleenor, in *Hoosiers* (Dir. David Anspaugh, USA, 1986). This film is about a high school basketball team from a small town that overcomes the odds to win a state championship. Fleenor, a teacher, is initially sceptical about the benefits of sport for schoolchildren and disdainful of basketball. Tudor identifies how her feelings are communicated by way of 'body and facial gestures [that] are very stiff and controlled'.[5] There is also a growing literature on the use of gesture in cinema more broadly. One of the most notable essays on the topic is by Giorgio Agamben. Agamben's argument, in 'Notes on Gesture', is that cinema 'leads images back to the homeland of gesture'.[6] He contrasts cinema with other forms of image, including the sports photograph, which he believes seizes gesture, stilling it.[7] The sports photograph nevertheless retains a trace of dynamism although its vigour remains checked. It becomes aestheticised, rendering sign as beautiful sight rather than locus of action. Cinema, the moving image, frees gesture from these restraints. For Agamben, this makes cinema, in contrast with other forms of image-making, a site of ethical and political activity.[8]

Agamben believes gesture in cinema comprises a means without ends. He describes it as 'the exhibition of a mediality, it is the process of making a means visible as such'.[9] Gesture 'allows the emergence of the being-in-a-medium of human beings and thus it opens the ethical dimension for them'.[10] Gesture in film is able to interrupt its function as visible utterance, as physically purposeful communication, becoming instead 'communication of a communicability', purposive without purpose.[11] It signals by not signalling, through the suspension of signification, that the subject is in language. It shows the subject's subjection to language.

The gesture is not located by Agamben. There are no specific examples of how communicability is communicated. It seems that gesture is not to be found in an actor's visible utterances or a camera's motions. Gesture, rather, forms another term for what Agamben elsewhere labels the inoperative or the messianic. Film as a whole registers, as this gesture, communicates communicability, thereby revealing being-in-language and assuming a political dimension through exposing what humankind has in common, a universal mediality: we all share the same communicative flesh.

It is arguable whether film is the sole arena where the potential for such a politics exists. In actual sporting activities, for example, purposive motions, gestures without purpose come into being. Agamben's abstract thinking avoids engaging with the concrete similarities between watching a film and our everyday perception of motion including sporting events. The political potential of gesture as understood by Agamben is possibly present in sport as well as cinema. Here, however, politics of a more concrete kind will be examined through a study of specific gestures in sports films. The gesture by Tory in *Personal Best*, for example, clearly signals a sexual politics that is grounded in culturally and socially specific circumstances.

Compulsive Athletes

Tory's gesture is plainly culturally coded as masculine. Luce Irigaray, in her classic essay 'The Gesture in Psychoanalysis', describes the in-out movement of masturbation as linear and manly.[12] Tory's and Jules's emulations of wanking motions go against the circular movements Irigaray associates with femininity.[13] Their behaviour would therefore be aberrant. In her essay, Irigaray explores the relationship between gesture and speech that occurs in Freud's example of the boy child playing a game with a reel on a string as a means to offset the absence of his mother. Her close attention to the relationship between gesture and speech, their co-expressivity, echoes the research of David McNeill which has identified a dialectical relationship between the gestural and the verbal in speaking.[14] In his essay 'Beyond the Pleasure Principle', which Irigaray approaches via ideas about cross-expressivity, Freud explains of the child:

> What he did was to hold the reel by the string and very skilfully [*geschick*] throw it over the edge of his curtained cot, so that it disappeared into it, at the same time uttering his expressive 'o-o-o-o-o'. He then pulled the reel out of the cot again by the string and hailed its reappearance with a joyful *da* ['there'].[15]

Freud reads the game as one of 'disappearance and return'.[16] The 'o-o-o-o-o' represents the German word '*fort*' [gone], making the game one of fort/da. The pastime was developed in response to letting his mother depart without protesting: 'he compensated himself for this, as it were, by himself staging the disappearance and return of the objects within his reach'.[17] The game enables the child to shift from a passive to an active position, demonstrating the boy's drive to master the situation rather than be mastered by it. It also enables him to express the hostility towards his mother which he felt because of her leaving him.

Irigaray uses the game to explore whether the boy is sexually neutral/neuter at this point. Her interpretation focusses far more on the significance of the words than Freud's. She attends to how the enunciation of these words contributes to their significance in the context of the game as a coping mechanism:

> In the economy of consonants and vowels, *fort* (or o-o-o-o-o as it is in his discontinuous signal) articulated by the mouth's forming a little triangle, a triangle formed by lips and tongue: the *o* is inside it, but cannot be swallowed. The far away is not introjected; it describes, in the mouth above all, a determinate space, a frame, framing, as it were, a space of departure and return, coming to a halt with the *t*, if the word is *fort*, or the discontinuity of the sound if it is the o-o-o-o-o. Whereas the *da* can be swallowed, a sharp, dry mouthful, thus inverting the *fort*, unless it [*da*] stays in the back of the palate.[18]

The words, like the reel, move through space, the vocal tract, the mouth. They are, however, more inhibited: 'both *fort* and *da* are closed up by the teeth'.[19] These words symbolise the mother. She is, therefore, 'held on to so that she is available to become articulation (*fort*) or she is inside, swallowed or closing up the throat at the back of the palate (*da*)'.[20] The mother in the fort/da game is therefore always split, 'she is in the cot, and she is also in the mouth, behind the teeth'.[21] The mother inside the mouth is also divided, 'by the teeth and by all the differences between the sounds'.[22] For Irigaray, then, the actions of the mouth echo the role of the reel, performing a processing of absence, simultaneously emitting sound and holding it in. Hearing the word *da* he has spoken also permits the boy to imbibe his mother through his ear.[23]

Irigaray concludes that a girl would not cope with the mother's absence using the same techniques, playing the same game, as the boy. She would not symbolise her mother using a reel and string as 'her mother's sex is the same as hers and the mother cannot have the objective status of a reel'.[24] Irigaray suggests that there are three stages to the girl's efforts to cope with maternal absence. Initially, the girl succumbs to distress. She then plays with a doll, a quasi-subject that resists objectification. Finally, she dances, a means by which she constructs a 'vital subjective space'.[25] This dancing may be accompanied by vocalisations but special importance is not granted to 'syllabic or phonemic oppositions'.[26] The utterances, if they can be so called, are rhythmic and melodic.

The girl's recreation is not dedicated to mastering the situation, the absence, through play. She cannot master what is already a part of her, is 'too familiar and too close'.[27] It is, however, a way of reproducing 'around her or inside herself a movement whose energy is circular, and which protects her from dereliction'.[28] In this circular reasoning, the girl cannot adopt the linear gestures of the boy because to do so would be to alienate a part of who she is. Her visible utterances, her dance, are in keeping with the proto-mother beneath her own skin. Irigaray does not negatively read this choreography as a coping strategy. For her, it demonstrates that women do not need the phallus. Their entry into language, symbolisation, is not premised on mastery, on the possessive. The phallus is only subsequently imputed to them as a need, a retrospective imposition.

The essay crucially links healthy psychic life for women with freedom of motion. Women's subjectivity requires the 'freedom to walk – that is, the freedom to go away and to draw close in all ways'.[29] For Irigaray, the emerging subjectivity of the girl child therefore differs from that of the boy in that he learns to endure loss from a sitting position, throwing an object, rather than himself, into space. The girl, however, withstands loss through her uprightness and spatial journeying. For Irigaray, this has important ramifications in analytic settings. The couch, for example, appears designed for male rather than female patients as it encourages a physical situation, static, supine, which is more reminiscent of the boy's early psychic life without perfectly mimicking it. The traditional analytic setting is also premised on the production of speech rather than motion, privileging the verbal over the gestural.

The gestures underlying Irigaray's analysis, the throw and the gyration (both, for her, gendered motions), merit further attention. It is noteworthy, although Irigaray does not remark on it, that Freud appreciates the skill of the boy, his aim and coordination. The analyst would not recognise the analogy but the crib appears, on one level, to act like a basketball hoop into which the reel is thrown. In *Woman Basketball Player No. 5* (Dir. Xie Jin, China, 1957), a Chinese film about the travails of a basketball coach, Tian Zhenhua (a former star of the men's game tasked with coaching the national women's team), the coach is shown in flashback giving instructions to his then girlfriend, Lin Jie, after she misses a basket. He communicates to her with his hands. His left hand is held horizontal, providing an analogue for the hoop, imaging it. His right hand is held vertically and makes a motion over the left, providing a pattern of action for how she should shoot. Tian's gestures could equally well illustrate, enact, the visible component of the fort/da game.

Freud's interpretation of the fort/da game includes an appreciation of motor skills. The mastery of absence is therefore bound up with mastery of the body, its capacities. There is also an aesthetic dimension inherent in this mastery. The way the throw is performed can be assessed, and qualitatively judged. The girl spins rather than pitches. Her dance of becoming, however, also possesses aesthetic potential. Agamben, for instance, recognises dance's aesthetic aspect. He lists the aesthetic judgment of dance as an example of how not to approach understanding gesture.[30] The production of the beautiful in dance, for him, is a purposeful action, an end enabled by kinetic means.

There are therefore underlying similarities between boy and girl. There is a shared aesthetic potential in their acts of physicality, there is also a shared physicality. In physical actions in adulthood such as sport and arts such as dance, the aesthetic aspect remains of interest to practitioners and spectators. The link between early infancy, with its initial refined athletic gestures, and later life is preserved via the aesthetic. The good eye-hand coordination of the boy child so admired by Freud persists, for example, in the measured force and angling required to shoot a hoop in basketball or in the quarterback's long, fast-paced throw to a receiver in American football. The girl's early rhythm and grace endures in the well-executed take-off, rotation and landing involved in a Lutz jump in figure skating and the agility and poise of the gymnast on the balance beam.

These actions are, however, not thought of as gestures in the common sense of the term. Gesture is, as already mentioned, a form of utterance, a communication. The shot, throw, jump and somersault may be significant, they are not, however, intentionally expressive. The boy child's throw and the girl child's dance are symbolic gestures and therefore seemingly of a different order to these other, later physical activities. There is, however, an aesthetic component which unifies these gestures from childhood and adulthood, from play and sport. This lends them significance. The desire to perfect the kinds of aesthetically pleasing physical actions involved in many sports may therefore be traced back to the archaic athleticisms discussed by Irigaray.

Pollock has suggested Irigaray's essay on gesture should be read philosophically rather than anatomically otherwise the philosopher's statements appear universalising and absolute.[31] It is, however, difficult to pare Irigaray's categorisation of gestures, of visible utterances, from the sexed bodies she associates them with. 'Gesture in Psychoanalysis' does appear to form a work that embraces essentialist ideas about sexuate identities. Following on from Irigaray's archaic gestural sexing, particular forms of visible utterance in adulthood become coded as aberrant. The woman who scores with a jump shot in basketball echoes Ernst's early man-making gestures with the reel. The man who spins off a defender to move past the three-point line follows the girl's choreography. Gesture in Irigaray affirms biological difference rather than forming a means by which to challenge it. Many films featuring sportswomen, however, employ gesture to contest such a vision of difference.

Gesture and Gender

In *Chak De! India* (Dir. Shimit Amin, India, 2007), a film about the fortunes of a fictional Indian women's national field hockey team, the central character, Kabir Khan, endures having his career as an Indian cricket player undone by a gesture. He misses a penalty stroke against Pakistan in the closing seconds of a World Cup match. The Pakistan Number 5 puts his hand on Khan's shoulder to console him, then shakes his hand and embraces him. Photographs of the handshake are circulated in the press as evidence of Khan, who happens to be Muslim, having engaged in match-fixing. This opening sequence reinforces how gestures are open to multiple interpretations and potential re-contextualisation. In this instance, a gesture of 'sportspersonship' is framed as an act of national betrayal. *Chak De! India* follows Khan's efforts to overcome the opprobrium generated by the media's reporting of the significance of the handshake through coaching the Indian women's hockey team to international success.

The film is instructive about the ways gesture provides insights into identity and background, and discloses politics. At one point Khan's social status, for example, is demonstrated by the dismissive gesture he gives to a man loading his belongings onto a removal truck. His minimal manual interaction with the removalist speaks volumes about the difference in standing between the two men. Later, in a meeting of Indian cricket's governing body, Uttamaji, a staunch supporter of Khan, is advised by the chair of the committee, Mr. Tripathi, that the women's team is a waste of resources. Tripathi's vocal disparagement of the prospects of the team is accompanied by a visible utterance, a swishing movement he makes with a biscuit. This minimal gesture, reminiscent of a broom sweeping away dirt, is one that ably captures his disdain for the female athletes.

Shortly afterwards, in discussion with Khan about the team, Tripathi suggests its existence is to be understood as 'a formality not a reality'. The negative in the statement is reinforced by the head official using a wave of the hand, a waving away of the idea the team might genuinely succeed. This sign is swiftly replaced by another gesture, in which Tripathi's initially cups his fingers then straightens them, leading him to display an open palm to Khan. This 'emptying' gesture, a letting go of any substance, reinforces the irreality Tripathi refers to. His contempt for the women's team is registered not only in the words he speaks but also through his gestures, the visible utterances he makes forming a supplementary, more subtle, expression of his sexism. For Tripathi, hockey is a man's game.

Chak De! India involves women playing a sport traditionally associated with men, including using the requisite gestures for it. In this, it joins many of the other films featuring women athletes discussed here. There are notably fewer films in which men engage in sports coded as feminine, and these are often comedic. The light-hearted *The Swimsuit Issue* (Dir. Måns Herngren, Sweden, 2008), for example, features a men's synchronised swimming team coached by a woman and the farce *Blades of Glory* (Dirs. Will Speck & Josh Gordon, USA, 2007) features men's figure-skating. Comedy is also employed as an element in some of the films about sportswomen playing 'men's' sports but does not define them. *A League of Their Own* (Dir. Penny Marshall, USA, 1992), for instance, has humorous moments but is not exclusively comedic. The film provides a fictional account of the founding of the All-American Girls Professional Baseball

League (AAGPBL), a real league established in the United States during the Second World War. It centres on the fortunes of one team in the league, the Rockford Peaches.

A League of Their Own begins with a sequence featuring a former Peaches player, the catcher Dottie Henson, in old age preparing to embark on a trip to reunite with her wartime teammates. She caresses a frame holding an old photograph and then drums her fingers on the chest of drawers it is placed on. These simple gestures capture Dottie's mental conflict, she is torn between a desire to meet old friends again, signalled by her 'touching' the past as it is indexed by the photograph, and her anxiety about what their reaction would be, marked by the drumming which indicates someone in thought and also, potentially, tension. Shortly after this, Dottie punches her old catcher's glove. This gesture, notably aggressive, is clearly a familiar one to her. Through these varied visible utterances, the importance of gesture to *A League of Their Own* is made obvious from the outset.

Gesture will subsequently become the weapon used in a battle of the sexes between Dottie and the official coach of the Peaches, Jimmy Dugan. Dottie has been coaching the team because of Jimmy's alcoholism. During one match, however, he decides to take over. He asks rhetorically, whilst pointing to his chest, 'Who is the goddam manager here? I am!'. In this scene, Dottie and Jimmy vie to deliver instructions to the batter, Marla Hooch, via a series of coded taps to different parts of their bodies. In baseball, instructions are frequently transmitted between coach and players through such gestures, the meanings of which are kept a closely guarded secret within a team. Jimmy will ultimately triumph in this gestural conflict and Marla, following his instructions, will successfully hit the ball that is pitched at her. This scene of visible actions as utterances forms a crucial turning point in the film as well as the specific game it relates to. It marks Dottie's demotion (she does not coach the team after this) and the beginning of Jimmy's redemption.

Gesture also features in the early skirmishes between Billie Jean King and Bobby Riggs in *When Billie Beat Bobby* (Dir. Jane Anderson, USA, 2001), a fictionalised account of the 1973 Battle of the Sexes tennis match between King and Riggs. In one scene in front of the media, Bobby tenses his left bicep and invites Billie to feel it. She does so. The arm gesture functions to provide evidence of Bobby's physical strength. His

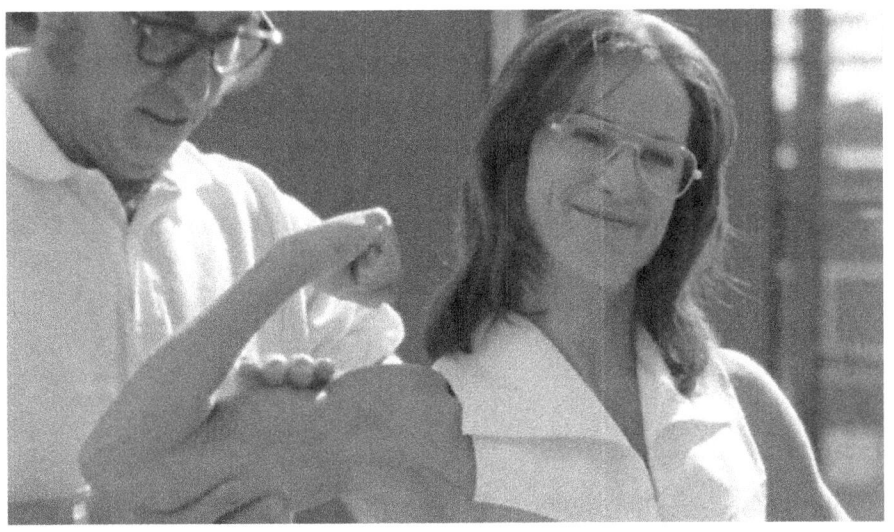

3.2 *When Billie Beat Bobby* (2001): Bobby's tentative touch

cotton polo shirt, however, conceals the muscle so much of the impact of the gesture is reliant on Billie's reaction. Smiling, she rapidly palpates the bicep through the cotton. Billie does more than feel it, she presses it. She exerts her own strength at the moment she should simply be sampling Bobby's. Billie then mirrors Bobby's invitation, flexing her right bicep and asking him to touch it: 'Now feel mine!' Billie's sleeveless tennis dress means her bicep is in plain sight. Bobby tentatively rests his fingers on the bulging muscle (3.2). The outcome of their tennis match later in the film is subtly prefigured here when Bobby is rendered passive by Billie's appropriation of his masculine gesture of strength. Billie's gestural gambit forms a powerful instance of 'one-upwomanship'.

There are, however, some gestures that are conventionally coded as feminine. These are gestures which men seldom make efforts to control or appropriate. In *Quarterback Princess* (Dir. Noel Black, USA, 1983), a fiction film based on actual experiences of a teenage girl, Tami Maida, who sought to join her high school American football team, Tami has to attend a high school meeting to argue her case to be allowed to try out for the team. She is shown seated on the front row at the meeting with her legs carefully positioned to preserve decorum. Her comportment, 'sitting like a girl' as Young refers to it, is conventionally feminine.[32] At one point in the meeting, she stands to argue her case for why she would like to be given a shot at the try-outs despite pressure to cheerlead instead. After making her case, she sits, smoothing her skirt as she does so, a gesture motivated by nervousness and the need for propriety. After this, her father reaches over and squeezes her forearm, a sign of encouragement and also a testament to the power differential between parent and child. It is an uninvited gesture, in contrast to the daughter's embrace with her mother later in the film in a scene in which Tami seeks reassurance for her decision to play ball despite the controversy and family tensions it causes. Tami's enclosed posture, her bodily timidity at the school meeting, is not one a man would usually seek to emulate or control.

At the school meeting, Tami is ultimately granted her wish to participate in the try outs leaving her footballing destiny in her own hands. Tami's hands are, in fact, repeatedly remarked on throughout the film. At one point, a teammate jokingly chastises her for doing DIY saying 'You could bust a fingernail or something. There go magic hands of Maida for the rest of the season.' After the final game of the season in which Tami overcomes injury to score a crucial touchdown, Mr. Caine, who has been vocally critical of her for the entire season, advises her, 'Maida, you are quite a guy!' He then extends his hand to shake hers. Tami, however, kisses him instead. She resists performing the gesture, the handshake, Caine's gendering of her dictates. The scene shows her as one of the guys, yet not a guy.

During the school prom, which forms the denouement to *Quarterback Princess*, Tami is presented with a signed football by the team who advise her: 'We'll miss your hands man.' Here, 'her' hands are gendered by association as masculine. Ultimately referring to Tami as a man invites a cross-gender reading. The film as a whole, however, discourages this. The title *Quarterback Princess* is intended as an oxymoron. Tami functions, however, as an undecidable. Deconstruction as event is embodied in 'her' actions, gestures that, cumulatively, refuse categorisation as either male or female. S/he provides a bodily challenge to the gestural binary identified by Irigaray. The football field provides the designated space in which binary categories of gender are placed *sous rature* [under erasure], Tami confides at one point: 'When I'm playing I'm not a male exactly but not a girl either!' Tami's free play, however, comprises a continual gestural refusal to present as either masculine or feminine, to presence either gender, which exceeds the confines of the sports field. Gesture in *Quarterback Princess* becomes a means by which to articulate and disarticulate gender oppositions.

Aggressive Gestures

Power disparities between the sexes are often registered through gestures, particularly ones involving touch. Touch is bound up with power and status.³³ Young discusses this in 'Throwing Like a Girl', suggesting that 'it is acceptable [...] for women to be touched in ways and under circumstances that it is not acceptable for men to be touched, and by persons – i.e., men – whom it is not acceptable for them to touch'.³⁴ In *A League of Their Own*, Jimmy's casual sexism is registered when he slaps Miss Cuthbert, the Peaches matronly chaperone, on the backside. Earlier in the film, Cuthbert has soil thrown at her by an aggressive coach driver. She is therefore repeatedly subject to gestural violence. In *When Billie Beat Bobby*, Billie witnesses an airline pilot patting the backside of an air stewardess. The film, set 30 years later than *A League of Their Own*, shows the continuing existence of sexist attitudes in the 1970s through uninvited gestures comparable to those in the baseball film. Men's wandering hands frequently signal their sexual objectification of women.

Cultures of violence towards women can also register through gestures. In *Forever the Moment* (Dir. Im Soon-rye, South Korea, 2008), a fictionalised account of the South Korean women's handball team's efforts at the 2004 Athens Olympics (where they won a silver medal and very nearly secured gold) a male coach, Kang, at one point pushes a ring-binder against the head of one of the players, Hyeon-ja. The aggressive gesture registers his disapproval at her underperformance in a training match against a high-school team. It subsequently transpires that she was menstruating, which her teammates decide is the reason for her poor showing in the match.³⁵ The scene captures casual aggression towards women.

South Korea is still a patriarchal society and *Forever the Moment* does not shy from exploring some of the detrimental impact this has on the lives of women in the nation. The struggles of single motherhood and the stigma of divorce are both sensitively examined. Through Kang's aggressive gesture, the film also acknowledges how patriarchal attitudes are manifested in visible utterances. In a Chinese context, in *Woman Basketball Player No. 5*, there is a scene in which Jie's husband, her cousin, realises that his wife is still in love with Tian and therefore flicks a lighted cigarette in her face. His cruel gesture marks him as villainous. The cousin is not, however, representative of Chinese men. Through his close relationship to Jie's father, he is marked as disreputable. Jie's father, who first appears wearing a fur-trimmed overcoat and a trilby, is aligned with America and its corrupt values. In a sequence featuring a basketball match between a Chinese team and an American team of sailors that takes place prior to the formation of the People's Republic of China, the leader of the US contingent is shown among the spectators smoking a cigar.[36] Jie's father, who is also smoking a cigar, is associated with the foreigner through this action and, by extension, with his values. Jie's father's clothing, particularly his hat, is also reminiscent of the garb landowners are shown wearing in the documentary *The Great Land Reform* (China, 1953).[37]

The cousin's gesture, and the disrespect for women it signals, is therefore tied to pre-revolutionary China and to foreign standards of behaviour. It contrasts markedly as a visible utterance with a moment later in the film, in the putative present, in which Tian affectionately puts his hands on Jie's shoulders as they discuss whether their daughter, also a basketball player, should have an operation for an injury she has suffered. His gesture, a gesture taking place many years later in the People's Republic, signals the shift in women's status that has accompanied the transition to communism. His respect for Jie is in keeping with a major theme of the film which is the enhanced opportunities for women that now exist in China. In this tender scene in the grounds of a hospital, shadows of the leaves of trees are cast on Tian's shirt. This image prefigures part of the lyrics of a patriotic song that the women's team will perform later: 'sun tree is rustling in the wind'. The song forges a vocal togetherness, echoing the closeness of the couple at the hospital. The individualism exhibited by Jie's cousin and father is ultimately rejected in the film.

In *Quarterback Princess*, aggressive tactile gestures towards women also occur. Once it is announced that Tami was successful at the try outs and has made the team, considerable media interest is generated. Tami's mother, Judy, opens the door of their home to a reporter who puts his hand on her shoulder and then, saying 'Excuse me, please', pushes past her into the house. This act of trespass is not only into the family residence but also, through the act of touching, into Judy's personal space. The touch is uninvited and unappreciated. It is not forceful like flicking the cigarette but it is invasive.

A Community through Touch

In his study of gesture, *Gesture, Race and Culture*, David Efron describes what he refers to as 'contactual gestures'.[38] These gestures involve physical contact between speakers. Touch as utterance occurs often in sport. Touch without any communicative intent even more so. The term 'contact sports', which refers to sports that involve varying degrees of deliberate or subsidiary physical connection, foregrounds the fact that tactile encounters between athletes, contactual gestures, are a common feature of many individual events and team games. Coaches also use touch in training to educate athletes about how and where to move.[39]

Deliberate contact occurs in sports such as boxing, that require participants to purposefully hit each other and rugby, which involves tackling. There are numerous other sports where subsidiary, incidental physical contact occurs during play including basketball, hockey and soccer. These sports all involve some element of touching between participants. Additionally, there are sports such as cricket, swimming and tennis that should require no contact between participants. Even in these sports, however, touch may have a role to play. The importance of communicative touch, of gesture, amongst members of the same team for their success has been studied in relation to basketball.[40] The findings of this research could conceivably also be relevant to teams engaging in non-contact sports.

Communal touch, touching encounters where the aim is to foster a sense of community, of common character and purpose, in a team, is evident in many sports films featuring male and female athletes and coaches. Tiffany Field defines touch as the social sense.[41] This sociality is particularly marked during the basketball huddle in which an entire team is joined by way of touch. The phenomenon of the huddle, in which the team, including the coach, gathers in a tight circle, involves participants putting their arms around each other. This can be interpreted as a show of unity. It also makes it easier for those in the huddle to lean in and hear each other as words of encouragement or strategy are exchanged. The huddle is often broken by players and coach putting their hands into the centre of the circle either at waist height or above head height and then shouting a saying. This occurs in a number of films featuring female athletes participating in team sports.

In *Forever the Moment* a huddle during a semi-final match against France in Athens is broken with a shout of '1, 2, 3, let's go get them!' Further huddles are featured in the final against Denmark. At one point, the camera provides a bird's eye view of the team with their arms outstretched, hands touching at the centre of the circle they have formed. A similar camera position is used in *Chak De! India* prior to the world championship final against Australia that forms the film's climax. It is, however, followed by a shot from below. As the team break to a shout of 'Chak De' [Make it happen!], the hands separate, ceasing to obscure the camera lens, and light is revealed. The breaking of each huddle provides a moment in which the coach and each of the athletes potentially all simultaneously touch. It is a moment of team unanimity embodied through touch and sound.

The combining of the sensory experiences acts as a valuable reminder that touch never functions in isolation from other senses at a given moment. Even when it is of great importance (as is the case in the huddle) it is accompanied by important acoustic or visual cues. The message of unity manifest in the huddle comes as much from the sight of hands joined together and the sound of voices raised as one as it does from the contact of skin against skin. In the huddles at the Olympics in *Forever the Moment*, barriers of age and gender that have manifested themselves earlier in the film dissolve in a powerful show of unity. In *Chak De! India*, class and ethnic prejudices between the players similarly disappear. Field has argued that touch as a form of bodily communication 'varies widely by gender, age, class, and culture'.[42] Touch, however, can also form a way to overcome difference. Rebecca Schneider has recognised this, arguing that 'the status of touch is problematic, not least because it suggests *bodies* at least partially merged across difference'.[43] The force of the act of breaking the huddle undoubtedly derives from how the senses of hearing, sight and touch mutually reinforce the message of communal determination, of indifference to difference.

There are, of course, gestures that do not involve touch which can foster community when numerous individuals perform them simultaneously. An instance of such gesturing is provided at the end of *Woman Basketball Player No. 5* when the plane carrying the women's team departs for an international competition and a crowd of people wave it off. This show of manual unity cements the film's communist message. Much of *Woman Basketball Player No. 5* is dedicated to working out sport's relationship to Socialism and to nationalism. In sport, egoism is shown to be detrimental to team success and, by extension, to the success of the nation. The waving hands of the collective at the end of the film reaffirm the condemnation of individualism which forms a key theme. In *Chak De! India*, the women have a narrow loss in a match against the men's team. The men clap in unison in appreciation of the sportswomen. They then raise their hockey sticks to salute the skill and tenacity of their opponents. The crowd also gives them a standing ovation. Here, again, shared gestures foster kinship without the need for touch. The sound of clapping, however, forms an acoustic commingling not dissimilar to contactual gesture.

The pluralistic dimension to touch discussed by Efron is what makes it a suitable impetus for Erin Manning's conception of a democracy to come. For Manning, if democracy is thought through touch then a more productive idea of the political emerges to one secured within the grids of intelligibility of statecraft. This different idea is one 'that speaks of aporias, of sensation, of movement, a notion of the political that is difficult to grasp'.[44] The handball or hockey huddles, as moving unions of individuals becoming together, like Manning's preferred example of the tango, form a useful model for formulating a politics of dissensus, one that refuses to silence disagreement and difference yet fosters communication and negotiation between self and others. The huddle as event comprises a crucial component to getting along together in team sports. In a gender-blind team, a team comprising of all sexes, the huddle would therefore provide a valuable means by which to communally feel difference as irrelevance. As this chapter has sought to demonstrate, gesture, whilst often overlooked in sports film analyses provides both a powerful individual and collective means of challenging gender stereotypes and restrictions.

4

Venus in Spikes: Track and Field Films

> Fascist aesthetics is based on the containment of vital forces; movements are confined, held tight, held in.[1]

Fascinating Fascism

The British film *Fast Girls* (Dir. Regan Hall, UK, 2012), about a group of professional sprinters aiming to succeed at the World Championships, was released in the United Kingdom in the same year as London 2012. The subject of *Fast Girls*, as it refers to a different, fictional sporting competition, is ostensibly not related to the XXX Olympiad. The timing of the film's world premiere, however, held in London in June, a month before the start of the Summer Olympics, suggests otherwise. *Fast Girls* is a spin-off. The film was produced to cash in on Olympic fever in the United Kingdom and comprises a feel-good message of national sporting success. It was initially meant to feature an Olympic storyline but the idea had to be abandoned because of trademark issues. *Fast Girls* is therefore a film about the Olympics in all but name. It joins a small, yet significant, pantheon of films featuring female athletes that are dedicated to the Olympic Games either as central subject-matter or as the endpoint of endeavour. This chapter focuses on these films in relation to the specific issue of sexualisation. Sexualisation is taken here to refer to a number of different issues. These include how depictions of sport in the films are frequently coded as sexual in nature, how the athletes are, at times, sexually objectified, and how aspects of athletic enterprise come to be sexually fetishised.

The archetypal Olympic film is, unlike *Fast Girls,* non-fictional. The documentary *Olympia*, directed by Leni Riefenstahl, records the 1936 Summer Olympics in Berlin. The film is composed of two parts, *Fest der Völker* (*Festival of the People*) and *Fest der Schönheit* (*Festival of Beauty*). *Olympia* was released in 1938 and has caused considerable controversy ever since. It is frequently coupled with Riefenstahl's earlier films, particularly her documentaries of the 1933 and 1934 Nuremberg rallies, *Sieg des Glaubens* (*Victory of Faith* (Dir. Leni Riefenstahl, Germany, 1933)) and *Triumph des Willens* (*Triumph of the Will* (Dir. Leni Riefenstahl, Germany, 1934)), and cited as evidence of her fascist outlook. The practical benefits Riefenstahl derived from her political allegiances in terms of access to finances, equipment and personnel have already been examined.[2] *Olympia* is therefore the film containing footage of sportswomen that has been most discussed and it must also rank as one of the most analysed motion pictures by a woman director. The aim of this opening section is to provide an overview of existing ideas about *Olympia*, starting with Susan Sontag's classic analysis, and to offer a fresh interpretation of the documentary which argues that there is something in the depiction of the athletic itself as it is filmed by Riefenstahl that precludes it being readily co-opted for propaganda purposes.

Sontag refers to the film as part of her well-known critique of Riefenstahl's fascist aesthetics in the essay 'Fascinating Fascism'. She accuses the film-maker of a complete identification with Nazism, one that renders her art incomparable with works by other fascist artists including Louis-Ferdinand Céline and Ezra Pound.[3] For Sontag, Riefenstahl's later project photographing the Nuba peoples in Sudan exhibits the same corrupt aesthetics, the same totalitarian taint, as the films she produced under National Socialism. This aesthetics is one that celebrates beautiful male bodies and has 'a preoccupation with situations of control, submissive behaviour, extravagant effort, and the endurance of pain'.[4] Fascist aesthetics 'endorse two seemingly opposite states, egomania and servitude'.[5] Sontag's identification of the self-aggrandisement and self-abasement that characterises Nazi mentality is evidently indebted to Theodor W. Adorno's discussion of fascist propaganda. Adorno's ideas merit briefly summarising as he adeptly teases out the erotic underpinnings of fascist movements.

For Adorno, 'the basic tenets of fascist leadership [were] to keep primary libidinal energy on an unconscious level so as to divert its manifestations in a way suitable to political ends'.[6] Fascism draws on the psychic mechanism of identification to transform 'libido into the bond between leaders and followers, and between the followers themselves'.[7] Identification possesses a strong narcissistic aspect and the leader therefore takes on the attributes of an ideal self, one that 'gets rid of the stains of frustration and discontent which mar [the follower's] picture of his own empirical self'.[8] The leader does not, however, take on every element of the follower's narcissistic ego and therefore 'must still resemble the follower and appear as his "enlargement"'.[9] The leader is both superman and everyman, big man and average Josef, a composite, a contrast. It is this individualism coupled with collectivism that Sontag identifies in fascist aesthetics. This aesthetics, mobilised in the service of propaganda, is easy to see in operation in *Triumph des Willens* with its footage of leaders and crowds of followers: Hitler is shot as if alone, stark against a cloudy backdrop, a thousand faceless soldiers are filmed from behind, grouped obediently before Nazi banners.

Adorno also importantly suggests that the fascist leader and their followers require a constitutive outside to enable them to belong. This outside in National Socialism was constructed from out of the figure of the Jew, the Gypsy, and the "degenerate" among others. The maintenance of fascist identity is therefore bound up with establishing and safeguarding borders between insiders and outsiders. The outsider is perceived as weak, deficient in comparison with those privileged enough to be on the inside. The anti-Semitic rhetoric of the 1935 Nuremberg rally, the introduction of the Nuremberg Laws, can be understood as forming a response to the need to clearly demarcate who was Jewish in Germany, to build a barrier from out of legal statutes. The boundary fascinations of fascism are also attended to by Sontag who describes the choreography of the huge rallies as an exercise in making the masses take on form and in 'the holding in or confining of force'.[10] The marches give groups of people edges, produce designer crowds, ordered, orderly. This constituent of fascist aesthetics is also clearly visible in the mass formations of people in *Triumph des Willens*.

The presence of these characteristics of boundary-making and dominance and submission in *Olympia* is, however, less obvious. There is brief footage of a mass athletic demonstration, an endeavour Sontag recognises to be a valued activity in totalitarian regimes, yet, as Michael Mackenzie has drawn attention to, it is peripheral to the film as a whole.[11] Mackenzie perceives a tension in *Olympia* between a more conservative conception of athletics associated with the Turner clubs (gymnastic organisations) and the competitive ethos of modern sports. He reads the athletics drill as 'an irruption of an older, specifically German physical exercise into a film and an event that otherwise efface that tradition'.[12] The opening of the film, which will be discussed in more depth later, is interpreted as an attempt by Riefenstahl to reconcile a discursive split in relation to athletic activity between the discipline of *Ausdruckstanz* (expressive dance) and those sports that embody its values, and modern goal-oriented sports geared towards competitive success and fair play. The mass athletic demonstration may visually echo the choreographed crowds at Nuremberg yet it is rooted in an earlier phenomenon.

It is actually more instructive to work back from the Nuba photographs reproduced as *The Last of the Nuba* and *The People of Kau*, rather than seeking parallels in the Nuremberg documentaries, to grasp how fascist aesthetics carry into *Olympia*.[13] Nuba societies are varied and complex, some matrilineal, others patrilineal. These intricacies are, however, lost in Riefenstahl's vision. Her photo essays do tell gendered narratives but these are not reflective of reality. Sontag has insightfully drawn attention to gender disparities in the photographic depictions of Nuba culture although she limits her analysis to identifying the differing tasks performed by men and women in the farming communities. In the photographs, women are shown as restricted to the roles of 'breeders and helpers'.[14] Sontag fails to consider, however, what the visible differences between the sexes at the level of accoutrements signal in relation to the photographer's aesthetics and its accompanying message. The men of Kau, for example, are often photographed wearing body paint, sometimes hair is brightly coloured, usually skin is white, but sometimes yellow. There are a great number of images showing men with their bodies coated in wood ash particularly in the sections on wrestling and on the *zariba*, a camp where herdsmen and wrestler's congregate, that appear in *The Last of the Nuba*. In some shots they are shown applying the pale powder. In others, their whitened bodies wrestle. Although the ash forms a crucial part of Nuba ritual, it is possible to read this repeated emphasis on the whiteness of their painted bodies as evidence of Riefenstahl's racism.

The racist dynamic of a film such as *Predator 2* (Dir. Stephen Hopkins, USA, 1990), for instance, can here be seen to work in reverse. In this film, set in the urban jungle of Los Angeles, the 'civilised' hero, black police officer Lieutenant Mike Harrigan, is contrasted with other black characters, a group of brutal Jamaican gangsters and the seemingly dreadlocked alien from which the film takes its name. Harrigan wears a suit which gives him a veneer of white-collar respectability. Ultimately, however, this respectability, his civility, is shown to be a masquerade. The film ends with a bloodied Harrigan, his clothes shredded, his face coated in dust, returned to his 'rightful' place. He looks 'savage'. The powder that clings to his visage, reminiscent of clay body paint, is the strongest indicator of his 'brutishness'. In his exhausted state he also walks stiffly, connoting the zombie. The scene forms the most obvious one of several in which Harrigan is associated with images of the 'primitive'.[15]

Riefenstahl's photographs also invoke the rhetoric of primitivism. Mackenzie traces her interest in the Nuba back to the ideas of Hans W. Fischer who saw the dances of African tribespeople as evidence of their lack of culture and closeness to nature.[16] It was 'free of the deadening effects of modernity (*Zivilisation*)'.[17] Tribespeople are to be viewed positively because they possess attributes, namely their sense of community and proximity to nature, which many German people have lost because of the perceived deleterious effects of modernity. In this sense, the whitened bodies of the Nuba encourage connection with the European spectators of Riefenstahl's book. The 'savage' is shown to be similar to the white viewer in terms of physical appearance and, by extension, in relation to a shared need for community and communion with the natural world. Cultural relativism is rejected by Riefenstahl in favour of universal communitarianism.

Taking a Shine

In her analysis of the Nuba photographs, bell hooks has also stressed how these works are informed by Riefenstahl's slavish adherence to, and celebration of, phallic masculinity. The racist mindset underpinning the images intersects with patriarchal ideology. hooks suggests that 'any onlooker who critically studies Riefenstahl's treatment of male bodies in the film *Olympia* can see that she continued to celebrate the tyranny of the phallic masculine in her representations of the Nuba'.[18] The firm, muscular bodies of the Nuba men are burdened by Riefenstahl with symbolising phallic potency. Her photographs invite comparisons and contrasts between the many dusty, matt male bodies that are displayed and the numerous oily, glistening bodies of women. The men are lustreless, their bodies dry. The women gleam, their bodies are slick. There is a photograph from *The People of Kau* (in the section on tattooing) of a young woman, her abdomen heavily scarified, ridged. A figure, seen only from behind, has coated the crafted welts with oil. She is in the process of adding to the pattern with a thorn. Scars are frequently used in Nuba culture to mark major life events.

Riefenstahl has composed this particular image, which forms part of a series detailing an act of scarification, so that the head of the woman is largely out of sight, only her chin and bottom lip is visible. The top of the woman's thighs and her pubis are in view, although the latter is in shadow, but her legs are invisible. Her arms are also only partly in shot. The way the woman is framed is therefore revealing. She is attenuated, reduced to a torso. Her body becomes breasts, unctuous midriff, and pubis. She is reduced to what is essential about her: bosoms, crotch, and sheen. It is this sheen which is most noteworthy. It is a recurrent motif in the images Riefenstahl chooses as representative of the Nuba in *The People of Kau* although it is also visible in *The Last of the Nuba*.

In *The People of Kau*, for example, there is another photograph of a woman's face and upper body. The woman, known as Jamila, is smeared in oil and ochre, her skin shining in the sunlight. There are also photographs of groups of women dancing the *nyertun*, a lover's dance, their bodies glistening russet or gleaming jet. Riefenstahl's photographs operate to forge a link between Woman and lubricity, and Woman and gloss, particular tactile and visual attributes that are interconnected. Riefenstahl is conscious of the visual effects the women display, writing of the *nyertun*: 'the girl's bodies glint as if gilded among the swirling clouds of sunlit dust' and 'shine as though coated with red or black lacquer'.[19] It is oil and sweat that makes the women's skin reflective, which causes the fleeting, shifting streaks and patches of shine that the viewer finds fixed in the photographs. The wood ash used by the men prevents specular reflection. It is lacklustre and absorbs perspiration. This is not to say that all the men or women display these characteristics yet there are marked tendencies particularly in terms of the images Riefenstahl uses to represent the Nuba.

Her selection makes gender differences visible at the level of lustre. Men are frequently pictured as lacking in sheen. Women, by contrast, are often shown as radiant. In Riefenstahl's vision of the Nuba, irrespective of whether it meshes with their lived reality, men are dry and women are lubricious.

Riefenstahl acknowledges that there is an erotic element to some of the subjects she photographed.[20] The taking of pictures possesses a frisson. She writes, for example, of photographing a knife fight:

> I now ventured closer to the arena and took my first action shots. I had slung my two Leicaflex cameras round my neck and fitted them with motordrives and powerful telescopic lenses. It was incredibly exciting. After taking a few general views, I moved progressively nearer the fighters until I was in the thick of the fray. Somebody shooed me away, but I dodged back in from the other side.[21]

Once the fight is over and Riefenstahl has ceased shooting, she is 'tired out, soaked with sweat and covered in dust but blissfully happy'.[22] The description could be one of post-coital pleasure. Riefenstahl gets off on taking pictures as is evident from her references to how stimulating photography is for her. Her pleasure is, however, often voyeuristic and implicitly violent. Riefenstahl, for instance, calls her Leica cameras part of her 'photographic arsenal'.[23] The reluctance of the people of Kau to be photographed means that she has to do most of her work 'with very powerful telescopic lenses'.[24] The frisson is bound up with furtiveness. Shortly after describing how lithe the bodies of a group of girls dancing are, and how erotic their movements, Riefenstahl explains: 'the dancers were unaware of my presence because I had hidden behind a tree and was photographing them with powerful telescopic lenses'.[25]

Riefenstahl's subjects frequently do not consent to their images being taken. The Nuba are used by her as unwitting canvases upon which to project her erotic desires. It is clear from the images of men and women that she appreciates compact backsides. She also links cicatrisation with lingerie in her imagination: 'the designs cut on the back can be very beautiful and give the effect of black lace on a dark body'.[26] It is also, however, obvious that she has a fetishistic interest in lustre. Freud's most extraordinary case of fetishism was the man who was aroused by a 'shine on the nose', or *Glanz auf der Nase*, which the psychoanalyst signalled was in reality a '*glance* at the nose'.[27] Here, for Freud, the nose acts as stand in for the missing maternal penis. His interpretation elevates a bodily protuberance to the status of the fetish object at the expense of the shine despite the fact this phenomenon seems central to the man's desiring glance to such an extent that, as Freud's account acknowledges, he endowed noses 'with the luminous shine which was not perceptible to others'.[28] The fetish comprises a combination of flesh and its capacity for reflection. Freud, however, disavows the man's lust for lustre. Laura Mulvey in her discussion of fetishism does not. She comments that in popular imagination the fetish 'glitters'.[29] It is a luminous phenomenon.

Riefenstahl appears to be a populist of the kind Mulvey refers to as she exhibits a comparable fascination with shining flesh to Freud's patient. This is evident in *Olympia* which, at times, can be interpreted as a paean to sweat. Sontag is right to detect a fascination with fluidity and its suppression in *Olympia*. There is a tension throughout the film between imagery of fluidity, of which glistening sweat is a central marker, and solidity. This substantial friction is set up at the start of the film. The classical vocabulary of the opening credits cements Germany's connection with ancient Greece. It also aligns film with Greek architecture and with sculpture as an art form.[30] The inscription of the film's title in stone, rendering it as part of an antique frieze, also works to emphasise timelessness and stasis. Stone is a solid, enduring material. These robust credits are, however, followed by a shot of descent through clouds, by an encounter with the amorphous and evanescent, accompanied by Herbert Windt's suspenseful music. The camera descends to earth, to overgrown fragments of a classical temple, the imagery transparently suggestive of a lost classical past. Once the architecture, the Parthenon, parts of the Ereichtheion and the Poseidon temple, on the Acropolis has been revealed, the preceding shot of clouds are open to retrospective interpretation as symbolic of the heavens, of Mount Olympus.[31] There is, however, more nebulous material located amongst the ruins.

I am thinking, for instance, of shots of classical statuary for which Riefenstahl employs special effects, mechanically engineering fog that rises from the ground partially obscuring the sculptures. This *mise-en-scène* links the lasting and the transient, the opaque and the diaphanous, solid melting into air. The contrast is brought out most strongly through a shot that dwells on a statue of a female figure, possibly Aphrodite. The conjoining of fog and female form links fluidity and motion, and also visual disturbance, with femininity. This connection will be reemphasised later when shots of a group of naked women dancing are presented against backdrops of wind through grass and waves breaking on a beach, visually establishing a relationship between femininity and flow. That this affiliation might be a cause of anxiety is suggested by the dissolve in which the women are overlaid and consumed by the Olympic flame. Sport is therefore visually allied with triumph over Woman or, even more disconcertingly, with her destruction.

The shots of nude men and women in the prologue to the film have been attributed to the influence of the painter Hubert Stowitts on Riefenstahl.[32] In 1936 Stowitts had mounted an exhibition of 55 tempera on masonite paintings called 'The American Champions' in Berlin. The series included depictions of African-American and Jewish athletes. The exhibit was closed either because of the ethnicity of some of the athletes portrayed or due to its homoeroticism. The show included nude portraits of sportsmen including the UCLA AAU lightweight wrestling champion Briggs Hunt shown wrestling William Golden, the diver Frank Kurtz, the decathlete Woodrow 'Woody' Strode, and the tennis player Bobby Riggs. It displayed the sexual appeal of the athletic male body. Riefenstahl's film also registers an erotic appreciation of sporting physiques. Rodriguéz has sensitively drawn attention to Riefenstahl's propensity to take 'leisurely pleasure' in athletic bodies.[33] She sees this pleasure as occurring in equal measure between male and female athletes. The film, however, does not bear out this perceived parity. It is the male athlete who is the primary recipient of Riefenstahl's licentious lens. Jesse Owens and also other anonymous male bodies are given greater screen time, more seen time, than the women. The temporal disparity, the editing, betrays Riefenstahl's erotic reflexes.

As well as affirming a heterosexual viewing dynamic, Riefenstahl also reinforces patriarchal ideology. In *Male Fantasies*, Klaus Theweleit reproduces a section of a triptych of the *Four Elements* (c. 1936) by Adolf Ziegler that used to hang over the mantelpiece in the Führer Room of the Brown House in Munich. The painting depicts water personified as a naked woman: a bowl of the substance is used to anchor her symbolism.

This picture reproduces a traditional alignment within Western culture of Woman with Nature. As aforementioned, Riefenstahl's prologue endorses this perspective through visually establishing water and wind, flow and motion, as feminine attributes. Theweleit discusses how the world's literatures frequently evince this choice of metaphor.[34] He interprets Woman's longstanding symbolic equation with fluidity as a form of underrated oppression. It denies particularity. Riefenstahl's sexually saturated vision of femininity continues this longstanding negative practice. Woman as aqueous, as a watery element within the film, exists not only in the Prologue but also, implicitly, in the second part of *Olympia*.

The beginning of the second part of the documentary holds echoes of the start of the Festival of the Nations. Festival of Beauty opens with footage of trees and water, oak leaves reflecting in a stream, ripples, dew on a spider's web, light streaming through trees to illuminate a morning mist. Silhouettes of runners appear, the figures growing in substance, emerging into view. These clothed athletes, presumably out on a morning training session, precede a sequence showing naked men swimming in a pond and then running in woodland. The camera remains fixed on the bank of the pond after the men have jogged out of view, pausing to catch the chaos of the water disturbed by their passing.

These male athletes are then shown having a sauna, beating each other with what are, presumably, birch boughs, massaging each other. The sequence delights in the naked athletic male body. One shot momentarily draws attention to a man's glistening buttocks, conspicuous in the bottom left corner of the frame (4.1). These are erotic and homoerotic scenes. Riefenstahl's thirst for Teutonic flesh is palpable. Rodriguéz has drawn attention to how only a woman could have directed such a brazen celebration of a male athlete's physical virtues.[35] There is also, however, a recognition of the role of the feminine in the construction of this female heterosexual desire. It is the sheen of sweat, for example, that provides the buttocks with their density, the gleam of perspiration that catches the eye. The fluid, the formless, the streaming sweat as it reflects light, serves to enhance definition.

This liquid secretion, like all fluids, all flowing places, is figured as feminine in the cultural context of Germany, and Europe more broadly, in the 1930s. There is a delight in fluidity even as, politically, solidity is being praised and privileged. The men in the sauna evidently take pleasure in their showering. They are shown as languorous. This pleasure

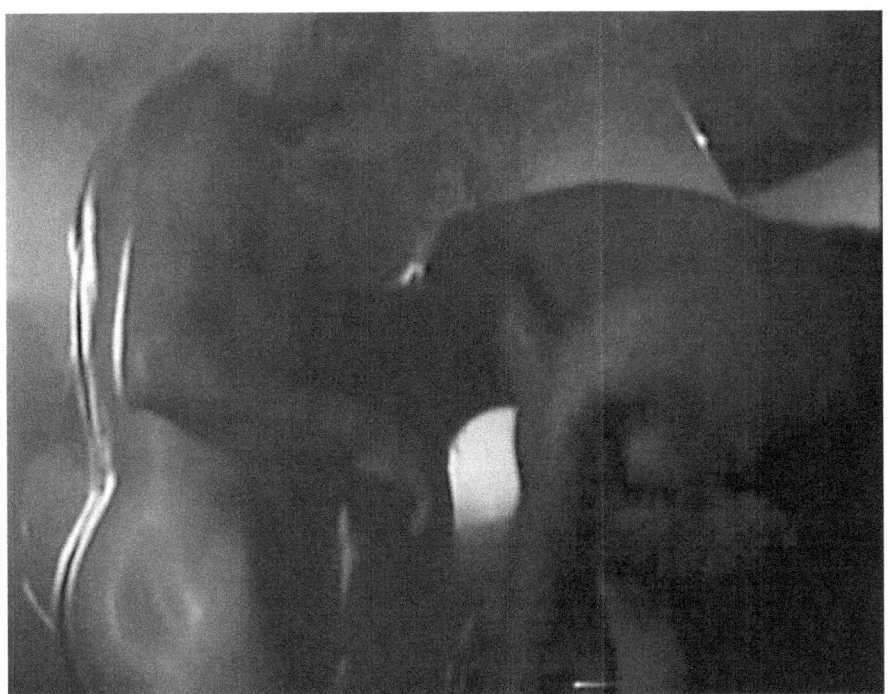

4.1 *Olympia* (1938): Gleaming buttocks

in water, as a form of enjoyment in fog and flow, potentially runs counter to the fascist aesthetic identified by Sontag. Sontag's identification of fascist aesthetics with containment resonates with Klaus Theweleit's eloquent exploration of the Nazi desire to inhibit fluidity: by way of its carefully choreographed formations of marching men: 'the threat of inundation had been eradicated'.[36] *Olympia*, however, fails to adequately excise this peril which appears at several junctures. There is an unresolved dialectic between the bounded and the unbounded running, flowing, through the film. The significance of this visual dialectic in relation to the political tenor of *Olympia* will be returned to.

Sporting Fetishes

In *Olympia*, sweat forms a substance that defines bodies but resists its own definition because of its unfixed and ephemeral qualities. Riefenstahl appears to appreciate its erotic potential. *Personal Best*, however, makes this possibility more explicit. The film has been described by Allen

Guttmann as 'a romantic combination of the aesthetic, the erotic, and the athletic'.[37] The two main characters are pentathletes Chris Cahill and Tory Skinner (whose appropriation of masculine gesture was discussed in the last chapter). *Personal Best*'s director, Robert Towne, studied the cinematographic techniques used by Riefenstahl in *Olympia* in preparation for filming. Two scenes set in a sauna in *Personal Best* can be seen to visually echo the sauna scene in *Olympia*. Here, however, it is women athletes that are relaxing surrounded by steam. Their association with haze and sweat is established through these sequences. The use of colour rather than black and white film reduces the amount of perspiration that can be seen. Tory makes up for this deficit, however, by stating at one point that she has come to the sauna to sweat.

The centrality of sweat to *Personal Best* is signalled when there is an artful shot of droplets falling onto a cinder race track. The camera then reveals the head of a runner, Chris. She is in her starting blocks waiting for a race to begin. Beads of sweat are dripping from her nose and chin onto the track. The scene is not, in itself, erotic. It does, however, draw attention to the phenomenon of perspiration. Sweating forms a means by which the body regulates its temperature. It can signal exertion as it occurs when muscles heat up through use. The substance, composed predominantly of water, is therefore associated with various form of exercise including sex. The sexual connotations of sweat are made obvious in the crime thriller *Tightrope* (Dir. Clint Eastwood, USA, 1984). The central character, police officer Wes Block, encounters rape prevention advisor Beryl Thibodeaux working out in a gym. Subsequently over a lunch of oysters, Wes suggests he would like to lick the sweat of Beryl's body. The initial impetus for this expression of desire appears to be their encounter in the gym. There is therefore crossover between health and fitness and sex. Reinforcing this, the role of the gym as a potential pick-up joint is a key theme in the film *Perfect* (Dir. James Bridges, USA, 1985).

Sweat can form a fetish. Salophilia is sexual attraction to salt or salty things such as body sweat. Wes in *Tightrope* appears to have a taste for this. He may also, however, appreciate the sight, smell and feel of perspiration. Sweat has multi-sensory appeal. Its olfactory potential contributes to fetishes for sweaty socks or pungent sneakers. These inclinations involve finding traces of the body, of its exertions, stimulating. They are intimate, requiring proximity to the object that incites desire. The erotic charge of sweat is also signalled in *Personal Best*. Guttmann singles out a scene of

Cahill and Skinner arm wrestling as particularly stimulating: 'lying on the floor, the two women clasp hands, strain, pant, sweat – and become sexually aroused'.[38] Here touch, exertion and perspiration combine to kindle desire. The way the sequence is filmed, the women weakly illuminated by flickering light from a television and table-lamps, is reminiscent of candlelight. The romantic meal is replaced by a passionate test of strength. The eyes of the two women meet over their tightly-clasped hands. Their intense connection established through repeated shots and reverse shots. Talk is minimal in this *tête-à-tête*. Chris does not speak at all. Their bodies are, however, in conversation, articulating effort and determination. Tory, in particular, sweats with effort. The scene exemplifies an androgynous eros of the kind discussed in the next chapter. Here it is sweat, muscle and strength that stimulate. The contest forms a microcosm for the nature of the relationship between Chris and Tory throughout the remainder of the film. Their competitiveness towards each other is bound up with their sexual attraction. The couple make manifest an erotic aspect present in all competitive sport.

Guttmann also draws attention to other, more conventional, sexual dimensions in the film such as a sequence in which the crotches and thighs of women high-jumpers are repeatedly focussed on as the athletes each leap backwards over the bar. Guttmann states that 'in slow motion, the sensuality of the movement is so explicit and so emphatic that some feminist critics have denounced the scene as the most blatantly pornographic sequence in what they condemn as a thoroughly sexist film'.[39] The rhythm of the sequence, the crotches continually rising towards the spectator, is here interpreted as suggestive of the coital. It also fragments the women into specific body parts. They are reduced to their legs and crotches. This conventional form of sexual objectification recurs in a number of more recent films featuring sportswomen including *Fast Girls*. It is evident, for example, in an early scene in that film in which main rivals, working-class Shania Andrews and bourgeois Lisa Temple, are shown at a UK Athletics training facility practising their block starts. The women are filmed from in front as they step into, and settle into, the blocks, carefully positioning their hands along the start line while the coach delivers instructions. The camera at this moment is static, positioned low to the ground, at a similar level to the bodies of the athletes. They are initially shot with their heads out of frame. Their faces subsequently drop into view.

A close-up shot of Shania shows her looking down as she carefully positions her hands which are out of shot. That this is what she is doing is clear from the motions of her shoulders and head, the pendulum like motion of her neck chain. The shot also reveals her cleavage. The next shot is from above and behind the athletes. As the coach instructs them to keep their heads down and their weight forward, they raise their bums to the camera. The shot is highly stylised with the lane markings bisecting the two individuals so they can be read as mirror images. It reinforces the parallel and contrasting lives of the two women that is a key theme of the film. The shot, however, also focusses on a particular part of their anatomy from a position rarely, if ever, employed in sports coverage because its atmospheric or informational value is minimal. This shot is about bums. It is chosen to titillate. In a repeat of this exercise, a shot from a similar camera angle focuses on the calves of the women as they position their feet in the blocks. Legs are, admittedly, what propel the sprinters out of the blocks so the shot focuses on the means to sprint. The camerawork, however, still appears overdetermined. It is followed by a shot from in front which provides another view of the cleavage of the two. The scene at the blocks appears to provide a pretext for getting up close to the bodies of the athletes.

This reduction of the women to particular body parts is not a one-off event. There is, for instance, a later scene involving the team physiotherapist Carl and Shania. This disturbing encounter reveals sexual power dynamics at work in the film. It begins with Shania waiting seated on a physiotherapy table as Carl writes. Once he is ready to begin his physical examination he gives vocal direction: 'Can you go and stand over there for me?' He then approaches Shania and begins to manhandle her, asking her to turn around and then, as he grips her backside and hips, extend her leg. Shania's expression during this examination of her lower body is one of bewilderment. Her pursed lips suggest tension, perhaps a degree of suspicion, in relation to Carl's manipulating. There is an exhalation of relief when he finishes this part of the examination. She was holding her breath, trepidatious. Carl then attends to her upper body, parting her hair and pushing it over her shoulders as he grips her clavicle. Carl looks down and then kneels, his hands sliding off her shoulders, shading into what seems like a fleeting caress of the deltoids. In an earlier scene Carl's 'brutal touch' is referred to by the coach, Tommy, as Shania's reward for making

4.2 *Fast Girls* (2012): Carl manipulating Shania

the relay squad. Here, through the physiotherapist's handling the nature of that brutality is revealed (4.2).

Shania's eyes widen as Carl feels her waist. He appears to be looking at her buttocks at a moment in which information should primarily be sourced through tactility. Carl feels yet he also observes. He then takes Shania's shoulder and turns her body to face him rather than asking her to turn around. She is shown to be manipulable. The way Carl approaches Shania, directing her movements, is reminiscent of the work of the film director, the individual currently out of shot yet dictating the action. Actors are bodies to position and choreograph. Flesh is there to be managed. The inspection of Shania's body also echoes the earlier close analysis of her and Lisa at the starting blocks. In that scene she was similarly reduced to body parts, scrutinised, caressed.

Despite Carl's manhandling of her, Shania makes a pass at him. He initially appears indifferent yet just before she leaves he commends her strong glutes. He is praising her buttocks using the guise of her athleticism. The remark, ostensibly professional, appears passional in the broader context of the examination and given that later in the film he refers to her 'arse' before correcting himself and saying glutes. Shania is consistently reduced to her bum in *Fast Girls*. The camera has also inspected it at close quarters as, by extension, have the audience. The sexual politics of the film are therefore reactionary. This contrasts with its genuine efforts to promote sport as a practice that can foster understanding across class and ethnic differences.

The film's treatment of sportswomen as instruments for sexual titillation, visual and tactile enjoyment, must be regarded negatively. Its carnal take on female athletes can also be seen as reflective of a general and persistent trend in culture to treat sportswomen as sources of voyeuristic sexual pleasure rather than physically intelligent individuals. The video of hurdler Michelle Jenneke performing a warm-up at the 2012 Junior World Championships in Barcelona which has been set to the song 'Boys' by Sabrina on YouTube forms a high profile example of the routine sexualisation of actual, rather than acting, athletes. Jenneke's warm-up is more exuberant than those of her rivals. It makes her bosom heave and her broad thighs quiver. The music, however, contributes significantly to framing Jenneke in insalubrious terms. Comments posted on YouTube frequently refer to the masturbatory potential of the footage.

Jenneke, although unlike most of the women in *Fast Girls* in that she is bulkier, more muscular, wears similar sporting apparel. She is dressed in a white Lycra cropped top and green sprinter shorts. This clothing is designed to maximise her capacity for speed. Sally Gunnell, another hurdler, has drawn attention to how 'state-of-the-art designs and fabric' can give a 'vital edge in performance'.[40] Jenneke's shorts and top weigh hardly anything and only minimally impede the movement of her body as she powers along the track. The material only slightly hinders her body in motion as Lycra is a stretch synthetic fibre. This stretch property is, Sarah Braddock states, 'vital in all sports clothing' and allows 'maximum movement'.[41] Lycra also wicks, draws away, sweat from the skin. The athletes in *Fast Girls* wear clothing comparable to Jenneke's yet in the film the camerawork in sequences such as the training session draws attention to Lycra's sexual dimension. The fabric has an erotic potency that *Fast Girls* continually exploits in ways that *Personal Best*, which also features athletes in Lycra, does not. One reason for the lack of attention to bodies in Lycra in the earlier film may be that Lycra had not become popular as a form of fetishism.

Since the rise of Lycra as an erotically charged material, athletics, as an activity in which the use of stretch-fabric is particularly pronounced, has provided a spandex smorgasbord for the fetishist. *Personal Best*, however, was released in 1982 which is the same year Jane Fonda produced her first exercise video. It is too early to register the effects of the rise of aerobics attire upon eroticism. The figure-hugging clothing worn by many 1980s workout devotees was, as Braddock draws attention to, not only practical but also aesthetic. It showed of an athletic physique. This kind of body became a beauty ideal in the 1980s and has remained so. Joy Mackenzie suggests that as it is an object of desire, 'most sports clothing today is designed not only to be technically efficient and increase a competitor's effectiveness but also to reveal the body beneath it'.[42]

Lycra, as close-to-skin clothing, functions as a second skin. The fabric's capacity to spring to accommodate diversely shaped physiques has led Judith Halberstam to interpret its popularity as symptomatic of the contemporary trend for fluid conceptions of identity and personal choice.[43] The fabric is democratic, equally expansive and capacious for all, rendering similitude in difference. Sexual attraction to Lycra is referred to as Lycra or spandex fetishism. The emergence of this phenomenon may lend credence to Freud's assertion that fetish objects, as substitutes for the absent female phallus, relate to 'the last moment in which the [mother] could still be regarded as phallic'.[44] Lycra, as Kaori O' Connor discusses, was frequently employed as the fabric for brassieres and girdles in the 1970s and for leotards and leggings in the 1980s.[45] The fabric was therefore prime territory for providing fetish material in Freud's terms.

Lycra fetishism can potentially take many forms. The fabric has diverse qualities which may possibly comprise its appeal. Its stretchiness is the most obvious, it expands and contracts, it is tumescent and detumescent. It can also, however, be felt as restrictive.[46] Lycra is used in foundation garments to alter the body's usual shape. As shapewear, it permits the wearer to look slimmer or more curvaceous. Lycra therefore has a bondage element. The spandex fetishist can take pleasure either in expansion or confinement. Michel Serres's remarks on the cords that comprise clothing are informative in this context. He writes that their 'limits invert the properties they enclose and protect: mobility inside and fixity at the frontiers, absence inside, sudden presence on the borders'.[47] The synthetic fibres enable motion whilst simultaneously securing the body, they restrain without constraining. Additionally, the fabric possesses marked tactile qualities which may also be a source of pleasure. It is smooth, silky, pliant yet tough. Lycra is sensuous. Knowledge of the feel of the material can be brought to representations of it in film.

The fabric also takes a range of dyes well and clothes therefore exist in diverse colours. Lycra's versatility enables a feminine apologetic to frequently be embedded in the design through colour, panelling and trim.⁴⁸ This rich colouring is evident in *Fast Girls*, in which a contrast between the sports clothing worn by male and female characters is often evident. In the first scene at the indoor training facility, Tommy wears a black polo-shirt with white stripes and matching tracksuit pants and Carl, whose lower body is not visible, wears a grey polo shirt with black stripes over a white tee-shirt. Two of the women wear turquoise. Belle sports a singlet in the colour and Lisa a crop top with black piping. Lisa's black Lycra running shorts are also embellished with turquoise stripes. Turquoise, the name of which derives from a precious stone, contrasts with the muted colours worn by the men and by Shania throughout the film.

In an outdoor training session shortly afterwards, Trix Warren is shown wearing a black floral patterned body stocking underneath her top and shorts. The design of this stocking is echoed later when Trix is shown at a fundraising party in an evening dress made, in part, with a similarly sheer and delicate fabric. The shots of the legs of several of the athletes running at the outdoor session are a blur of black Lycra with pink stripes. The fine bands of colour form a 'feminine' touch built into the design of the shorts that is equivalent in purpose to the body stocking. The need for the sprinters to look feminine is later reinforced by Belle Newman who, whilst applying lipstick, advises a hung-over and retching Shania "Look good and run fast girl – that's how it works". Sports clothing is frequently coded as feminine through its colouring even, as with running shorts, when it has the potential to be unisex.⁴⁹

If Lycra clothing is sexually stimulating it is often because its colour or function genders it. *Fast Girls* exploits this. It is filmed in ways which appeal to the erotic connoisseur of women in stretch fabrics. The contours of each of the athletes are frequently made easy to see. They are clothed in their nakedness. The potential for sports clothing to reveal the female body is already evident in *Olympia* which includes a scene in which the Italian hurdler Trebisonda Valla's nipples are clearly visible through her top. Riefenstahl, however, does not search for transparently erotic moments whereas *Fast Girls* actively pursues Lycra's sexual appeal. *Personal Best* does not exploit clothing in this way but it does capitalise on similarities between athletic activity in sexual and sporting contexts, taking advantage of sounds and sweating to connote both types of activity at once.

Spent Politics

Olympia, *Personal Best* and *Fast Girls* are all, however, united in their focus on sheens, either of sweat or of light reflective synthetic materials. There is a common fetish across the films. Fetishes, as Mulvey explains, do more than substitute for the missing maternal penis. They also commemorate it.[50] The fetish is a memorial to 'the original moment of castration anxiety' and 'also a mark of mourning for the lost object'.[51] Mulvey suggests that this commemorative dimension means that the fetish as sign includes 'a residual knowledge of its origin'.[52] It is therefore a potential source of anxiety as it indexes the traumatic event that comprises recognition of the mother's lack. In *Olympia*, the fetish as sign of feminine difference, of a perceived missing part, works to trouble the drive to secure form that Sontag sees as comprising the fascist aesthetic of the film. The sheens of sweat and water on athletes bodies both provides an assertion of their figures, their crafted flesh, and, as a fleeting and diffuse phenomenon, undercuts it.

Mulvey argues that 'the fetish is always haunted by the fragility of the mechanisms that sustain it'.[53] In *Olympia*, the fetish for holding tight and holding in, for grasping and constraining, is challenged by an accompanying fetishisation of the dispersed and the amorphous. The gleam in Riefenstahl's film troubles its imagery. It functions like glare as it impacts on visual clarity in photography. There is another register at work in the film to the one Sontag focuses on which prevents *Olympia* from fascinating only in fascist terms. Shimmers and sparkles caused by light and liquid also draw the attention. This amorphous aspect reveals the formlessness required for any process of forming to take place, the ancestry, and potential future, which form disavows. Riefenstahl's avant-gardism, as exhibited in her visual style, made her an outsider in the film industry of National Socialism.[54]

For Sontag, fascist aesthetics flow from 'a preoccupation with situations of control, submissive behaviour, extravagant effort, and the endurance of pain'.[55] She goes on to suggest that: 'the fascist dramaturgy centers on the orgiastic transactions between mighty forces and their puppets, uniformly garbed and shown in ever swelling numbers. Its choreography alternates between ceaseless motion and a congealed, static, "virile" posing'.[56] Sontag's priapic description draws attention to the phallic pretensions of fascist aesthetics. The carefully choreographed marches in *Triumph des Willens* form parade ground exercises in group tumescence. Through the machinations of National Socialism, the masses, the unruly crowd, are morphed into the determined cohort. In her Nuremberg films, Riefenstahl celebrates multitudes of people conforming to a singular design. The fascist aesthetic forges sense, cohesion, and discretion, out of the chaos and tumult of the crowd. Sontag perceives what takes place at a macroscopic level, the well-defined, designed, groups of marching bodies, to be reduplicated at a microscopic level as well, in the rigid and regimented body of the individual. The solitary body engaged in sporting activities such as gymnastics can also exhibit the same drive to control and constrain. The gymnast exhibits a 'holding in or confining of force; military precision'.[57] In this context, a comparison made between elite gymnasts and Navy Seals by Haley in *Stick It* is not far-fetched.

Discipline, for Sontag, always operates in support of fascism, enabling the production of solid form. *Olympia*, however, demonstrates that disciplinary practices create subversive side-effects, such as beads or rivulets of sweat. Efforts to curtail flow are undermined by flow. The fascist aesthetic of the film is also undercut by a parallel visual fascination, what might be termed, in this context, Riefenstahl's decadent aesthetic. She is unable to resist the beauty of water, the chop and spray in the yachting sequence, bubbles and ripples during the diving. In the documentary, these phenomena are all produced by sporting activities. The water in the pool and the sea is linked with physical exertion. The clue to Riefenstahl's continual fascination with turbid water is provided in the juxtaposition of the scene of the swimmers in the pond and the sauna discussed earlier. Water throughout *Olympia* is metonymically linked with physical action and, by extension, perspiration. Riefenstahl is fascinated by the rough surface of the empty pond or a seethe of bubbles in a pool as these both index physical exertions. The pond continues to reflect the actions of the naked swimmers, their vigorous efforts.

The artistic fascist body is supposed to be untainted by toil, an immobile ideal. Riefenstahl, however, is seduced by athletic labour. Sontag concedes that the documentary includes what she identifies as imperfections, the depiction of effort and strain, of physical exertion.[58] This effort and strain marks the erogenous aspect of the film. It is one Sontag fails to register as she perceives the erotic in National Socialism to be 'women' as temptresses. Riefenstahl, however, is enticed by the athletic male body. That the male physique in action is her core concern is made evident by the different ways she approaches directing the filming of events such as the discus. The precision she dedicates to recording the men's efforts is abandoned when it comes to representing the women. The filming here is clumsier, with female athletes frequently disappearing out of frame whilst making their attempts. This contrast might be explained by the obedience of Riefenstahl and her cameramen to the gender hierarchy instituted by fascism in which virile masculinity functioned as the ideal. Another reason for the differing attentiveness exhibited here is, however, that the men held more allure for Riefenstahl and, possibly, some of her entourage. The camera betrays desire for the male body.

Thomas Elsaesser has written of Riefenstahl's abstraction of the human figure, her voiding of the specific in favour of empty generality.[59] This is largely the case, although sometimes specific athletes are singled out for more attention, such as Jesse Owens, and this emphasis particularises them. The human figure is also not abstracted from gender. Men are the prime concern as the cinematography and editing affirms. *Olympia* manifestly celebrates heroic masculinity. In this, its aesthetic fascination with the athletic male body, it resonates with Arno Breker's sculptures of muscular figures. His work *Der Zehnkämpfer* [*The Decathlete*] was designed for the 1936 Olympics. It portrays a naked make athlete standing with his arms by his sides. Breker also produced another sculpture, *Der Siegerin* [*Victory*], for the Olympics which shows a naked woman holding a laurel. It is telling that the female figure forms an allegory, an embodiment of an abstract concept, whereas the male represents an athlete associated with a specific sporting event. *Der Siegerin*, was however, modelled on an actual woman javelin thrower. A skilled sportswoman hides behind the symbolism.

In *Olympia* there is another dimension to the film behind its primarily masculine subject-matter. This dimension is traditionally culturally coded as feminine. Riefenstahl's documentary possesses a prettiness that is at odds with the fascist aesthetic it is frequently held to embody. Rosalind Galt equates the pretty as it manifests itself in film with qualities such as 'arabesque camera movement, detailed mise-en-scène, and [...] emphasis on cinematographic surface'.[60] Galt tracks how the pretty as an aesthetic category has frequently been denigrated through a critical vocabulary that aligns it with femininity. She suggests that pretty films are also frequently criticised for their fetishism. In her book *Pretty*, Galt wishes to recuperate the pretty as a political resource. Here, however, I want to briefly examine what it meant, and means, for Riefenstahl to have produced a film with a strong aspect of prettiness to it at a time when to do so risked condemnation. Galt, for example, examines Hugo Münsterberg's condemnation, in *The Film, a Psychological Study* of 1916, of melodramatic light effects.[61] The flawed visual effects, which dazzle the spectator, include lights, glare and flashes. Riefenstahl, as already indicated, was a connoisseur of luminous effects throughout her career. Sheen, however, would have aroused Münsterberg's aesthetic suspicion.

The visual style of *Olympia*, its delight in plays of light, in sweaty sparkles, would have been even more politically suspect in the 1930s. The attention to ephemeral glister threatened the political coherence of the film although, evidently, not sufficiently for it to be disparaged. The film strives to glorify the male body yet its obsession with glistening sweat and its metonyms undercuts this message. The sequence in the sauna, in which sweat functions as erogenous ornament, is the most explicit rendering of what comprises an overarching preoccupation. Riefenstahl's vision is ultimately too drawn to the 'stain' that is shininess, too impure in form, to embody the fascist politics she embraced and sought to lionise. Sheen, as it is manifested in motion pictures, is fleeting and changeable. It resists rigidity. It was only subsequently, with the photographs of the Nuba, that Riefenstahl was able to fix her visual effects, bring them into line with her fascist sympathies. She was still seduced by gleaming bodies yet the use of still images enabled her to suppress luminous modulations, to arrest shift and flow.

Riefenstahl wrote of the Nuba: 'I was fortunate to get to know them whilst their traditional way of life still existed, and to be able to fix this in pictures, films and recordings.'[62] Fixing is indeed central to understanding her projects in Africa. The pictures fix and repair, the 'damaged' vision of *Olympia*. They provide Riefenstahl with an opportunity to make reparation to National Socialism for her aesthetic failure in documenting the Olympics. This is because the subversive potential of luminosity is held in check. The ephemeral and unsettled is secured. It is only in these later works that the fascist aesthetics identified by Sontag, the containing principle of fascism, finally triumphs. The Nuba photographs display a more controlled eroticism. Riefenstahl's fetish is no longer given free play.

The pictures are cold. They freeze sunlight and sweat. Bodies and places are contained. Riefenstahl, in those moments when she abandons the movie camera, has now got a hold of her desire and of her subject. Practice has led her to perfect her artistic methods, allowing a purer expression of her fascination with fascism.

5
Muscle Pictures: Bodybuilding Films

Warm-up

A woman's face is shown in close-up: the bodybuilder Gladys Portugues. Her lush, dark curly hair fills the right of the screen. It is mirrored to the left by a sizeable black barbell disc which obscures the background. Her right hand, with its manicured nails, is just visible gripping the bar. She takes quick, deep breaths, preparing to lift. The camera now cuts to a shot filmed from side-on and slightly behind her. It reveals Lydia Cheng, the woman 'spotting' Portugues. Cheng will provide assistance during the lift if it is needed. As Portugues bends her knees, lowers herself, Cheng mirrors the movement. Her hands lightly clasp the leather weightlifting belt fastened around Portugues's midriff, the grip loose enough so as not to impede movement. She then raises herself in tandem with Portugues. The camera is steady, centred on Cheng's toned upper arms and then, as their lower bodies rise into view, on the glutes of both women. Portugues lets out a gasp of effort as she comes to a standing position. The sequence is one that emphasises symmetry and paralleling at the levels of motion and visual appearance (5.1). Cheng's red and black striped leotard echoes the pink, purple and white stripes of Portugues's.

The brief scene just described occurs as part of a much longer sequence of gym-related activities in the semi-documentary *Pumping Iron II: The Women* (Dir. George Butler, USA, 1985). This film is the sequel to *Pumping Iron* (Dirs. Robert Fiore and George Butler, 1977, USA), which centred on the build-up to the 1975 International Federation of Bodybuilding and Fitness (IFBB) Mr. Universe and Mr Olympia competitions. *Pumping Iron* features Arnold Schwarzenegger and contributed to his

5.1 *Pumping Iron II* (1985): Working out in tandem

becoming famous beyond the world of bodybuilding. *Pumping Iron II* follows a similar format to its predecessor, in that much of the film presents preparation for a bodybuilding contest, the 1983 Caesar's World Cup organised by the IFBB. This contest, which was held specifically for the film, was not a regular event. It was never repeated. *Pumping Iron II* focusses on the physical fortunes of four competitors in particular, the Americans Lori Bowen, Carla Dunlap, and Rachel McLish, and the Australian Bev Francis. It differs from the earlier film in that it explicitly addresses gender issues, specifically what kind of physique should form the benchmark for femininity. Douglas Aoki suggests that the film sets up the winner of the competition as someone who 'will figure the standard posed by the judges for future sex/future woman'.[1]

This reading of the film, in which the debate about femininity is seen as the central concern, is echoed by most writers who critically engage with it. Jocelyn Robson and Beverley Zalcock, for example, interpret the film as interrogating which body images are appropriate for women.[2] Alan Mansfield and Barbara McGinn suggest that the competition the film centres around is 'a contest over definitions of women's bodies and what they do or should look like'.[3] Cindy Patton argues that the viewer is asked to adjudicate between two concepts of femininity, 'beefy Bev, the defeminized woman, versus Rachel McLish, the naturally muscled paragon of femininity'.⁴ This chapter, however, draws on the corporeal philosophy of Belgian athlete and novelist Nathalie Gassel as a means to supplement these earlier interpretations, drawing attention to how *Pumping Iron II* explores sexuality as well as gender.

Gassel's Corpus

Nathalie Gassel's writings provide a crucial template for thinking about bodybuilding's potential as a means by which to move beyond gender binaries and genital-centred conceptions of sexuality. She also provides crucial insights into how to write athleticism, how to compose sports related texts differently. Gassel does more than provide accounts of her bodily accomplishments. Her prose is, at times, inhabited by her physicality: forceful and substantial. She brings to the fore the continuum between action and its notation, between athletic endeavour and accounts of it, disrupting differentiation between the two. Bodily insights are carried into her prose, the vigour of physical actions lifted into written words.

Gassel has authored eight books to date. Her work has not been widely translated into English although some short pieces were published in *Picturing the Modern Amazon* in 2000.⁵ Gassel's writings, frequently sexual in content, are difficult to classify. Hybrid in style, they form a kind of prose-poetry, and shift genre between autobiography, pornography, essay and photo-essay.⁶ Previous commentators have focussed on how her work redefines the genre of pornography or provides a conceptualisation of identity that is grounded in physicality rather than personality.⁷ Jan Baetens and Juan Jiménez Salcedo credit Gassel's corpus, particularly through its repeated emphasis on the eroticisation of muscle and of strength, with providing a manifesto for thinking sex beyond the penis-vagina coital model of sexual gratification.⁸ The descriptions she provides of her physique have also been praised for the queer potential they hold, portraying a body no longer bound by gender norms and their accompanying imperatives.⁹ Both these aspects of her writings are useful for making sense of *Pumping Iron II* and the practices it documents.

Gassel's writings often detail her sexual exploits. She derives carnal pleasure from physically intimidating and dominating men and also from admiring and fantasising about the hyper-muscular physiques of women bodybuilders. Her descriptions of these activities allow her work to be categorised as muscle erotica. She is also, however, a philosopher of muscle. Her ideas primarily take form in her muscles. These comprise her preferred mode of thinking. She articulates her ideas through flesh as well as words. Gassel theorises the 'pump', the pleasurable feeling that accompanies a muscle becoming engorged with blood, as a mode of being. In *Pumping Iron*, Arnold Schwarzenegger famously characterised the pump as 'better than coming'. This pleasurable sensation of expansion forms the principle topic of Gassel's book *Éros androyne*. Baetens reads it as a work that is ultimately about getting hard.[10] This swelling and stiffening is, however, not linked to the penis but to muscle. In this it is similar to Joanna Frueh's conception of the pump as a sensation that need not be figured in phallic terms: erection and engorgement are bodily states that both men and women can experience.[11] For Gassel, the pump signals more than mere physical expansion, it also figures expanded horizons of being in the world. Her built body enables her to break with dominant ideals of female corporeality, as her muscles stiffen she feels she escapes 'woman's body'.[12] Her built body argues for biological indeterminism, her muscled form questions sex as ontological substrate. In this, Gassel's physique is comparable to some of the bodies that appear in *Pumping Iron II*.

Women bodybuilders are often described as practising a kind of drag. Alan Mansfield and Barbara McGinn, for example, read the feminine apologetic frequently manifested by hypermuscular women bodybuilders in this way: 'it is as though, when pushing at the limits of gender identity, lipstick and blonde locks are as necessary for the woman bodybuilder as they are for the female impersonator'.[13] The feminine apologetic comprises compensatory actions adopted by female athletes who are 'entering a traditionally masculine domain (sport in general)'.[14] In bodybuilding it takes the form of 'exaggerated use of feminine accoutrements such as makeup, jewellery, breast implants, and the like'.[15] The commonness of this cosmetic contrition in women's bodybuilding lends credence to Eve Kosofsky Sedgwick's sexing economy, in which investment in particular attributes, such as muscularity, can engender qualitative differentiation.[16] The muscle mass of the woman bodybuilder renders her qualitatively different from physiques circulating as feminine. The appliance of make-up, the attention to coiffure, the breast augmentations, as cosmetic alterations, all serve to quantitatively increase 'beauty' in an effort to nullify the emergent qualitative difference caused by heightened muscularity.

These efforts can, nonetheless, lead to what Cynthia Lewis describes as 'a curiously hermaphroditic look'.[17]

In *Pumping Iron II*, however, the hypermuscular Francis is unapologetic about her physique, she does not possess implants to conceal her compact pectorals, and her use of makeup is not overstated. Gassel also makes use of make-up but does not regard it as compensation for a lack of femininity. She believes it produces an abstract eroticism, at a remove from flesh.[18] When she does fantasise about wearing it paired with her massively muscled arms and shoulders, it renders her androgynous.[19] She does not use cosmetics to try and reassert femininity but, coupled with her powerful physique, to figure as male and female, hence neither male nor female. The event of deconstruction present in her body can also be read in Francis, particularly in her posing routine which is discussed later.

Gassel's writings conceive of muscle as a marker that is not bound to either masculinity or femininity. This is made clear when she describes the muscular buttocks, shoulders, and biceps of women bodybuilders, features that arouse her sexual desire, as hermaphroditic body-parts.[20] Here the fragmentation of the body, the fetishisation of parts, is found enabling. It is not that having highly muscled bodies (a type of physique often culturally coded as a masculine) turns women into hermaphrodites. Muscle as material that is shared by both sexes is what is always already hermaphroditic. This choice of description echoes that of Alphonso Lingis who also refers to a bodybuilder's muscles as hermaphrodite.[21] Gassel's own muscled figure, one that exhibits these hermaphroditic traits, can therefore be understood to 'think' gender in a non-traditional way. She shows, by way of her body, that muscularity and strength are not attributes that are bound to male bodies. They are potentially available to any body.

At this level, Gassel's project and Francis's practice in *Pumping Iron II* both appear to resonate with Judith Halberstam's in *Female Masculinity*. Halberstam foregrounds how masculinity should not be equated with being male. She cites Francis as an example of a masculine woman.[22] Masculinity can also be produced by women. Gassel, like a drag king, can be seen to potentially destabilise notions of the male body's realness and naturalness.[23] Indeed her choice of language sometimes seems to celebrate female masculinity. She writes, for example, of the woman bodybuilder as practising a 'cult of superman within woman, a hyper-strength'.[24]

This implies an appropriation of kinds of masculinity, a demonstration of the exchangeability of male attributes, their openness to cultivation by women, yet one that is coupled with the retention of the gendering of masculine attributes, a maintaining of the binary of male and female as a means of making sense of such practices.

Muscle, for example, remains a manly substance throughout Gassel's corpus. Her physical argument appears to depend upon pre-existing categories of male and female in order to make sense. It is because 'she' is muscular that she reveals muscle not to be an exclusively male attribute. Gassel's point is, however, that by becoming muscular 'she' escapes woman's body, leaves behind femininity. S/he becomes a body that is no longer capable of being categorised as female or male. Gassel writes in *Musculatures* that 'a woman athlete who is tremendously strong is no longer a woman. She is transformed, a third sex, androgynous'.[25] This androgynous physique, muscled body, articulates generally practised oppositions and disarticulates them, practising a fleshly deconstruction. In this context, the idea of an androgynous eros advanced in *Éros androgyne* and her other works can be understood as desire for undecidability. Gassel fetishises the event that is deconstruction as it manifests itself in hypermuscular 'women' and highly submissive 'men'. She eroticises, fixates upon, lack of gender fixity.

Writing the Body

Salcedo has argued that Gassel 'perceives her body to be modelling material – a blank sheet of paper upon which she can write her own sexual hagiography – which she situates at the centre of practices of seduction, positioned not as male or female but as Nathalie Gassel'.[26] His insight that Gassel refuses to occupy the positions, the oppositions, of male or female is well made. The use of the analogy of the blank sheet of paper is, however, questionable. Elizabeth Grosz, for example, has suggested that, 'in feminist terms at least, it is problematic to see the body as a blank, passive page, a neutral "medium" or signifier for the inscription of a text'.[27] It is obvious that Gassel also recognises the body is bound to texts that pre-exist and produce it. She works from within these. The connection that Salcedo makes between body and text here, whilst misplaced, is, however, not indiscriminate. He evidently recognises that, for Gassel, her writing takes place in body as much as word. She perceives the two kinds of writing as connected. It is this aspect of her project, rather than the relative merits of her philosophy, that is vital. For her, there is continuity between physical and prosaic bodies. This has ramifications for writing about sporting bodies and sports films.

Gassel's earlier works frequently include reflections upon the process of writing, about composing prose that words the physical, lifts the feel of muscle and the exercise of strength into the literary. This does not simply mean providing elaborate description, using highly wrought metaphors. It involves enfleshing the ink. In this literary vein, Salcedo, as part of a brief discussion of Gassel's style, detects formal similarities between her lifestyle and her thought: 'the text is short and sharp, like repetitions in a weightlifting exercise, and hard and lean, like an athlete's body'.[28] This echoes Gassel's identification of a profound resonance between word and muscle. She writes of a time in her life in which 'bodies and books were one, my everyday concerns were focussed on pursuing these two paths, my muscles set me to listening for the verbs which could sing their fleshy contours. I wanted to give them ample volume. Writing produced words that fleshed out sensations, defined muscle mass, turned the analytical eye inwards.'[29] Gassel knowingly cultivates a kind of writing that performs her corporeal arguments. Her bodily rhetoric carries her philosophy of the flesh into a more conventional philosophical format, verbiage. This is illustrated by a passage expressing the pleasure of the 'pump':

> *Quelque chose se dresse dans une fierté d'acier, l'entraînement devient fougueux, ardent. La crispation d'une volonté s'acharne sur l'acier des poids à lever, multiplie dans la suer les exercices. Et gonfle, gonfle, gonfle, se concentre, se centre entièrement sur la sensation de l'engorgement, la plaisir du sang qui afflue, de la puissance qui grimace; notre esprit est traversé d'images qui relatent d'autres moments où des corps furent dans cette même jouissance, transportés par elle.*[30]

> Something rises up in the conceit of pumping iron, training becomes mettlesome, ardent. A willed tension unremittingly applies itself to the weights to be lifted, enhanced by the sweat of exercise. And swells, swells, swells, concentrates, focuses entirely on the sensation of swelling up, the pleasure of blood that flows, of grimacing potency; our spirit is crisscrossed by images that relay other instances when the body was given to this same joy, moved by it.

This passage, an individual fragment of text from *Construction d'un corps pornographique*, begins with two sentences of similar length and concludes with a much longer one. There is therefore repetition followed by difference: the unvarying initial sentences, constancy, replaced by change, dynamism. The expanded final sentence contains a notable repetition of the word 'gonfle', 'swell'. This works to affirm the temporal duration of the swelling, it is not instantaneous but proceeds by degrees, comprising a pulsing inflation. It also draws attention to what becomes the focus of attention in lifting weights: sensation as something that supersedes sense.

It is this phenomenon that Kathy Acker refers to when she suggests that 'in a gym, verbal language or language whose purpose is meaning occurs, if at all, only at the edge of becoming lost'.[31] Acker believes that bodybuilding is antagonistic to conventional language. Words are incapable of getting a purchase when it comes to lifting weights. Gassel, however, through distending her last sentence, labours to carry the feel of pumping iron, of blood pumping, into her prose. The repeated words perform the swelling that they also refer to, become vascular. This passage therefore moves beyond mere description. It embodies aspects of the experience of weight-lifting. The passage provides an example of what Peter Schwenger refers to as 'syntactic imagery', which involves the shape and rhythm of sentences articulating a non-verbal perception.[32]

Additionally, the passage possesses marked alliterative elements, the first sentence through the repeated, hard 'd' and the final sentence through an initially sustained use of sibilance. After the semi-colon in this last sentence there is a notable shift in register to a more reflexive, less sibilant or sensory prose. This might suggest an acknowledgment of the separation of mind and body yet the opening sentences resist such an interpretation. In them will and weight, thought and action, are forcefully fused. All Gassel's text is carefully constructed. Her decision to write in fragments such as the one just analysed, for example, is not haphazard. Baetens describes her technique as one that produces a series of short fragments which are 'at once related to each other and forcefully closed in on themselves'.[33] The text progresses by way of singular repetitions, cementing themes, ideas, sensations through their distinct reoccurrence. This continual coming back to the same, the feel of muscle, pleasure of the pump, joy of sex, removes any sense of narrative progression.[34] There is a similar technique of return to the same at work for much of *Pumping Iron II*. Gassel tells stories but she is not telling a story. She is endeavouring to communicate physicality, the repetitions, thick descriptions, fibrous musings, bringing particular body parts and sensations to prominence.

One physical experience Gassel revisits is the act of writing itself. In *Éros androgyne*, after a prolonged passage transcribing, sensuously describing, memories of love making held not in the mind's eye but in the mouth and the lips, Gassel draws attention to the process lying behind the composition, a physical procedure subsequently camouflaged by the paragraph's transition to typeface. She writes: 'My hand is tired from noting down. It is weary from reliving a distant scene, observing the ball-point's travels, simply performing the gesture and act of writing.'[35] Elsewhere, Gassel refers to the rapid motion of inscription and to its material impact: 'My hurried writing bruises the paper.'[36] These instances draw attention to the athletic aspect involved in putting pen to paper. The practice involve the use of the extensor muscles of the wrist, flexor muscles of the wrist, and the lumbricals, four worm-like muscles that have the special ability to flex the metacarpophalangeal joints of the hand whilst simultaneously extending the interphalangeal joints of the fingers thereby producing the precise pressures and motions required for penmanship (and, to a lesser extent, typing).[37] Notations about athletic activity are in themselves athletic, the difference is only one of degrees of exertion. The same can be said of camerawork. Its physicality is discussed in the final chapter in relation to *Whip It*.

Gassel also regards cursive action as closely connected to the cardiovascular system. She recounts composing prose between exercising so that she is congested with blood.[38] She desires her writing to hold 'the full impact of blood swelling the senses, spreading through the muscles'.[39] Her conception of writing is therefore a vital one. This aspect of her project is potentially enabling for writings 'about' athleticism. Such writing does not merely have to be about the subject of the athletic. It can itself become athletic, performing what it describes. This has significant implications when it comes to cinematic representations of athletes, particularly in relation to sexual politics. In my descriptions of *Pumping Iron II* in this chapter, I have also sought, at times, to infuse my prose with something of the vitality of the bodies on screen.

Future Sex

There is a sequence in *Pumping Iron II* that features shots of different competitors working out at Eiferman's gym in Las Vegas in training for the Miss. Olympia competition. The gym is named after former Mr. Universe

George Eiferman. The sequence begins with shots of Francis, wearing a red and white striped singlet, lifting dumbbells as Steve Michalik, who is training her, continually talks to her. Francis twists the 10 pound dumbells working her biceps and triceps. Her aquiline features are lean and taut. The bulk she carried earlier in the film at the start of her training has, to a large extent, disappeared: there is less fat and more muscle.

McLish is shown immediately afterwards. Patton has described the rivalry between Francis and McLish as a 'catfight' and here it is possible to see how this brawl is constructed by way of the editing, the conscientious combination of shots that couple the women.[40] McLish is not working out. She is outlining why she is a bodybuilder. She states she wishes to perfect a physique like that of Wonder Woman. This forms her ideal. It is an ideal that requires considerable effort on her part to achieve. In a later gym scene, McLish is shown lifting heavy weights, the veins on her arms protruding. Her face contorts, exposing her teeth as she grimaces with effort. There is no smile for the camera. This scene exemplifies Michelle Bridges's assertion that 'what really changes bodies is grunting and sweating'.[41] The labour involved in building a body such as McLish's, her body as it labours, is not conventionally attractive. This scene presents a different McLish to the one seen earlier primping and posing during a photo-shoot. For the shoot, in which she models with handweights, she presents her trim and toned body as finished.

Woman presented as spectacle in this way is rendered inactive. The reality that McLish must spend hours in the gym, lifting, straining, sweating, frowning, gasping, to become the posed object of desire is absented from the resultant still images. The taut, toned body appears as an expression of effortless grace. *Pumping Iron II*, by contrast, shows the built body as a perpetual, painful process rather than an achievement. It works to undo the illusion of effortless glamour, of relaxed desirability of McLish in the photographs. Whilst she is working out, pumping iron, McLish, like Francis, does not look attractive in a conventional sense. Both women can be seen to embody a new erotic, one *Pumping Iron II* strives to formulate and promulgate.

Gassel's writings have been interpreted as sexually revolutionary. They can be read as forming an extended manifesto for a sexual future that is not reliant on male and female identities and coitus. The film can be seen to prefigure this corporeal philosophy although this dimension is usually neglected. The erotic potential of *Pumping Iron II* is acknowledged by Claudia Schippert, who describes how the film 'could be found in the pornography shelf at my local gay video store albeit in "lesbian pornography"'.[42] She does not, however, explore this pornographic content in detail. Cindy Patton's analysis of the parody of *Pumping Iron II*, the overtly pornographic *Pumping Irene* (Dir. C.C. Williams, USA, 1986), points towards the erotic potential of the former film but does not pursue it.[43] This inattention occurs despite the fact the call for a new form of eroticism is given equal prominence in the film to its feminist message, albeit through the cinematography and soundtrack rather than the dialogue.

The sexual message of *Pumping Iron II* is made clear from the start. The documentary begins with footage of the Hoover Dam. This introduces a central theme, that of technological triumph over the natural world, be it the Colorado River or the human body. Early on there is a shot of some bas-reliefs carved by the artist Oskar Hansen in the classical style. These images, which are coupled with text, are situated on the North Elevator Tower. The words 'Water Storage' accompany a sculpture of a male figure, his right arm upraised. The camera then pans down revealing the words 'Power' above a bas-relief of a man flexing his biceps. These sculptures cement the relationship between masculinity, muscularity and dominance. The dam is used to generate electricity, it is a power source, and the images of the men therefore also figure the strength of Nature. The camera pulls back from the relief to reveal the back of a broad-shouldered figure. This person is looking up at the artwork. It then cuts to other architectural features including Hansen's Winged Figures of the Republic.

This footage of the dam is soon replaced by fixed and tracking shots of power lines, one of which includes lightning bolts in the background as a thunderstorm is in progress. The film cuts from these shots of cables against the evening sky to night time in Las Vegas, a city of lights. One message produced by these editing choices is that the dam powers this city, provides the electricity that sustains it. It becomes clear, however, that the earlier footage is also included to form a visual analogy. There is a close-up shot of a heavily veined hand. A figure is lying on a tanning bed. The camera tracks from the hand up the person's arm, further prominent veins appearing diagonally, the shot is reminiscent of the earlier ones of power lines. The analogy is clear. These veins carry power through the body. They comprise its natural grid.

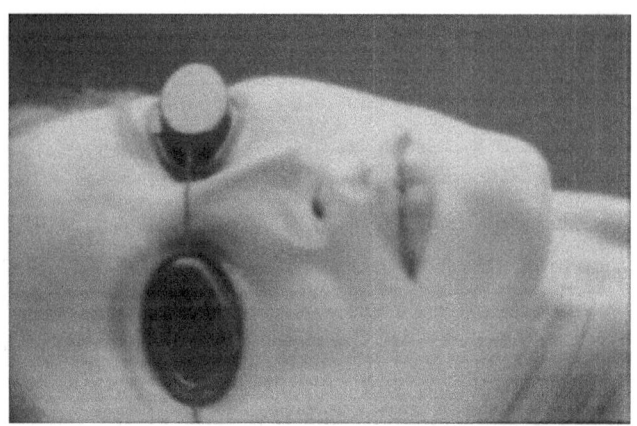

5.2 *Pumping Iron II* (1985): Lips as sex

The camera continues its journey, reaching a bulging bicep and, visible behind it, the figure's compact chest, nipples invisible, protected by cotton wool. It ends at the head of the figure, feminine features and pierced ears. The film then cuts to a shot of the woman rubbing the skin near her navel, followed by one of her licking her lips. The soundtrack to the sequence features the song 'Future Sex' which includes the lyrics: 'I am the future, beyond your dreams / I got the muscles / Future Sex / I got the motion / Future Sex / I got the body / Future Sex / Touch this body / Feel this body'. These lyrics are described as 'suggestively seductive' by Chris Holmlund.[44] The shots of the navel and lips are accompanied by the lyrics 'perfection, desire'. The camera then cuts to a shot of her right bicep. The future of sex is visually indicated to be muscle.

Later on in this sequence there is also a shot of a different woman's firm calf muscle, the gastrocnemius, followed shortly after by a shot of her turning her head to face the camera, her lipstick-lips viewed at a vertical. Her lips in this shot signal her sex (5.2). This works to reaffirm that the sequence as a whole is about sexuality. It signals, however, that the future of sex is not bound to the genitals. It is located elsewhere in the body. This woman's hands gesture to one of these areas when she is shown rubbing oil into her firm buttocks, massaging her dense gluteal muscles, as the lyrics pronounce 'touch this body / feel this body', inviting the viewer to share her tactile experience. The buttocks have, of course, long functioned as a site of erotic interest. Here, however, their desirability is tied to their muscularity. It is their status as muscle, as glutes refined, perfected in the gym, as testaments to physical exertion, that renders them part of the future sex extolled by the film. It is the attractiveness of gym-inspired glutei maximi that the spectator is encouraged to get a handle on.[45]

The sequence in the tanning salon ends with a shot of the head of a bodybuilder fading out, to be gradually replaced by a neon heart. The message is simple: love this physique. Holmlund reads the sequence as betraying 'the film's preference for a male-oriented, heterosexual eroticism' through combining 'the suggestively seductive lyrics with slow pans of a woman's naked body'.[46] That the eroticism is heteronormative is questionable given the film's lesbian audience reported by Schippert. If it is accepted as tailored to a male audience, then the celebration of muscle as erotic matter, the camera's focus on, fetishisation of, specific muscles, still breaks with the conventional cartography of male desire.[47] Male sexual attention as mapped in heterosexual pornography is predominantly distributed across the breasts, buttocks and vagina. *Pumping Iron II*, by contrast, redistributes desire to biceps, deltoids, abdominals, glutes, quadriceps and triceps surae. Holmlund's description of the camera movements, editing strategies, framing and lighting as reminiscent of 'softcore pornography' is apposite. This is, in fact, not a film that seems to be like pornography. It is, like Gassel's writings, pornographic.

Skin as Film

The tanning room sequence, with its sexual electricity, like the sequences of women working out in the gym, mirrors the muscle fantasies articulated by Gassel in her writings. *Pumping Iron II* proffers the palpably muscled female body as sexually appealing.[48] The film encourages its audience to engage in synaesthesia, to look with tactile feeling.[49] It is a film that foregrounds skin. Skin clothes the muscles that contract and extend, flow and ebb, beneath it. It parallels their shapes and movements. Muscle fantasies are therefore always also skin fancies.

This focus on skin as a key pathway to sexual satisfaction is rare in non-sports related films. There are, however, notable exceptions including *Crocodile Dundee* (Dir. Peter Faiman, Australia, 1986), *Cruising* (Dir. William Friedkin, USA, 1980) and *The Piano* (Dir. Jane Campion, New Zealand, 1993). In *Crocodile Dundee*, a comedy about an Australian adventurer Mick Dundee, the sex appeal of skin is most obvious in the party scene in New York. This sequence represents a smorgasbord of skin.

The dishy cocktail dress worn by Dundee's love interest, Sue Charlton, is seemingly 'vapor wear'. It prefigures the black Versace dress Elizabeth Hurley famously wore to the premiere of *Four Weddings and a Funeral* (Dir. Mike Newell, UK, 1994), forming an off the shoulder number that includes several panels down one side revealing exposed patches of skin.

The sexual import skin assumes in this scene is reminiscent in scope, if not in tenor, to that in *Cruising*, which also accords the cutaneous its erotic due.[50] The film uses the sadomasochistic subculture of the gay community in New York as a backdrop for a murder investigation. There are a number of instances in which camerawork directs the viewer to the skin as sexually stimulating surface. *The Piano,* a period romance set in nineteenth-century New Zealand, includes a notable scene in which a small patch of skin visible through a hole in some stockings becomes a powerful locus of desire. Skin as it is eroticised in *Pumping Iron II* is, however, qualitatively different from these other films which usually reveal, foreground, isolated expanses of epidermis. The bodybuilders, by contrast, tend to display large expanses of skin. The appeal here is not of a patch of skin as microcosm of nakedness. It is of cuticle as the representative for force and action, as the messenger for muscle. Skin mediates between muscle and the eyes and, in particular, hands that desire it.

This is brought to the fore in the documentary *Highway Amazon* (Dir. Ronnie Cramer, USA, 2001) which explores the phenomenon of muscle worship. At one point the bodybuilder Christine Fetzer, who fulfils muscle fantasies for clients, says of her customers: 'They want to feel your strength, they want to feel that they're small and weak and that you're like, you're like superwoman. They want to like feel all that.' As she describes what her clients desire, she clasps her hands together twice in a gesture that emphasises the importance of feeling, of tactility, in these encounters. She then signals her strength through tensing her biceps, demonstrating how she is used to speaking with her body. These desired feelings, of strength, and of powerlessness in the face of it, are all communicated through the skin. In the documentary, there are shots of men massaging Fetzer's biceps, glutes, quadriceps, and trapezius. Here skin, theirs and hers, forms the conduit to muscles. There are also scenes of massage in *Pumping Iron II* although these manipulations of muscles are ostensibly for pain relief and relaxation. The film, however, through its close-ups of manicured hands kneading flesh, invites vicarious, potentially sexually motivated touching from the spectator. In *Éros androgyne*, Gassel draws attention to the tactile pleasures offered by a lover's body, describing the joy she takes from frisking flesh, 'endlessly searching it from top to bottom'.[51] Her fragmented prose acts like the camera, focussing attention on specific surfaces, textures, the bristly hairs of a man's bottom, the soft flesh of a sphincter.[52]

Patton suggests that cinema audiences employ imagination as well as identification as a means of connecting with persons on screen. She suggests of watching pornography, in which viewers are often 'tightly positioned as the person who owns the penis', that 'it is quite easy to imagine that this is your penis, regardless of your anatomical configuration'.[53] For Patton, therefore it is possible to become intimate with an individual on screen even if physical similarities are absent. This requires leaving behind the lived body and, instead, fantasising another's body, possessing their physique, performing their actions. Imaginative adoption of this kind differs from identification in that it involves becoming another rather than acknowledging likeness to another, seemingly offering the possibility of changing sex. The woman viewing pornography in Patton's scenario takes possession of the penis. A man watching the masseuses at work in *Pumping Iron II* might comparably take their hands. Biology ceases to be destiny, if it ever was conceived of in these terms, for the duration of the viewer's imaginative tenure in the body of another sex. Camerawork that dwells on actions, be they sexual or sensual, invites fantasies of this kind. The mind needs time to settle into another's flesh.

Muscle forms a powerful attractor for this kind of imaginative labour as most muscle groups occur across the sexes, are already shared. Marcia Ian suggests that muscle has form rather than gender.[54] Muscle is, as discussed earlier in relation to Gassel's writings, hermaphroditic material. It therefore transcends identity categories despite the fact that its development and forms of usage varies across identities. A man's muscles, another woman's muscles, will differ from those of either masseuse yet also be the same. They may not know the motional techniques of massage, the artfulness of a masseuse's physical actions, but they will be able to imagine them rudimentarily. They will be able to share in the actions of this already communal material, potentially recognising a muscular commonality of force and motion.

The only muscles men and women do not share are those of the genitalia. Men for instance, possess the bulbospongiosus muscle and the vagina is fibromuscular. To imagine these muscles is therefore to potentially take on markers of difference rather than embracing similarities. These sexually differentiated muscles are not hermaphroditic. They do, however, have comparable qualities to the others. They possess an equivalent capacity for movement and engorgement. It is therefore possible for a woman to imagine herself a penis as muscle, as force, rather than as object. She is, however, not becoming man through this action, she is, like the man or woman becoming a masseuse's motions, leaving sex, although not necessarily sexuality, behind. The viewer who imagines their way into film not through becoming a character, but through adopting the forces and motions underpinning a character, all characters, does not trespass on identity. They cease to watch a story and, instead, embrace dynamism, energy. The experience is reminiscent of Gassel's description of apartment wrestling. She pins her lover against a wall: 'There only exists the pleasure of the situation, the relationship of forces.'[55]

The viewer does not become one of the masseuses. The give of flesh as it fans beneath their fingers, the density of the muscles they feel through cuticle, the rippling tactile pleasures they take are not bound to another's identity. Gassel's contention that power is also hermaphroditic is therefore informative here.[56] Power is not conceived of as authority possessed by a particular individual. Power is force, physical strength. This corporeal capacity is not bound by identity. The viewer who identifies with energy and action transcends difference. Their visual pleasure, bodily delight, is not bound to a specific sex. It is a way of seeing, of feeling, of sharing another's skin. This resonates with Gassel's androgynous eros and is, similarly, not bound to gendered identity. Such a form of hermaphroditic spectatorship is only skin deep, it samples and skims, rather than subjugates.

Muscle Erotica

The pleasure in muscle, its forms, movements and capacities, is the film's key message. The eroticism of muscle, its revolutionary sexual potential, is, however, downplayed. This is because muscle resists definition at the same time as it renders it possible. The issue of definition runs throughout *Pumping Iron II*. As already mentioned, the film is usually interpreted as being about what comprises femininity, how to define it and establish its limits. The issue of outlining femininity, of whether women should strive for high-definition in relation to their muscles has vexed many women bodybuilders. One competitive woman responding to a questionnaire about how female bodybuilders perceive themselves stated: 'Who is to define what too much muscle is? The sport is bodybuilding, not body-semibuilding.'[57]

Definition is, however, also a term from within bodybuilding as practice. It means having muscle groups that are separate and distinct from one another: the biceps, for example, should be plainly distinct from each other and from the triceps. Definition is therefore bound to what might be called visible physical clarity. The defined body is one in which the location of specific muscles, their contours, are clearly discernible, demarcated. It is an exercise in clear outline. The quest for the 'definition' of femininity in the film forms an example of the everyday understanding of the term. Here definition refers not to ideal conditions of muscle display but to the meaning of a given word or phrase. There is, however, crossover between these two kinds of definition. Both involve instituting boundaries. The bodybuilder strives to produce a physique that displays clearly bounded muscles and muscle groups. The lexicographer who provides the signification of a particular word, through differentiating its meaning from that of other words, also engages in a process of bordering.

Pumping Iron II repeatedly calls attention to both forms of definition. In the bodybuilding competition at the end of the documentary, for instance, the initial posing requires the athletes to display specific muscles to their best effect. They are called upon to show their double biceps, side chest, back double biceps, side triceps, abdominals and legs. There are also sequences throughout the film showing the women in training working with, or admiring, specific muscle groups. In terms of linguistic significance, what should constitute the definition of femininity is also a theme referred to more than once. Dunlap, for instance, states of femininity at one point: 'We've got to put some kind of perimeter around the word.' There is, however, a third kind of definition, linked to the other two, that is also present in the film. This is the definition of what is erotic. The film forms a manifesto for muscle, and accompanying attributes, being sexually attractive.

The allure of muscle is alluded to through the repeated sequences of women working out in the gym. The early gym scene that shows Cheng, Portugues, Mclish, Inger Zetterqvist and other bodybuilders spotting each other, forms a series of brief glimpses of different exercises, muscle groups in action. There are repeated shots of straining, pulling, lifting, and recurring sounds of grunting, gasping, bumps, clangs of weights.

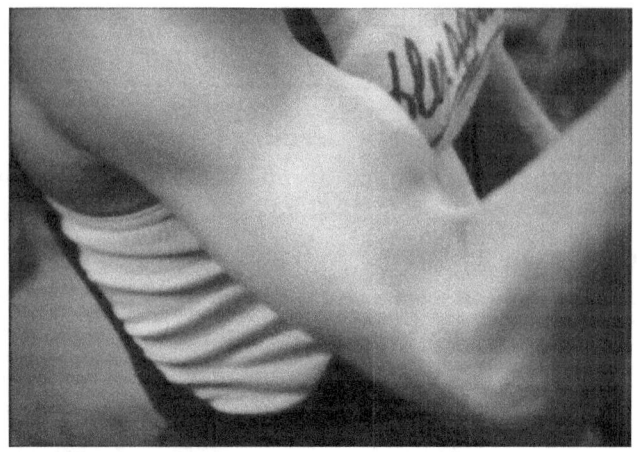

5.3 *Pumping Iron II* (1985): Bicep

These work cumulatively to emphasise muscle and strength. The aesthetic here, repetition through fragments, is reminiscent of Gassel's writings. The sequence is followed by a shower scene which Holmlund describes as 'a fetishist's delight: the camera pans and cuts from torsos to biceps to necks to breasts to heads'.[58] The footage of the women lathering and washing themselves, steamy, soapy, is, however, not meant to be read as stand-alone. The camerawork Holmlund uses draws attention to repeats that are used in the gym sequence. The shower scene is the 'cum shot' which follows the orgy of exertion that preceded it. There is also only a brief shot of a breast in the scene. The camera predominantly focuses on biceps, buttocks, abdominals, sternum, thighs, and calves (5.3). This is hermaphroditic cinematography.

The sexual aspect to the gym, its openness to being read as muscle erotica, to stimulating the bodybuilders and their audience, is reinforced by the second major sequence of the women working out near the time of the contest which can be read as another orgy of exertion. This footage ends with all the women spent, leaning against each other or lying down. Bowen is shown close to crying. The athletes all possess the appearance of having just had sex. *Pumping Iron II* shows its flex-rated credentials at this point. The flex, the demonstration of muscle in action, of substance and strength, is what is erotic. In her discussion of *Pumping Irene*, Patton argues that the film 'makes full use of the sexual undertones of gym language and weight-lifting apparatuses'.[59] The erotic potency of the built female body is, however, already clearly signalled in *Pumping Iron II*. Marcia

Ian has recognised bodybuilding's 'salacious' dimension, suggesting that the cheering for hypermuscular women at bodybuilding competitions is sometimes lustful.⁶⁰ The reality that desire for muscle may motivate audiences to attend bodybuilding contests is, however, one the judges of such competitions cannot contemplate. This is evidenced by the result of the competition featured in the film. The reasons behind Dunlap's victory can be ascertained by closely studying the posing routines.

Francis is constructed as a larrikin by the film. She is introduced to the audience playing a practical joke on two of her friends. Her routine for the contest that forms the climax of the film, in narrative and, arguably, sexual terms, is also mischievous. It appears indebted to a 'playful routine' parodying the sex-gender binary system that she performed in front of family and friends slightly earlier.⁶¹ She strikes powerful poses yet is alternatively coquettish, flirt of foot, swinging her hips. Francis presents a corporeal text that refuses to securely signify the gender categories of feminine or masculine.

The routine begins with an acoustic reference to *2001 A Space Odyssey* (Dir. Stanley Kubrick, USA, 1968) therefore forging connections between technology and possibility, foregrounding the built body as technological achievement. Francis begins the routine emphasising her monumental physique. She is the monolith in *2001* (5.4). Her gym-chiselled body, like the monolith, constructed as the trigger for a new ways of thinking, this time in relation to the female form. This powerful force for change, however, is soon replaced in the routine. Francis morphs into a parody of the coquette. She prances and sashays to lyrics heralding a new dawn sung by a soft voiced woman: 'morning is calling, pushing and pulling [...] body moves, spirit flies'. This is a light routine which seeks to question assumptions about femininity, or a perceived lack of it, through the use of humour. It echoes Francis's earlier parodying of female bodybuilders which she performed for close friends. This routine encourages the kinds of readings usually provided for the film which focus on the debates over femininity rather than possible futures of sex. McLish's pop funk routine, by contrast, is sedate and conservative, assured in its reassuring vision of the feminine.

Dunlap's posing routine is performed to music by Grace Jones. She enters the stage accompanied by an audio-track of confused noises. Jacqueline Brady reads this acoustic commotion as 'a jungle soundtrack' that encourages primitivist fantasies. The routine does not start with music but

5.4 *Pumping Iron II* (1985): Bev Francis as the monolith

with noises, screeches, roars and howls. Dunlap appears lost, anxious, and uncertain. Her movements are those of someone in confused and fearful flight, Brady suggests she is behaving like a 'hunted animal'.[62] The live and film audience are therefore initially presented with carefully choreographed chaos. This is, however, soon replaced by a performance of poise and purpose. Once the music begins, Dunlap's body becomes controlled expression, a graceful and fastidious display of her muscular definition. Dunlap crafts order from out of disorder. Her routine comprises undefined sound and motion, followed by a bringing to definition, and, at the end, a return to disorder. She leaves the stage covering her ears to the animal, to sounds that figure the unwanted, the unknown and ill-defined. Chris Holmlund interprets the performance as one of 'passing from mystery and bewilderment to flashy self-confidence to mystery again'.[63] It is, however, more a passing from unruliness to command and back again.

Dunlap's performance will be echoed later on by Steve Michalik's time-filler as the final results of the competition are being calculated. Michalik enters the stage wearing a baggy, black silk cape, shapeless. Gradually, however, he removes the robe to reveal his sculpted physique. Michalik's act, which leaves him stripped and ripped, again displays a passage from formlessness to form. It is the perceived power of the bodybuilder to arrest

5.5 *Pumping Iron II* (1985): Lori Bowen as muscle temptress

incertitude, to delineate, shape and hold the body in place, which forms a key aspect of their appeal. Dunlap's routine, which provides the illusion of attaining control over the unruly whilst also signalling the danger of not achieving it, taps into modern anxieties. Michalik's striptease reaffirms her message.

The bodybuilder nearest to Dunlap in terms of physique, Bowen, gives explicit expression to the new muscular erotic the film proposes in her routine. Through her sultry athleticism, she provides an open display of the value of muscle as erotic capital (5.5).[64] The song that accompanies her performance includes the lyrics: 'Don't mess with me, 'cause I'm dangerous'. Her curves are indeed so. Her lithe and lissom body coupled with her style of posing draws too great an attention to her physical desirability. She reveals the competition for what it is: an erotic spectacle. It is for this reason that she cannot be chosen as a corporeal compromise between Francis and McLish.

The eventual winner of the competition, Dunlap, forms not just a bodily compromise between the physiques of Francis and McLish but also represents a toned down version of the film's central message about the sex appeal of muscle. This message is given its most forceful articulation by Bowen, usually the forgotten competitor in discussions of the film, who openly gives 'voice' to muscle fantasies, giving voice to the hard body as erotic through her sensual performance. Bowen's routine comes closest to embodying Gassel's carnal prose, expressing a similar joy in corporeal power and strength. She openly invites the audience to worship her muscularity. It is Bowen who most obviously heralds the future of sex as proposed by the film.

6

Shaping the Self: Martina Navratilova and the Tennis Film

Game, Set, Age

In 1999, Martina Navratilova came out of retirement having given up competitive tennis in 1994. In 2004 at the age of 47, she won her first round match at Wimbledon beating 25 year old Catalina Castaño 6-0 6-1. She then lost in three sets to 19 year old Gisela Dulko in the next round. In 2006, partnering Bob Bryant, she won the mixed doubles title at the US Open at the age of 49. She was already the oldest ever Grand Slam champion having won the mixed doubles with Leander Paes at Wimbledon in 2003.

Navratilova's singles victory over Castaño was, however, reportedly described as 'a terrible thing for women's tennis' by former men's champion Michael Stich who believed the win revealed a lack of depth and quality in the women's game. Stich's remarks appear to represent ageism interacting with sexism. The achievements of older male sports stars are seldom interpreted as revealing failings amongst their younger peers. The golfer Jack Nicklaus's victory at the 1986 Masters tournament at the age of 46, for example, was attributed to his immense stamina and overall proficiency in all aspects of the game rather than to playing against weak opponents. In tennis, John McEnroe's triumph, alongside Jonas Björkman, in the doubles final of the SAP Open in San Jose in 2006 at 46 years of age was also not interpreted as symptomatic of a crisis in the men's game. The ageing yet athletic female body appears to be a source of anxiety for Stich. He demonstrates the same response as the promoter upon learning Jane's age in *The Gymnast*. Navratilova's triumph, accomplished with energy and flare, shows a body subverting ageist ideology. Through it she challenged the cultural norm of the ageing female body as in decline. Her argument was, like that of the bodybuilders discussed in the last chapter, one made through the flesh rather than in words.

Navratilova paved the way for more recent ageing women players such as Kimiko Date-Krumm who, in 2012 at Gifu in Japan, beat 20 year old Noppawan Lercheewakarn 6-1, 5-7, 6-3 to win an International Tennis Federation singles title, to demonstrate that it is still possible to be competitive at over 40. Date-Krumm would subsequently reach the third-round of Wimbledon in 2013 at the age of 42 defeating 18 year old Carina Witthoeft in the first round and 23 year old Alexandra Cadantu in the second. Date-Krumm's achievements build on those of Navratilova. Navratilova used her body, her athleticism, as a physical rhetoric to contest dominant beliefs in society about ageing as it intersects with femininity. Rhetoric is the art of persuading. Navratilova's argumentative artfulness was articulated through her agility and strength, her muscles and sinews. It was with these that she made her points. Bodies are not usually regarded as treatises. They are not conceived of as investigating issues and formulating opinions. Speech is, however, frequently supplemented by gesticulations. Gestures signal that thought is bodied. Navratilova brought the power of the body as a mode of expression and as a kind of oratory to the fore.

Stich was ostensibly dismayed at her spectacular physical argument because this triumph by an ageing athlete had revealed the poor quality of the younger female tennis players. Ageing, however, is sometimes interpreted as emasculating. This is hinted at in *When Billie Beat Bobby* (Dir. Jane Anderson, USA, 2001). In *When Billie Beat Bobby*, Riggs, the game's elder statesman, has to continually prove his sexual magnetism and his ability to win tennis matches. His masculine identity also appears tied to his continuing physical prowess. There is a similar anxiety about ageing present in *Wimbledon* (Dir. Richard Loncraine, UK, 2004). This film centres on a budding romance between an up and coming woman player, Lizzie Bradbury, and a fading player on the men's tour, Peter Colt. Peter is shown at the start of the film fretting about his position as 119th in the men's singles world rankings which means that there are '118 faster, stronger, younger' players he is competing against. The theme of ageing returns in a later discussion with his practice partner Dieter Prohl. Dieter believes the tennis court provides the stage for an oedipal scenario in which younger players kill their fathers, the older professionals on the tour. Tennis is therefore bound up with castration anxiety. The man who is beaten loses his manhood. Peter, however, wins the men's singles at Wimbledon, defeating a young American player, Jake Hammond. He shows he can still live up to his surname. In the final, he acts his cognomen not his age. By winning against Hammond, Colt affirms his masculinity, becoming a symbol of national pride in the process.

The male athlete who shows their age (age here being determined through a capacity for physical activity) is in danger of losing their masculinity. Growing old and becoming uncompetitive in sport is culturally coded as a becoming feminine. The woman who refuses to grow old and rejects slowing down, challenges this convention. Through her athletic body, she argues against any unified idea of how a woman should act her age. In this context, Navratilova refused, and refuses, to age quietly. Older women are stereotypically expected to cease to display intellectual and physical agility.[1] Navratilova, however, maintains an active lifestyle and a high media profile. She continues to comment on political and sporting issues.

The Seniors tennis age category also begins at 35. Navratilova could have participated in the International Tennis Federation's Seniors Championship in 1992. The term senior usually refers to an elderly person and frequently implies someone who has retired. To participate in senior's tennis is therefore to announce your retirement from tennis proper. Thirty-five has been identified as the appropriate retirement age for female and male players. This is because 'athletic ability is supposed to fade after the age of 30'.[2] Navratilova, however, refused to collect her pension and continued to play in the standard International Tennis Federation competitions until 2006. By winning a number of competitions when she was over 40 years old she demonstrated that it was not necessary to be 35 years old or younger to be successful. She voiced this challenge to ageing preconceptions through the flesh. The body is the most appropriate forum for making such arguments as the effects of ageing are felt physically as much as mentally. Corporeal ageing is also often highly visible, registered in wrinkles, solar lentigo and greying hair.

Contemporary medical research shows that the impact of ageing upon our physical capacity varies. Our muscles do not have to substantially shrivel and our joints do not have to significantly stiffen if we do not wish them to. Muscle does reduce with age yet this may, in part, be attributable to the elderly living out stereotypes about the ageing process including increased inactivity.³ Physical activity in ageing people is associated with enhanced psychological wellbeing.⁴ The idea that ageing is a process we undergo involuntarily is the product of medical studies that have examined sedentary people. It is now known that people who exercise a lot change far slower physically than those who do not. The idea that ageing as physical decline is just a fact of life, the perception that our lived bodies somehow operate beyond culture and that ageing occurs outside of ideology, can, however, function to make such deterioration an accelerated reality. Perception, as Young's work demonstrates, informs how we think about ourselves. The body that perceives itself as in steady and uncontrollable decline will, like the female body exhibit an inhibited intentionality. The body made spectacle, rather than in feeling with itself, is detached. It looks its age rather than handles ageing. As discussed in earlier chapters, Young argues that objectified bodily existence means 'a woman cannot be in unity with herself but must take a distance from and exist in discontinuity with her body'.⁵

This being out of sorts with one's body is communicated forcefully in a sequence from *Pat and Mike* (Dir. George Cukor, USA, 1952), a film about an exceptional athlete, Patricia Pemberton, whose performance suffers whenever her fiancé, Davie Hucko, watches her in action. Davie's appraising and critical gaze makes Patricia self-conscious and inhibits her talent. This is graphically underscored in a tennis match she is playing against Gussie Moran. Patricia begins in commanding fashion, her hard-hitting play, aggressively coming to the net, keeps Moran on the defensive. Once Davie arrives, however, her confidence falters. Under his watchful eye and in earshot of his tittering companions, she begins to drop points. The psychological impact of Davie's presence is communicated through the net seemingly raising itself to prevent her shots getting over and then growing bigger. The size of the racquets also alters so that the head of Patricia's is miniscule and Moran's is enormous. The sequence ends with Patricia swooning as a ball that is coming towards her continually multiplies until her visual field is filled with balls. The special effects in the sequence operate as a metaphor for the impact of the objectifying gaze as Young envisages it.

Navratilova's refusal to perceive herself as culture dictated she should, her refusal to objectify, provides a physical and visible argument against

6.1 *Pat and Mike* (1952): Patricia's shrinking racquet

the stereotype of inevitable decline. Her media visibility means she has intervened, and continues to intervene, in the self-perceptions of other women. Susan Brownmiller writes in *Femininity* of how society offers the ageing woman 'few ways to *look* successful as she enters her middle years'.⁶ Navratilova has expanded this realm of visible opportunity. There may, however, have been something else about Navratilova, beyond her visible age and refusal to age, that motivated Stich to find her out of place at Wimbledon. His criticism was ostensibly related to her age, framed in that register, yet it also seems possible she did not look right to him. Women's tennis has never been entirely about competitive success. It is also bound up with appearances in ways the men's tour is not.

Easy on the Hawk-Eye

Looking good has been a feature of women's tennis since its inception. In the 1920s, for example, France's Suzanne Lenglen and America's Helen Wills were praised as much for their glamour as their on-court achievements. Susan K. Cahn suggests that 'Lenglen's appeal lay precisely in the way she fused athletic ability with heterosexual allure'.[7] The Frenchwoman set a fashion trend with her sleeveless outfits and her matches drew previously unprecedented numbers of spectators to watch women's tennis. From the 1980s onwards, cultivating the femininity of players became crucial to the business strategy of professional women's tennis and, indeed, other sports such as badminton and squash. The female sporting body is frequently sexualised. This can be seen, for instance, in promotional campaigns and in advertising. In 2001, for example, the Women's International Squash Player's Association (WISPA) orchestrated a PR stunt at the 2001 British Open. The then professional player Vicky Botwright was persuaded to wear a thong and claim the clothing commonly used in the sport was too restrictive. Botwright, who was then ranked as fourteenth in the world in squash, became known as the Lancashire Hot Bot, a pun on the traditional English dish of Lancashire hotpot. Botwright became associated with foodstuff, equated with a substance to be consumed.

Botwright's experience demonstrates how the promoting of women's sports is bound up with sex. Sex rather than ability sells sport. In tennis, Anna Kournikova's striking commercial success during a career in which she never won a Grand Slam in singles demonstrates this. It is possible to extrapolate from this that Stich is also upset because Navratilova does not display the body ideal he would like to see on the court. Her lack of perceived femininity is, however, not only related to her physical appearance. While Navratilova was on the women's tour she often behaved in ways that were not considered ladylike, she did not conduct herself in a manner deemed appropriate to the tennis court.[8] She was, however, not the first to comport herself in a fashion out of keeping with the values tennis saw itself as upholding. Althea Gibson, for example, the sport's first leading African American player, had an explosive style of play that was not perceived as appropriate for a lady.

During his discussion of Gibson's tennis achievements in the book *Sportsex*, Toby Miller quotes Billie Jean King who describes tennis as 'a perfect combination of a violent action taking place in an atmosphere of total tranquillity [. . .] almost like having an orgasm'.[9] The most outwardly violent style of tennis is serve-and-volley, of which King was an exponent. Serve and volleyers, unlike baseline players, are risk-takers. They are willing to lay it all on the line at the net. Serve-and-volley is an aggressive style of play. It is the style of play that Navratilova favoured. Her greatest rival during her career was Chris Evert who was a baseline player. The baseline player waits for their opponents to make mistakes before then exploiting them.

Mike Estep, one of Navratilova's former coaches, has said that 'the baseline player is the counterpuncher, and women are taught to be counterpunchers, to react to things'.[10] Young suggests that one piece of evidence that the feminine movement is inhibited is the tendency of a woman playing a ball sport 'not to move out and meet the motion of a ball, but rather [. . .] stay in one place and react to the ball's motion only when it has arrived within the space where she is'.[11] The baseline player waits for the arrival of the ball like this. The serve and volley player, by contrast, moves onto the court, up it, outwards towards where the ball will come from. The serve-and-volleyer takes full possession of space. Tennis, like boxing, is partly about controlling space. Navratilova suggests that 'when you know how to defend your territory, the court will seem much smaller to you, much simpler to play one'.[12] The serve-and-volleyer defends through attack. They seek to finish each point as swiftly as possible. Navratilova has stated of her chosen style: 'I hated the idea of waiting around on the baseline for my opponent to make a mistake, or to rally with her endlessly, patiently tiring her out of the match'.[13]

Evert, who played a waiting game, is one of the most successful tennis players ever to have competed on the professional women's tour. She won the Australian Open twice, the French Open seven times, Wimbledon three times and the US Open six times. Navratilova won the Australian Open three times, the French Open twice, Wimbledon nine times and the US Open four times. Evert and Navratilova therefore have won eighteen Grand Slam titles each. It is there, however, that in many ways their similarities can be seen to end. Evert was feted as much for her looks as her tennis. She was the sport's main 'poster girl' in the late 1970s and early 1980s. Navratilova, by contrast, was viewed with some hostility. Evert joined the professional tennis circuit at the age of 16 in 1971 making her the youngest player at that time. It was soon decided by the tennis establishment that she had the 'look' the sport needed. She was conventionally feminine, wearing pinafore dresses and ribbons in her hair. She was slim and prim.

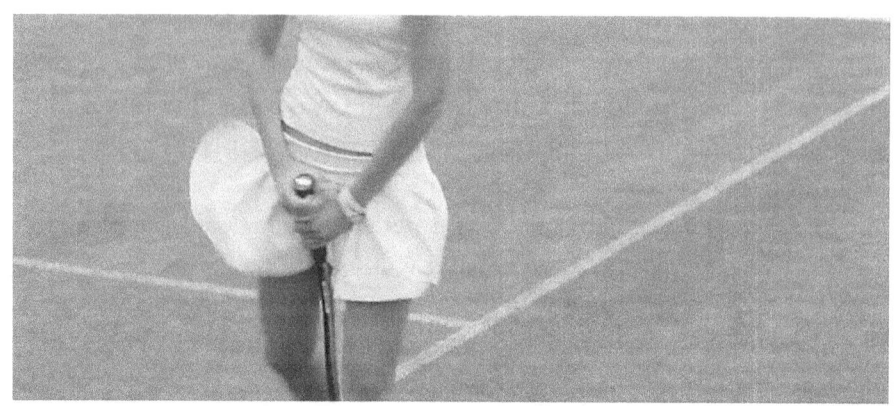

6.2 *Wimbledon* (2004): Lizzie's sexualised grip

Her contemporary film equivalent is Lizzie in *Wimbledon*. Lizzie, with her svelte figure and movie-star looks, is depicted as a pin-up of the women's tour. The romance with Peter that develops during the film echoes Evert's relationship with British tennis player John Lloyd in the late 1970s and early 1980s. Lloyd reached one Grand Slam singles final but did not win. His highest ranking was number 21 in the world. Evert was world number 1 when the couple married in 1979. The connection between Lizzie and Evert is buttressed for the audience by the former tennis player's presence in the film as a sports commentator. There are, however, differences between Evert and her double. Evert, for example, seldom got emotional in matches. She had no John McEnroe type outbursts. She was serious. Some called her the Ice Princess because she was so unflappable on court.[14] In *Wimbledon*, however, Lizzie does display some of McEnroe's attitude. She is shown at one point contesting a line call with an umpire. He rules against her and as she walks away she places her racquet handle between her thighs so the grip becomes a substitute erection and briefly slides her hand up and down in a simulation of masturbation indicating that she feels the official is a 'wanker' (6.2). This kind of 'unladylike' behaviour was not associated with Evert. It was, however, a trademark gesture of her one time beau Jimmy Connors.[15] It was Navratilova, rather than Evert, who was more prone to argue the toss with umpires.

When Navratilova arrived on the professional circuit, she was big and tough, possessing a physique that contrasted markedly with Evert's. Navratilova was nicknamed the Great Wide Hope for a time because of weight gains in the early years of playing in the States. In America, Evert was viewed as the girl next door whereas Navratilova was regarded as an outsider. The polarising effect that Navratilova had on tennis fans in the States was caused, in part, by her nationality. As a Czech player she was associated with Communism. After her defection to America in 1975, Navratilova was still viewed as a foreigner because of her Czech accent. She was also unapologetically athletic in a way that contrasted markedly with Evert. Her arms and legs were muscular. She was aggressive in her play and towards officials. Her appearance and her comportment did not conform to the wholesome look women's tennis wished to portray. Navratilova was marginalised because her 'image' was not right. She gradually recognised this, recounting in her autobiography that in the States: 'Your image seems to count more than what you do.'[16]

In the early years of her career, Navratilova's image was that of Navrat the Brat. She says that at that time she was 'doing my Billie Jean get-on-the-officials imitation on the court, and wearing five bracelets and three necklaces off the court'.[17] She was building a reputation as belligerent and a big spender. This behaviour, and her physical appearance, was continually contrasted with Evert's. Evert was the ideal woman player. Navratilova was the constitutive outside to this ideal. Hers were the necessarily excluded body and actions that confirmed Evert's as the norm. Navratilova was, however, featured in a 1982 *Time* magazine cover story on new concepts of femininity. She states that the idea of the article, in which she was photographed alongside Olivia Newton-John, was to suggest that being in shape was fine for a woman. Newton-John's song 'Physical' had been released the year before.

In the video for 'Physical', set in a gym, it is noteworthy that after Newton-John is portrayed taking a shower she is shown wearing a tennis outfit. The erotic potential of the clothing is obviously being exploited in the film. It is a video about sex. The gym is sexy. Tennis, by extension, is also sexy. Newton-John is presenting herself as an Evert, an object of mainstream heteronormative desire. She flirts with chiselled hunks (who have been magically transformed in, or by, the gym) whilst in her tennis gear. The video, however, signals alternative forms of desire to heterosexuality through its closing scene of two of the men leaving the gym hand in hand. It is noteworthy that this scene was frequently cut when the video was shown on MTV. The video was also banned in its entirety by some broadcasters in Canada and the United Kingdom.

The acknowledgment of homosexuality was obviously not permissible on a trendy music channel on cable television or suitable for a British or Canadian viewing public in the early 1980s.

Navratilova's homosexuality, rumoured and then confirmed, was, of course, another reason why she was not initially greeted with open arms by the tennis establishment despite her brilliance on court. In the US in the 1970s and early 1980s being gay meant being silent or using euphemisms to discuss your sexuality. One of Navratilova's former lovers, the basketball star Nancy Lieberman, writes about her relationship with the tennis player without once mentioning the terms gay, lesbian or homosexual. Her autobiography confirms the pressure there was, and is, to keep sexuality a secret. In *Wimbledon*, the presence of lesbians on the women's tour is acknowledged. There is a scene in which Peter is shown looking for Lizzie and asks an Italian player Billi, who is breakfasting, if she knows where he can find her. The player is with her lover, Sophia. In *When Billie Beat Bobby*, however, King's sexuality is sidestepped.

Navratilova was not good at denying or hiding her desires. She felt her sexuality should be unimportant. The connection between sport and homophobia is longstanding. It is still rare to encounter elite athletes who are openly gay. In 1981, however, Navratilova publicly acknowledged her sexual orientation. For a considerable length of time this had a negative impact on income from sponsorship.[18] Navratilova was also depicted three times less frequently than her main rivals Evert and Steffi Graff in *Sports Illustrated*.[19] She was *imago non grata*. The women's tennis sponsor Avon ceased supporting the game in 1981 in response to Navratilova's declaration and to King's 'galimony' suit. King was sued by a former girlfriend for a share of her wealth. After Navratilova's declaration, as Miller has observed, television cameras would often focus on the reactions of boyfriends or husbands of women opponents such as Evert during matches but not on her girlfriends.[20] The choice of camera shot embodied the conservative moral values of the time.

The tennis tours inability to address sexual diversity was still evident in 1990 when Margaret Court announced that tennis was full of predatory lesbians seeking to seduce young players. In response to this, Gabriela Sabatini was reported as saying: 'I don't even like to take my clothes off in the dressing room.'[21] Hannah Mandlikova suggested that Navratilova and, by extension, other lesbian players 'must have a chromosomic screw loose somewhere'.²² This homophobic comment, couched in pseudo-scientific terms, is interesting because it shows that gay people are quite capable of articulating anti-gay views. Mandlikova is reported to have entered into a civil ceremony with Jana Novotna in the same year.²³ She condemned Navratilova, however, to conceal her own sexuality and escape judgements of the kind she voiced. Amélie Mauresmo also experienced abuse after she came out to the media during the 1999 Australian Open. Mauresmo defeated Lindsay Davenport at the Open and the American said afterwards: 'A couple of times, I mean, I thought I was playing a guy, the girl was hitting so hard, so strong [...] Women's tennis isn't usually played like that.'²⁴ Mauresmo played against Martina Hingis in the final of the Open that year. Hingis, named after Navratilova, stated before the match that Mauresmo 'came to Melbourne with her girlfriend, I think she's half a man'.²⁵

These comments by Davenport and Hingis were obviously not tied to Mauresmo's appearance as the Williams sisters and Mary Pierce, also playing at the time, had comparable physiques.²⁶ The remarks were bound up with Mauresmo's sexuality. Navratilova's and Mauresmo's courage in being open about their sexuality is obvious in the light of these kinds of statements. During her career, Navratilova supported Renée Richards when she took the tennis association to court over their refusal to let her play on the women's tour and would later employ her as a coach. Richards is sometimes labelled a transsexual although it is obvious from comments she makes in the documentary *Renée* (Dir. Eric Drath, USA, 2011) that this is not a term she agrees with. Born Richard Raskind, she had sex reassignment surgery in 1975 and was subsequently denied entry into the 1976 US Open. In *Renée*, Navratilova explains that she felt affinity with Richards: 'I think being gay I felt like an outsider already, you know you're not quite part of the mainstream and maybe that was the empathy I felt for Renée because I knew what it felt like not to be welcome.' Through her support of Richards, Navratilova showed her sexual politics were embodied in deeds as much as words.

Second Serve

Richards entered and won the La Hoya tennis championships in 1976. Her former identity was soon discovered. In *Renée*, Herb Fitzgibbon attributes her detection to the style of play she adopted in the tournament suggesting that 'a tennis stroke is like a fingerprint'. The choice of analogy is worthy of comment as referring to fingerprints in this context encourages reading the tennis court as a crime scene. The style of play becomes the incriminating evidence by which Richards's 'sex crime' is uncovered. Sex, however, cannot be effectively determined from the visual appearance of a print. Its ridge density can be measured to determine biological sex but this has a considerable margin of error (as does measuring peptides present in traces of sweat left in prints). Such tests also work on the reductive assumption that sex is, in any simple sense, fleshy. The remark, however, is not entirely negative. It locates Richards's identity not in her body but in something derived from, but not equal to, it: the way she handles a racquet.

Styles of play form distinctive manners of engaging in a given sport. These can be gendered as the discussion of baseline and serve and volley has already demonstrated. Richards is a serve and volley player. Fitzgibbon, however, is not referring to style in these general terms. Within the style that is serve and volley, there is another level of style, a way of playing serve and volley, which is unique to each individual. It is this personal expression within a style of play that 'undoes' Richards. The sex changes but the style remains the same. Richards, however, did change her personal style. After her surgery, challenging Fitzgibbon's implicit assumption that players possess innate tennis styles, she altered her approach to the game to fit with how she perceived a woman should play. She knowingly embraced the inhibitions in relation to bodily comportment that Young observes are usually unwittingly cultivated by women. Sheila Jeffreys has drawn attention to transsexuals subscribing to traditional feminine stereotypes of behaviour.[27] Richards, however, cultivates stereotypes knowingly rather than unwittingly embodying patriarchal ideology. Her actions reveal that flesh is acculturated. Through retraining her body to comport itself 'girlishly', Richards also demonstrates that style, *modus operandi* as Fitzgibbon might see it, is variable. The problem is that Richards's coach still believed specific styles of play are bound to certain sexed bodies. He wanted Richards to embrace her 'natural' style, regarding that 'mannish' style as inborn.

It is also less often remarked that, at least initially, Richards's sex change was accompanied by an age change. The ramifications of this are noteworthy in relation to Navratilova's refusal to act her calendar age. The reporter Dick Carlson, upon uncovering Richards's previous identity, remarked '31 year old Renée Richards is actually 41 year old Dr. Richard H. Raskind.' This asinine statement is followed slightly later in the documentary by Carlson observing that 'chromosomes make you a man or a woman'. His views on sex are rooted in a particular conception of biology, and of the capabilities of sex-testing, which explains why he feels he can 'actually' deduce who Richards is. He ignores the plural in Richards's surname, the nominal recognition that individuals potentially manifest a plurality of identities. Carlson, however, purposely does not restrict himself to revealing Richards's 'real' gender. He also adjudges her proper age. This age reassignment cannot be linked to chromosomes. It is, rather, bound up with documented dates and the calendrical. Richards turned back the clock ten years as 'for most female athletes, 30 is the age at which you should be retired'.[28] Carlson, however, assesses age by date of birth. Richards did not resist this age fixing continuing her career using her certified age rather than her chosen age at her rebirth. Her career after this point can therefore be interpreted as akin to Navratilova's in that it demonstrated competitive tennis can still be played after the age of 40.

The film *Second Serve* (Dir. Anthony Page, USA, 1986) also explores aspects of Richards's life story. In it, Richard Raskind is replaced by the character of Richard Radley. The actor Vanessa Redgrave plays both Radley and Renée Richards. The name of the film, drawn from the subtitle of Richards's autobiography, foregrounds the importance of tennis to her story. This is despite the game featuring only briefly and intermittently until the film's final 20 minutes. Using the second serve in tennis as an analogy for Richards's rebirth as a woman is, however, problematic. Second serves in tennis are usually more cautious and weaker than the first. The rebirth is therefore figured as feebler. The centrality of sport to it is, nevertheless, clearly signalled.

Second Serve does not follow Richards's actual life story in that the reporter who reveals her previous identity in the film is a female reporter. During a phone call in which she is invited to comment on her past, Renée advises the reporter 'You'd make a very good detective.' This links with the remark in the documentary about fingerprints. The language of crime that is invoked can be heard as indicative of a society in which transgender is conceptualised as wrongdoing. It is, however, not the uniqueness of Renée's style of play, her individual technical fingerprint, which causes her personal history to be investigated. In *Second Serve*, it is the power of her forehand drive, rather than its panache, that is remarked upon. Her boyfriend, known only as Bill, comments: 'Where did you get that forehand drive? – I have never seen a woman with a drive like that!' The forehand can involve immense racquet head speed if legs, hips, shoulder, arm and wrist combine effectively and fluidly in preparation for and execution of the shot. Renée's forehand is too powerful, too 'manly'.

Once Renée's former identity is publicised, reporters congregate at the apartment complex where she is staying. The press pack jostles her when she appears. Bill intervenes, pushing them back. He has only recently learnt of Renée's past on the television news. When Renée asks if they will meet at the apartment later, Bill demurs. He is unwilling to continue the relationship. Bill does not, however, demonstrate anger or disgust. There is no abject moment of the kind portrayed in *The Crying Game* (Dir. Neil Jordan, UK, 1992) when Dil's transvestism is revealed. Bill reaches out to Renée, puts his hand to her chin, in an affectionate gesture of support. This brief moment of physical contact is significant. In *Politics of Touch*, Erin Manning suggests that 'there is no sensation of touch that remains alert without reinstantiation'.[29] Touch is a feeling that is of the moment. It is 'very much in-time'.[30] Bill's before and after touching, his restating of tenderness, pointed towards a potentially loving future for Renée (even if with someone else). Touch is transitional. It challenges dichotomy, 'creating not a self and an other, but a third space, a reciprocal body-space that challenges the limits of both self and self as other'.[31] In their touching encounter, Bill and Renée are open to each other. The gesture is, however, noteworthy in that Bill's hand is closed in a loose fist. This promising openness is still combined with reserve and, possibly, aggression. Shortly before, Bill had firmly, over forcefully, gripped Renée's arm, urging her to leave. In this context, there are seemingly mixed messages embodied in the circumscribed reaching towards.

Second Serve, with its numerous scenes of therapy and depictions of Richard Radley's and Renée Richards's personal torment, does not provide many moments of respite from psychological pain. The cinematography is also conventional. There are no instances in which a transgender gaze comparable to the one identified by Halberstam in *Boy's Don't Cry* (Dir. Kimberly Peirce, USA, 1999) occurs. In that film, there is a judicious use of the shot/reverse shot technique which produces a situation in which 'the *sufficiency* of the transgender subject' is affirmed.[32] *Second Serve* involves no comparable camerawork. It points instead to insufficiency. There are instances in which visual and acoustic editing is used to suggest flashbacks. One such arrangement occurs towards the end of the film when Renée is shown waiting in a locker room for a match to begin. The soundtrack features reporters voices although she is alone in the room. These sounds carry over into a series of flashback images from Renée's past. These varied images, fragments, appear in quick succession. The flashbacks end with Renée lying in recovery after her sex reassignment operation.[33] The babble of the reporters is replaced with her screams of pain. This confusion of images and sounds suggests mental turmoil. Renée is depicted as traumatised. The sequence ends, however, with Renée resolutely putting on her cloth hat ready to play, the images and noises banished.

Tennis is represented as providing a means of escape from social pressures and the psychological strain that accompanies them. The game offers flight into motions and gestures, exertions, which temporarily exceed sexual politics. Tennis provides respite from, if not a solution to, the hurts and indignities Renée encounters in everyday life. There is continuing controversy over transsexual participation in sport. In this context, Jayne Caudwell has explored the deleterious effects of a sports system that relies on an exclusionary two sex understanding of gender.[34] This controversy, however, is peripheral to sport in practice. The golfer Mianne Bagger, the Muay Thai boxer Parinya Charoenpahl, the martial artist Fallon Fox, the mountain biker Michelle Dumaresq, for example, leave violence and misunderstanding behind when they compete and excel in their chosen fields.[35] Like the two transgender athletes interviewed by Caudwell as part of her research, they participate in sport not to reinforce a gendered subjectivity but to be active and enjoy themselves. Sport provides a venue in which to revel in physical ease, feeling it in the sinews. Gendered subjectivity is not an issue as Bagger, Charoenpahl, and Fox take swings and Dumaresq lifts a wheel. Sport provides a means by which to leave behind a world in which thinkers such as Jeffreys label trans people violators of human rights.[36] It is this message of bodily comfort that *Second Serve* seems to make when Renée exits the locker room calm and focussed.

Pushing Boundaries

Judith Butler has drawn attention to Navratilova's athletic activism. She emphasises how Navratilova showed 'just how radically gender norms can be altered through a spectacular public restaging'.[37] Through her actions, Navratilova transformed an unashamedly powerful physique from being outside the corporeal norm to being perceived by Butler and others as 'some of the most progressive instances of the norm'. Butler explores Navratilova's physical significance in the essay 'Athletic Genders' which uses a series of photographs by athlete Cindy Collins as its starting point. She contrasts these photographs of sportspersons with the imaginary body of an athlete. This latter, fantasised body lacks fixity, finish. The photograph, however, secures and stills. Efforts to think about athletes usually mirror photographs in that they conceive of the athlete's body as 'motionless, as a sculpted body, one whose contours bear the marks of achievement'.[38] Butler suggests that 'the athlete's body is thought of as a finished or completed accomplishment, as the effect of its labor, but it is rarely thought – or thinkable – in motion'.[39]

This voiding of motion is motivated by a suppression of the reality that the athletic body is, like any body, never an accomplished one. Through repetitive practices the figure of the athlete is always striving to attain an ideal of corporeality that remains forever out of reach. The athlete's body is perpetually tenuous in the sense that 'it is always in the process of being made, it is never quite the ideal that it seeks to approximate, and so the reflection of itself that it receives through visual form is precisely not the same as the kinesthetic movement that we think of as proper to athletic activity'.[40] There is a disjuncture between the body felt as a continuous process of becoming, a perpetual deferral of being, and the inert body-image, the lifeless ideal, such as the sports photograph or fantasised look, that it seeks to live up to.

Butler draws attention here to deconstruction as lived event. Her conception relates to the athlete's body as iteration. The physique repeatedly seeks to cite the ideal (an ideal that is in flux). It is a tissue of quotations.[41] Citation has its etymological roots in motion and it could therefore be said that athleticism is inherent to it. It is a kind of athletic writing. This writing, however, is engaged in a race that is never won: the ideal, the finish line, remains forever out of sight. The body always differs from this always deferred model it seeks to write into being. There are, however, other ways than this of thinking about athletic writing in relation to deconstruction. There is, for instance, an accord between skeletal muscles, which always function in combination. These muscles operate as agonists and antagonists, abductor and adductor, for example, biceps and triceps. Each requires the other to act in opposition to it, the pull of one counteracted by the pull of another: when the agonist contracts, the antagonist relaxes, when the antagonist contracts, the agonist relaxes. Motion is a continual muscular give and take, a series of negotiated tensions, perpetual efforts at co-operation. The action of the biceps cannot be explained without acknowledging the triceps, the influence of which can be traced in every flexion.

Every muscle is incomplete, beholden to another. No muscle is present in itself. Muscles supplement. They are also supplemented. Muscles cannot move us without drawing on other materials. They adhere to joints which act as hinges between bones. These articulations work in harmony with muscles to enable movement. Movement therefore does not originate in either the actions of joints or muscles, its beginnings cannot be apprehended. It is also never accomplished, always instituting further fleshly contractions and extensions. The language of the body, its motions, actions, articulations, signals 'that the signified is originarily and essentially [...] trace'.[42] There is differential play within the body as writing. Sport, through its physical demands and the athletic physique it often requires, is a particularly bold form of bodily writing. Sports films translate this somatic text into acoustic and visual spectacle. Motion pictures are therefore of a different order to photography as Butler conceives of it.

Photography, 'the ideal that governs athleticism becomes visible only on the condition that that very athleticism is visually suspended in time'.[43] The image here is conceived of as motionless, un-athletic, yet not inactive. The sedentary photograph acts upon the athlete, possesses a force, impresses their physique, even though it is immobile. Representations move. They also alter in another sense. They are changeable, shifting. These variable representations comprise 'cultural norms that govern the limits of the imaginable'.[44] They provide athletes with ideals to aspire to yet in endeavouring to assume such ideals the athlete takes part in 'their rearticulation and transformation'.[45] The relationship between ideal and athlete, like that between agonist and antagonist muscles, is one of unavoidable overlap, interdependence.

Figures in films, like those in photographs, form ideal bodies that athletes may aspire to. There is, however, greater slippage in cinema. The images of athletes, unlike those in photographs, are not hard and fast. They can shift. Motion pictures resist fixity. In *Hard, Fast and Beautiful* (Dir. Ida Lupino, USA, 1951), for example, the character of Florence Farley, a tennis ingénue, develops from naïve prospect, to tough businesswoman, to loving fiancée. Farley's physique does not alter noticeably throughout the film but her demeanour, her comportment, changes markedly. The ideal Farley aspires to initially, one created by her mother Millie, is that of tennis champion. Millie strives to live out her own dreams of wealth and status through the competitive successes of her daughter. She is constructed as a femme fatale who callously manipulates Florence for her own ends. The use of lighting, of strong shadow effects, particularly in some of the apartment sequences on a visit to London, evokes film noir.

Early in the film, Millie joins forces with Fletcher Locke, a coach and promoter, to mould Florence into a successful competitor. Locke's approach exemplifies dismembering teaching methods as they are identified by Bruno Rigauer. Rigauer argues that in modern athletic training 'the learning process is divided up like the division of labour into single movements and elements of behaviour'.[46] Fletcher therefore subjects Florence to the sporting equivalent of Fordism. When working on her backhand, he advises Florence: 'Let's do it until it is automatic!' During a session devoted to improving her backswing, he urges: 'Let's do it until it is mechanical!' Fletcher's coaching seeks to mould Florence into an efficient, unthinking machine. This is his ideal player. His methods initially pay dividends with Florence becoming national amateur champion after an aggressive match that she wins with a score of 7-9, 6-4, 6-4. Florence's improvement shows she is not hard, her technique is malleable, her style of play flexible. Once his methods have made Florence a winner, Locke, acting in connivance with Millie, uses her success as a means to surreptitiously secure money from firms in return for endorsements. When Florence discovers this, she confronts her mother: 'I've been beating my brains out on a tennis court while you were playing it dirty for money.' Millie's behaviour here is, as Mandy Merck has recognised, equated with that of a prostitute.[47] She is, however, more a pimp who has prostituted her daughter.

The director Ida Lupino focuses frequently on Millie's fingernails throughout the film. Towards the beginning of *Hard, Fast and Beautiful*,

6.3 *Hard, Fast and Beautiful* (1951): Millie's beautiful nails

the mother is shown painting her nails. Millie is concerned with perfecting a beautiful appearance (6.3). There is a scene a short time later in which Millie is shown smoking, the camera again drawing attention to her neatly manicured nails. Soon after Florence confronts her mother about her financial dealings, Millie's nails are again in the foreground. Through this repeated emphasis on her long, polished nails, Millie's phallic credentials are foregrounded. Wendy Dozoretz argues that these credentials are also cultivated in her daughter who is encouraged to be 'aggressive, ambitious and triumphant'.[48] Millie's nails also pointedly indicate her castrating potential. She has emasculated her husband. When they talk, he struggles to make himself heard and he has no say in his daughter's future. She steals his voice just as her voice, her voiceover, will ultimately be stolen by the radio commentator Arthur Little Jr.[49] The long nails therefore signal her domineering nature.

Painted nails also connote waywardness. In *A League of Their Own*, Mae Mordabito, nicknamed 'All the Way Mae', paints the farm girl Kit Keller's nails. Mae is concerned Kit's elder sister will disapprove, implying that the polish indicates impropriety. In *Flying*, Robin's sister Gillian's

6.4 *Bend it Like Beckham* (2002): Paula's polished superficiality

close attention to her nails, she is shown in separate scenes putting on polish and filing, is used as a means to contrast her with her gymnast step-sister. Gillian is superficial whereas Robin is dedicated and complex. Fingernails are also used in other sports films to indicate the psychic state of a specific character. In *Apflickorna* (Dir. Lisa Aschan, Sweden, 2011), for example, which explores the rivalry between two teenage competitors in equestrian vaulting, the chipped nails of the character Cassandra, as well as her forename, figure her fragile temperament. In *Bend it Like Beckham*, Jules's mother Paula wears a variety of garish shades of nail polish, coral, fuschia, lilac, during the film. Her extravagant nails are designed to signal her tawdry superficiality (6.4). This shallowness is also indicated through dialogue. After wrongly confronting Jules over her perceived lesbianism, Paula remarks: 'I was cheering for Martina Navratilova as much as the next person.'

Additionally, long fingernails have pedigree as a fetish. There are numerous websites dedicated to long nails and to hands more generally. Their status as erotic material means that a woman's nails can frequently become the focus of attention in media coverage of her achievements. Florence Griffith Joyner, the American sprinter, was almost as renowned for her long, frequently colourfully painted nails as for her achievements in athletics. She explained her penchant for lengthy nails and figure-hugging leotards as motivated by the fear she would otherwise be viewed as manly.

The clothing and manicured hands formed a feminine apologetic designed to counteract any manly associations caused by her immense success on the track. Joyner was on the cover of the February 1993 edition of *Nails* magazine. The publication named her the 'patron saint of nail artists'. She is depicted standing behind a brocade covered chair, her hands resting on top of its back, posed to display her red painted nails to maximum effect. The colour of her nails mirrors the brocade. Woman and chair are to be seen as equally richly ornamented. Joyner's nails often became a similar focus of attention when she spread her hands at the starting blocks before a race. The sprinter Gail Devers, who rose to prominence in the 1990s, was also renowned for her long nails. Devers, however, had fingernails which went well beyond the norm and, rather than forming a feminine apologetic, might actually have contributed to intimidating her rivals given their talon-like quality.

At the 2013 World Championships in Athletics held in Moscow, Swedish high jumper Emma Green Tregaro exploited the allure accorded to nails by painting hers in rainbow colours. This nail art referenced the pride flag, representing gay pride. It comprised political activism, forming a visual challenge to recently introduced legislation outlawing the promotion of homosexuality to minors in Russia. Tregaro posted a photograph of her painted nails on Instagram and her actions were much publicised in the media. The Swedish sprinter Moa Hjelmer took similar action yet received much less attention. Tregaro was subsequently forced to repaint her nails after receiving a warning over her conduct from the International Association of Athletic Federations (IAAF). She chose the colour red, which she felt signalled love. Long nails, however, whatever colour they are painted, have, in the past, connoted wantonness as the colloquial expressions 'hooker nails' and 'whore hands' demonstrate. Millie's hands are framed in this way. They signal her transgression.

Millie's independence, her betrayal of marital values, is ultimately punished. The film closes with Florence turning her back on tennis to be with her man. She hands her last tennis trophy to her mother and then walks out on her. Millie is left spectating an abandoned court, listening to the imaginary sounds of tennis balls striking racquets whilst crumpled, discarded newspapers, tumbleweed, blows across the grass. It is a scene of desolation. The absence of on court bodies at the end of *Hard, Fast and Beautiful* coupled with the sounds of a match in progress suggest

Millie is experiencing a hallucination. The phantom players exposing the cleft between the fantasy of her American dream and the reality she cannot transcend either her sex or her lower-middle class life in Santa Monica. The imagined future that Millie constructed for her daughter and, by extension, for herself drifts away with yesterday's news. Ultimately, the message of *Hard, Fast and Beautiful* is conservative. It supports the 1950s Middle American status quo. Florence's sporting achievements made no impact as far as her imminent life of bourgeois domesticity was concerned.

The Shock of the New

Butler uses Navratilova as an example of an athlete whose appearance and achievements fostered change. She expanded athletic ideals and helped 'spawn a new generation of women tennis players'.[50] Navratilova moved from being outside the ideal to exemplifying the ideal. Butler explains that 'such a move could not be possible if gender ideals were not capable of transformation, of becoming more capacious, of responding to the challenge of what is excluded from their terms by expanding the very terms of gender themselves'.[51] This transformation is dependent upon the circulation of new representations of the athletic body that enter into competition with existing ideals. In tennis, it is therefore possible to see Navratilova's aforementioned rivalry with Evert as forming a contest between corporeal ideals. Evert was in the ascendant in this clash long after she began to consistently lose to Navratilova on court. She was constructed as embodying a 'dainty feminine ideal' in contrast to the aggressive 'unfeminine' body-type of her opponent.[52] Pat Griffin suggests that the rivalry between Evert and Navratilova had 'an unspoken subtext of Beauty (Queen) versus Butch (Lesbian)'.[53] Evert's representation as the epitome of athletic femininity was enduring even as her potency as a player waned.

Navratilova's own image throughout her career was not, however, as uniform as Butler's account implies. It is true that in the Eighties she was characterised as 'a bionic marvel to be placed in a unique gender category of not-woman and not-man'.[54] A classification of Navratilova, as a third-sex, that foreshadows the revolutionary corporeality envisaged by Gassel which was discussed in Chapter 5. Her physical appearance in that period has been described as 'hard to put into words – clearly female, but not frilly and willing to compromise her athleticism for the conventions of femininity'.[55] In the 1990s, she refused to display traditional markers of femininity such as long hair, jewellery, and cosmetics as a means to counteract perceived masculine attributes such as aggression and muscularity.[56] Towards the start of her international success, however, despite an unapologetic athleticism, Navratilova was often bejewelled and wore make-up. She also sported the seemingly mandatory tennis skirt until 1993 at Wimbledon when she opted to play in shorts. Navratilova's style of play remained consistent throughout her career (although her repertoire of strokes increased and her serve improved) yet her public face shifted with time. This change has been interpreted by Gilda Zwerman as representing Navratilova's growing confidence in her lesbian identity as manifested through 'becoming more "butch"'.[57] It is this corporeal identity which Butler draws on for her representation of the tennis star.

Butler ends her reflections on the athletic body in positive terms, seeing sport as a distinctively public way in which to enact and attest to 'dramatic transformation' in relation to the category 'women'.[58] For her, tennis players such as Navratilova and Richards demonstrated that 'the proper contours of gender were no longer easily marked or known, one in which gender itself proved to be more historically contingent and malleable than popular consciousness might have thought'.[59] Navratilova and Richards both unsettled taken for granted knowledge.[60] Butler reads the emergence of players such as Conchita Martinez as powerful evidence for the successful transformation of the athletic ideal, a change initiated by Navratilova. Butler's optimism, however, needs to be qualified in the long term. The progress she identified in 1998, as is obvious from the media treatment of Mauresmo a year later, is provisional. Navratilova's later experiences after emerging from retirement in 1999 also demonstrate that efforts to expand, or move beyond, the category of 'woman' are continual.

In *Female Masculinity*, Halberstam lists Navratilova alongside Bev Francis as providing images of strong women yet laments that despite their visibility 'there is still no general acceptance or even recognition of masculine women'.[61] One reason behind the failure of these images to change perception is precisely their status as images. As previously mentioned, Butler has drawn attention to the inertia of the photographic image and its lack of athleticism. Many of the images of strong women are of this kind.

A photograph of Francis or Navratilova may display their athleticism yet cannot substantiate it. Susan Sontag's insights into photography are informative here. She suggested that photographs are unlikely to actively mobilise people against a war in the way a piece of prose can. For her, narratives are more effective than visual images. The latter are too immediate: 'it is a question of the length of time one is obliged to look, to feel'.[62] Drawing on this observation, it is obvious that films, like prose narratives, can prolong observation and, by extension, feeling. Photographs, in their abruptness, tend to require minimal attention and to lack emotional impact.

The superficiality of the feelings experienced when viewing photographs that Sontag recognises can be expanded to encompass a superficiality of sensation as well. This is evident from the art historian Adrian Rifkin's reminiscences about Maria Bueno winning Wimbledon in 1962. Bueno was renowned for her artistry and the beauty of her stroke play.[63] Writing in 2009, Rifkin states that whilst his ardour for the Brazilian has waned, his passion for other spectacles that he encountered in that year has persisted. This appears to be because Bueno's appeal was tied to seeing her 'in movement'.[64] Still images of Bueno, such as the one Rifkin uses to illustrate his essay, do not seemingly convey her on-court magnetism. Footage of Bueno or photographs accompanied by narrative would, however, potentially carry traces of her aesthetically athletic appeal. That tennis possesses a strong aesthetic dimension is implied by Merleau-Ponty's decision to compare painting to playing the game: 'the rules of anatomy and design are present in each stroke of [the] brush just as the rules of the game underlie each stroke of a tennis match'.[65]

Navratilova's physical attributes, her revolutionary corporeality and kinesthetic intelligence, are best communicated through archival footage of her in action. Jennifer Barker has drawn attention to how in any cinematic experience 'we and the film have a muscular empathy for one another'.[66] This empathy involves inhabiting the bodies of figures on screen, becoming in fellow feeling with their gestures, motions, and also acknowledging the energy of the medium itself, its cinematographic athleticism. In filming sport, as will be discussed in the final chapter, the camera also exerts itself. The double partnership of the body being filmed and the body of the camera carry their play of forces through time.

Unlike the photograph, they are not bound to a given moment. This means Navratilova's corporeal activism continues into the present not only through her contemporary achievements but also through archival footage of her competing on court. She continues to shape women's ideas of who they can be through her past actions.

ically, a solitary layer
7

Surfing Aesthetics: Towards a Matrixial Reading of Sports Films

The Waves

Point Break (Dir. Kathryn Bigelow, USA, 1991) begins with images of waves, distant memories of storms. Waves initiate in far off squalls, each carrying an energetic message, continually instructing the water surface 'to go round in an orbital motion', from the storm to where it eventually arrives.[1] The first shot in *Point Break* is of receding water flowing rapidly, glistening in early morning sunlight. The backwash is met, engulfed, by an incoming wave which breaks as it reaches shallow water, causing a messy mass of roil and spray. The camera remains steady as the wave dissolves, replaced by foam and ripples. This scene is accompanied by diegetic and non-diegetic sound. The plunging wave that breaks causes a crashing noise as it traps and compresses air. There is also a musical score, a solitary layer of sound, thin, ethereal, that is distantly reminiscent of plainsong. The sea is acoustically anchored to a spiritual register.

There is another crash and the scene shifts to a shot of a surfer entering the sea. Some droplets of spray hit the lens, reflecting the light of the rising sun and causing small golden orbs to appear in the image. The film cuts to a shot of the surfer riding a wave, approaching the camera. There is significant lens flare, a string of hexagons visible close to the centre of the shot. The surfer turns, sending a wall of water towards the camera so that the lens is soaked, the cinema screen becoming a sight of froth, distortion. The sea veiled by itself. The film cuts from the beach to an FBI facility at Quantico. It is raining heavily. A recruit is preparing

7.1 *Point Break* (1991): The sea as cast member

to undertake a training exercise in a shooting gallery. The rest of the opening credits involve rapid cuts between this location and the beach, as shooter and surfer engage in their chosen activities. The shooter is Johnny Utah, the hero of the film.[2] The surfer's identity is left unclear. Given his actions run parallel to those of Utah, however, the audience is encouraged to retrospectively infer that this is Bodhi, *Point Break*'s antihero. *Point Break*, directed by Kathryn Bigelow, is the story of an FBI undercover investigation to catch a gang of bank robbers known as the Ex-Presidents who are presumed to be surfers.

The opening credits introduce the film's two main characters in Bodhi and Utah. There is, however, arguably a third character also being presented: the sea itself (7.1). The ocean has a central role in the film and, indeed, in most surf films. In films such as *Point Break*, *Big Wednesday* (Dir. John Milius, USA, 1978), and *Blue Crush* (Dir. John Stockwell, USA, 2002) the sea forms more than simply a physical phenomenon. It also has a psychical dimension. In *Water and Dreams*, Gaston Bachelard suggests that the fondness for landscapes and, by extension, seascapes does not derive from their objective characteristics. The love of nature is forged elsewhere. Nature, in fact, forms a projection of the mother.[3] The sea, in particular, is associated with the maternal. Its song is that of the mother's voice. For Bachelard, unconscious memories are activated through encounters with the sea.

The song that Bachelard refers to is a familiar source of pleasure. The seethe of sea upon sand possesses a gratifying lyricism to anyone listening. There is a satisfying cadence to the interplay of beachface and water.

The varied hiss as waves exhaust themselves along the swash zone, their sibilance dissipating as they disappear, can acquire a poetic quality, the sounds assuming the character of a soothing lullaby. The recurrent roar of breakers, crash and hush and crash, equally fascinate yet generate anxiety rather than enjoyment. These varied feelings sound the unconscious, reminiscent of early interactions between mother and child, echoing archaic tempos, temperaments.

Bracha Ettinger has written of matrixial bordertime and borderspace, of prenatal time and space, that it exhibits an affect that is 'suspended like a rotating sea-wave between its fading and a next birth'.[4] The analogy is revealing, demonstrating the connotative potency of the sea. Waves, their rhythms, motions, their ebb and flow, potentially provide powerful reminders of the pre-subject's psychic beginnings, its affective past. Ettinger's psychoanalytic theories provide a means by which to begin to approach this archaic aspect of psychic life, the subject's 'singular prehistory'.[5] Her ideas, which extend theories advanced in Lacan's late work, will now be summarised prior to exploring their relevance for the study of *Point Break* and other surf movies and the contribution they can make to the future of feminist film theory.

Ettinger proposes that there is a matrixial psychic sphere that exists subjacent to the phallic sphere. The matrixial, which relates to 'the prenatal, the intrauterine, gestation and pregnancy', can 'deconstruct and dissolve the concept of the unitary separate phallic subject split by the castration mechanism, rejecting its abject, and mourning its m/Other'.[6] The matrixial therefore provides scope for thinking through reconciliation within culture with the maternal. This differentiates her ideas from those of, for example, Julia Kristeva. In *Powers of Horror*, Kristeva describes early psychic life, the Real, as a source of fear and loathing.[7] Like Kristeva, Ettinger suggests that the Real is a 'Thing' that is never left behind. It still resonates in the subject alongside the Symbolic. For Ettinger, however, it is not a locus of anxiety but rather an ethical resource. Judith Butler explains that the matrixial provides an ethical framework through which to (re)think our relation to 'those to whom we are bound, prior to contract and will, whose lives are not only next to our own, but with whom we are linked through the border'.[8] The idea of the border, the matrixial as borderspace, will be returned to later. Artworks which exhibit an aesthetic that fosters encounters with borderspace therefore possess ethical potential.

Ettinger uses the term m/Other to distinguish the maternal of the matrixial from the Mother or Other of postnatal existence, the psychic figure involved in the oedipalising scenario. The little m/ stresses that this is a becoming mother rather than an accomplished entity. This mother-to-be comprises a generative subjectivity and 'subjectivises the I (to begin with a prenatal *becoming-partial-subject*)', distinct from the subjectivising operations of the phallic domain.[9] The matrixial therefore supplements psychic identity. Ettinger also uses the m/ to reinforces that the matrixial stratum of subjectivisation is 'feminine': 'is shaped by feminine difference that is linked to the female body and relates to *her* "hole" in the Real and to the originary matrixial times and spaces that differentiate themselves before repression'.[10] This feminine difference, however, is not of the order of sexual difference which is produced and regulated during the Oedipus complex.

Ettinger argues that in the matrixial, the infant's synesthetic capacity and affectability enable it to be responsive to 'affects, mental frequencies, waves, and resonance'.[11] The child receives and emits communications prior to being born. It processes and responds to energies. The m/Other also reacts to transmissions from the child. Links, provisional lines of communication, are established. Through these energetic connections partial subjects co-emerge. Ettinger writes that 'the matrixial is modelled on a certain conception of feminine/prebirth psychic intimate sharing, where the womb is conceived of as a shared psychic borderspace in which differentiation-in-co-emergence, separation-in-jointness, and distance-in-proximity are continuously reattuned'.[12] The womb as described here is not to be confused with the reproductive sex organ of that name. In the manner of Lacan's phallus, which, as image or symbol, is distinct from the penis, the matrix, as locus of energetic affective exchanges, is distinct from the biological uterus. Griselda Pollock explains that 'we must dismiss any sense of the uterus as organ, and replace it with the idea of a *spatial subjectivising condition enduring over time premised on encounter with an unknown, sensed otherness*'.[13] Ettinger's language, her repeated use of hyphenation, is a symptom of the difficulty of catching the 'differentiation-in-co-emergence' that characterises the matrixial within the detached terms and rigid structures of phallocentric language. The matrix is typified by flow, resisting fixed terms. It is exemplified by exchange and transformation, accommodating.

The matrixial is also distinguished by its shifting intensities which contrast with the controlled stability, the enforced order, of the phallic. Ettinger explains that 'the originary metamorphoses in the field of joint matrixial sensibility are connected to oscillations of touch and pressure, fluctuations of motions and balance (kinaesthesia), changing amplitudes of voices and light-and-dark variations – diffuse, shared sensorial impressions that enable the construction of partial object-relations and their loss, and that subjectivize the partial-subjects (partial *I* and partial others) as matrixial'.[14] I will argue in this chapter that the matrixial register of subjectivity, this economy of oscillation and fluctuation, is recognised and attested to, brought to bear, by way of *Point Break*'s cinematography, registered at the levels of chromatics, luminosity, repeated motifs and recurring vibrations. The visual field of the film, in particular, is at odds with the tighter focus maintained by many mainstream modern and contemporary action films.

Reading film through Ettinger's ideas forms a predictable extension of her thinking given the importance of another form of cultural production, art, to her. Ettinger's psychoanalytic theories are closely bound up with her artistic practice which can be understood as an extension of her philosophy. For her, aesthetic experience as prompted by an artwork forms one way in which the matrixial is still registered by the subject. In aesthetic experience, through a process termed metramorphosis, matrixial affects can 'infiltrate the nonconscious margins of the Symbolic'.[15] Ettinger believes there is an aesthetic dimension to subjectivity. She describes it as the 'matrixial stratum of subjectivization'.[16] It carries traces of the subject's pre-subjective intrauterine interactions with the maternal, residues of the co-emergence of partial subjects, vestiges of archaic linkages and connections. It can therefore be positioned in contrast to the castration paradigm which, centred as it is upon the phallus, is grounded in experiences of separation and loss.

Ways in which films that superficially promote a feminist message can be seen to ultimately reinforce phallocentrism and the castration paradigm are exemplified by *Charlie's Angels 2: Full Throttle* (Dir. McG, USA, 2003). This film embraces emancipatory sexual politics at a surface level. *Charlie's Angels 2* is a work which exemplifies so called 'Girl Power' and is designed to appear empowering for women. The three angels are exponents of the 'physical feminism' discussed in Chapter 2.[17] Their self-defence skills

7.2 *Charlie's Angels 2* (2003): Madison, Natalie and the sea

form a corporeal challenge to entrenched ideas about physical prowess as a masculine attribute. There are, however, strict limits to the feminist message of the film. These are made particularly obvious by the title with its male possessive, Charlie owns the angels. He is, in fact, figured as their heavenly father in that he never appears physically, only communicating with them through ethereal, disembodied speech via an intercom. The narrative therefore, through the male voice-box of Charlie, already opens up ways of problematising the ostensibly emancipatory message of the film for women.[18]

It is a former angel, Madison Lee, who, in a highly symbolically charged moment, shoots the intercom which vehicles this commanding voice thereby silencing it temporarily. Madison is first introduced to the audience at the beach where she has been surfing (7.2). She approaches a current angel, Natalie Cook, to say hello. Madison gets extremely close to Natalie as she is talking to her, making her uncomfortable. There are indications that Madison is physically attracted to the younger woman which are confirmed in the film's denouement. As she is the main villain in the film, her lesbian desire becomes tainted by association. It is a further sign of her immorality as well as of a homophobic subtext to the film. Ultimately this 'bad' angel is symbolically punished for her transgressions, her rejection of male acoustic authority and of heterosexuality, by being condemned to a pit of hell-fire by the three 'good' angels who unquestioningly obey the Adam's apple of their vocal puppet-master.[19]

The sequence in which Madison receives her come-uppance also functions, at the level of cinematography, to pass judgement on a particular

7.3 *Charlie's Angels 2* (2003): Madison is sent to hell

way of seeing, uncertain, imprecise, and indiscrete: 'in which perception *founders*'.[20] Madison's bad angel is defeated in a showdown with the trio of good angels. She plunges through the floor of an abandoned theatre, rupturing a gas pipe in the process, firing her pistol as she falls. The shot causes an explosion, leading her to tumble into a fiery annihilation, engulfed by a billowing upsurge of flames (7.3). It is noteworthy that her adversaries do not use guns in the sequence. They refuse to appropriate this symbol of phallic potency. Madison does adopt this phallic attribute. It is one which triggers the blaze that consumes her. Her phallic designs are, however, not the only thing being condemned. Madison also serves to inscribe that explosion, to foreground it by association as bad like her.

The rumbling outflow of fire, a hot golden seethe that briefly fills the screen, forms an unfixed, diffuse phenomenon which is coded, by way of its connection to the bad angel, as cruel and undesirable. Madison is also linked to the sea. It forms the rippling, shimmering, unfocussed backdrop to her first encounter with Natalie. She acts to anchor particular visual phenomena as, like her, aberrant. *Charlie's Angels 2* ultimately celebrates strong contours, clear outlines, identifiable boundaries which are reasserted and reaffirmed. The Lacanian subject – all edge – is bolstered here.[21] The scene ends with quiet shots of the three 'good' angels in sharp focus against an unfocussed background. They decide it is 'party-time'. What they, and the film, ultimately celebrate is a triumph of the castration paradigm registered at the level of cinematography. The image has to have its clarity, its discrete perfection, returned to it. The brief scene referencing surfing, however, points towards how the sea, its waves, its motions and noises, possesses a potential to disrupt the dominance of this paradigm.

Vision is Overrated

Alongside the classic cinematic fields of identification and fantasy, structures of phallocentric subjective formation, there are supplementary pleasures and desires related to connectivity and encounter. These form an additional dimension within the Symbolic that resonates within the subject by way of specific aesthetic moments which restore a sense of borderspace. Borderspace, intrauterine space, comprises a locus of touching perceptions that leads to '*relations-without-relating* to the other based on attunement to *distances-in-proximity* (and not on *either* fusion *or* repulsion) [that] reflect and create *differentiation-in-co-emergence* accompanied by shared, diffused *matrixial affects* of minimal pleasure-with-displeasure, like those of awe, alertness, astonishment, or compassion, which move us beyond sentiments of "love" or "hate"'.[22] Ettinger's language here is one that clearly rejects a logic of oppositions and also that emphasises the matrix as process. The m/Other and child, conjoined in difference, are continually traversed by waves of affects, fleeting feelings that signal twin energies.

The sea is characterised by repetitions, the recurring tides, the groups of waves that are similar in size known as swells. Ettinger argues that 'the rhythm of repetition created by alternations of absence/presence stands for the disappearance/return of the archaic mother, notched and burned in the kernel of the Thing'.[23] The Thing here refers to what Jacques Lacan calls 'dumb reality'.[24] It is dumb because experience of it precedes the entry into the Symbolic register of psychic reality, the linguistic dimension of subjectivity. Lacan terms it 'the beyond-of-the-signified'.[25] The Thing is the maternal, the psychic figure that is the Mother.[26] This Mother, as the Thing, is a part of the Real so outside language, inaccessible to thought, yet it still 'commands and regulates'.[27] The Mother spurs desire, and is its cause. This figure, as something figured, is, however, always out of reach. Language bars access to the Real, the existence of which can only be postulated retrospectively from within language.

Ettinger, however, believes that 'the Thing finds incarnation in the aesthetic art object'.[28] She suggests that aspects of the matrixial borderspace are preserved in cultural productions writing that 'something of this co-emergence and co-fading in the Real is delivered to the Symbolic's margins by way of covenants hidden in art'.[29] The artist is able to bear 'wit(h)ness' to the Other, the Mother, through 'borderlinking'.[30] This wit(h)nessing occurs by way of 'traces of vibrations and resonations'.[31]

Ettinger describes the incarnation of the matrixial in acoustic and tactile terms. Tactility is a proximate sense and reinforces the intimacy of encounter embodied in the matrix. The subject is touched by the matrixial through what Ettinger refers to as art's capacity to trigger a potential for 'co-spasming'.[32] A spasm is an involuntary contraction of a muscle group. It is a cramp. The spasm, as physical phenomenon, is therefore associated with a freeing of the body, the musculature, its means of action, from predetermined acts.

Ettinger, drawing on Merleau-Ponty, writes that the spasm 'is a celibate "state of birth"'.[33] This is reminiscent of Merleau-Ponty's discussion of Paul Cézanne in which he suggests that what the artist expresses 'cannot [...] be the translation of a clearly defined thought, since such clear thoughts are those that have already been said within ourselves or by others'.[34] The artwork is an immaculate conception. It is a thought that emerges from out of an act of artistic execution rather than being the motivation for it. There is only action rather than thought married to action. Thought, in such artistic practices, is afterthought. For Merleau-Ponty, Cézanne paints 'to make *visible* how the world *touches* us'.[35] He is therefore open to the world, exposing himself to its impressions, rather than subjecting it to his ideas, reducing the physical environment to passive materials to be worked upon and through. In this sense, Cézanne as a painter demonstrates a similar sensibility to the environment as some of the climbers discussed in the first chapter.

Cézanne's art practice is one that does not seek to control the outside world but rather cedes control to it. André Leroi-Gourhan has described how the use of symbols forms a means of dominating surroundings and 'coming to grips with reality'.[36] This approach to the environment, through language, symbolisation, reverses the tactile encounter envisaged by Merleau-Ponty. In language's controlling dynamic, the world is what is touched rather than what does the touching. The surfers in the films under discussion here frequently reject the symbol-driven, dictatorial attitude towards the world. In *Soul Surfer* (Dir. Sean McNamara, USA, 2011), for example, a biopic about competitive surfer Bethany Hamilton who survived a shark attack in which her left arm was bitten off, Hamilton is shown feeling the sea as she strives to locate where a strong wave will build (7.4). This foregrounds her oceanic literacy, a rare skill. It is one not possessed by contemporary mariners who rely too heavily on technology. It also represents Hamilton's openness to the sea's energies. Her father advises

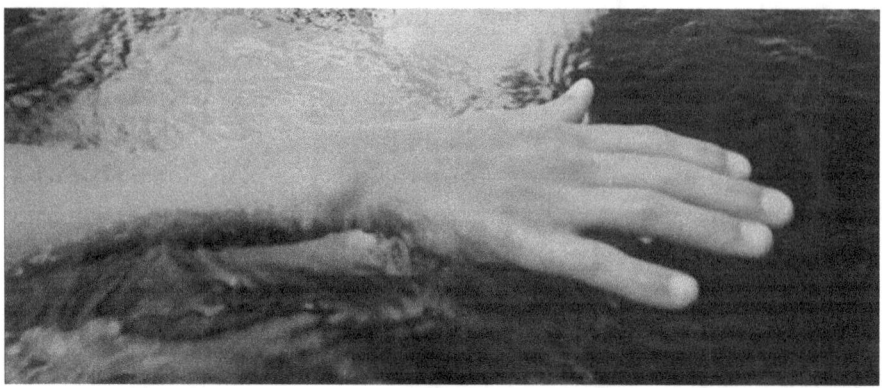

7.4 *Soul Surfer* (2011): Bethany in touch with the sea

her that the most talented surfers 'know when the best waves are coming [as] they can feel it'. The best surfers allow themselves to be sought out by waves rather than vice versa. In this sense, surfing becomes a letting go of control. It is conceived of as a channelling of forces from elsewhere. This brings it close to the spasm as that which is celibate. The surfer does not think their way into the wave. They form a conduit for it. As artists, the surfers strive to become open to the sea's embrace. They interlink with its energy.

The camera in films can also either grip or be gripped by a given scene. Rosi Huhn has suggested that the eye that seizes space exhibits phallic thinking and is associated with power and oppression.[37] There is, however, a repeated tendency in *Point Break* to surrender control of the visual field. The anti-ocularcentric tenor of the film is evident throughout starting with the visual fields disturbed by rain and sea as the film begins. Early on, the idea of looking beyond vision is broached when Angelo Pappas, Utah's partner in the Los Angeles robbery division of the FBI, is shown diving for bricks in a swimming pool blindfolded. The first bank robbery by the film's outlaws, the Ex-Presidents, that is shown occurs in an interior bathed in blue light, leaching the image, the environment, of clarity, sharpness.

Vision carves the world into sights. It detects objects, differentiates between things. Vision, as Milena Marinkova explains, usually operates at a distance, it is 'premised on the presence of a gap between the seer and the seen'.[38] The optical is associated with isolation.[39] The bank interior, however, has been lit in such a way that discernment is impeded, edges are dulled. This is also the case in a later scene in which Bodhi takes Utah night surfing. Utah is concerned by his inability to see clearly. Bodhi, however, is unperturbed. He invites Utah to connect with water, or more specifically the energy it translates, to be at one with natural forces. If such a linkage occurs, Bodhi explains 'You don't need to see!' Utah is sceptical, replying 'Yeah right, vision is highly overrated!' After they have finished surfing, however, the agent is transformed, elated. This sequence is crucial to understanding the psychic undercurrents of *Point Break* as a whole.

If a purely phenomenological approach is adopted, the night surfing could easily be read as an effort to encourage haptic visuality of the kind identified by Laura U. Marks.[40] The scene is, however, also about de-spectacularisation. It encourages a seeing beyond the castration paradigm, a paradigm established through cutting understanding out of the world, towards a less detached outlook. This comprises the matrixial gaze, a gaze distinct from the scopophilic and spectacular. Ettinger writes that 'in the field of vision, and in the dimension of the scopic drive and the desire to see, in the move from Thing to Object and into representation, the Woman-Other-Thing is in fact constituted as a fetish'.[41] In spectacular cinema, the m/Other is therefore symbolically excluded, substituted for by signs. *Point Break*, by contrast, regularly obscures signs. The reduced visibility it fosters, however, cannot impede the communicative force of the waves. In the night surfing scene, through his loss of sight, Utah becomes one with the waves, is traversed by them. His experience gestures towards something beyond spectacle. This thing features in other surf films as well.

Surfing and Trauma

Trauma is a theme in many surf, and indeed sports, films. Several of the boxing films discussed in Chapter 2, for instance, featured women who had been subject to potentially traumatising violence in the home. The traumatic events referenced in surf films are varied. In *Point Break*, the parents of Tyler, the woman surfer Utah befriends as he seeks to locate and catch the Ex-Presidents, died in a plane crash in 1984 when she was 20 years old. In *Soul Surfer*, as already mentioned, Hamilton survives a shark attack. It is, however, her friend Alana Blanchard who is represented experiencing symptoms of PTSD, suffering from nightmares about sharks. *Blue Crush* is also a film about overcoming trauma. The main character,

Anne Marie, has been severely affected by a near drowning incident after a wipeout, and suffers from flashbacks. This has destroyed her confidence and negatively impacted on her surfing career. Ultimately, however, she is able to surmount her fears and successfully surf competitively again. *Beautiful Wave* (Dir. David Mueller, USA, 2010) features a woman grieving for her father, who drowned to death, learning to surf. *Puberty Blues* (Dir. Bruce Beresford, Australia, 1981), a coming of age film about teenage girls who become 'surfer chicks' and then realise how sexist and vacuous the surf scene can be, features the death of a surfer, Garry, by drug overdose. This event is felt keenly by his girlfriend Debs. If not a trauma, it is a tragedy.

The films *Big Wednesday* and *Soul Surfer* also feature collective traumas which encompass large numbers of people.[42] *Big Wednesday*, a film about three very different men with a shared passion for surfing, spans the period 1962–1974. The Vietnam War is therefore strongly in the background. The central trio of surfers in *Big Wednesday*, as a group within a group, foreshadow Bodhi's gang in *Point Break*. The actor Gary Busey, who plays Leroy "The Masochist" Smith, one of the three central characters, in *Big Wednesday* also appears in *Point Break* as Pappas. The differences between the two films are, however, also noteworthy. In *Big Wednesday*, the identity of the women characters derives from the men. To return to Forster's terms from Chapter 2, they are flat rather than round. Tyler in *Point Break* is permitted a depth and complexity not afforded them. The men in *Big Wednesday*, like Tyler, derive their identity primarily from their relationship to the sea.

Big Wednesday moves through distinct time periods and also distinctive winds and waves that are bound up with those periods. It begins with the South Swell in 1962, moves through the West Swell of Fall 1965 and the North Swell of Winter 1968 and ends with the Great Swell of Spring 1974, specifically with Big Wednesday. The film is about the effects of the passage of time, about how times change people, and also about how the physical world produces changing times. In relation to the three main protagonists, the differing swells are associated with discrete periods of their lives. The Great Swell of 1974, for example, provides the heroes with an opportunity to regain the esteem in which they were held in their youth. The sense of self of each man is bound up with the sea and their relationship to it. The earlier North Swell of 1968, however, is linked to the death of a close friend of the trio, Waxer, in Vietnam. One of the three, Jack Barlowe, is himself a Vietnam veteran. The other two dodge the draft.

In *Blue Crush* and *Soul Surfer* water is the source of traumatic experience. This is not the case for the other films. Turning to other common themes in the genre, the quest for the perfect wave and for a prelapsarian, paradisiacal existence, demonstrates, however, that all the films relating to trauma share common psychic concerns. The desire for the perfect wave and/or world symbolises the search for *jouissance*, the *objet* (*petit*) a, residue of the Real. *Jouissance*, coming to enjoyment, will always elude the subject in the Symbolic. In Lacanian psychoanalysis, the Thing that motivates desire, the maternal, cannot be returned without descending into psychosis so *jouissance* for the subject, the surfer, will always remain a pipe-dream. This means that there is a traumatic core to subjectivity, the inassimilable Real, which can never be mitigated. The Real, as 'missed encounter', forms an archaic trauma which later traumatic events are mapped onto.[43]

In all the surf films that feature catastrophic events, despite their differences, the underlying trauma that motivates their narratives is the originary one that enabled the self to become, namely separation from the Mother, separation from the Real. Pollock suggests that art cannot represent but can allude to this trauma. She writes that 'the original creative gesture of art [can become] an originary site for an encounter with the affective ripples around the non-experienced, hence, absent traumatic pool, so that we know about trauma rather than reducing it to a representation it cannot but evade'.[44] Butler also states, in reference to Ettinger, that the traumatic Thing 'can be presented in ways that do not belong to the order of the signifier'.[45] Trauma is, Butler goes on to suggest, by its very nature something that breaks the bounds of signification 'which means that trauma has to find another mode of presentation, one that is not reducible to existing signifiers'.[46] Signifiers are too detached from what Ettinger refers to as the 'corpo-Real' to attest to it. The corpo-Real is, as Pollock' explains, 'unthought and unrepresented' producing effects 'which we cannot know directly'.[47] This is not to say, however, that it cannot be registered. Aesthetic practices which generate borderspaces of the kind discussed earlier permit the corpo-Real to resonate in the subject. In film, this occurs at a sub-narrative level.

In this respect, *Big Wednesday* (which only fleetingly depicts a woman towards the beginning of the film, her presence being labelled an invasion of privacy by the men), and *Point Break* (in which Tyler assumes a supporting role), possess greater feminist force as challenges to mainstream cinema's spectacular phallocentrism, than more obviously liberatory films such as *Blue Crush*, *Puberty Blues* and *Soul Surfer*. In these films, the story is feminist but the hegemony of the castration paradigm is never unsettled. *Puberty Blues* provides a good example of this. It explores the experiences of two teenage schoolgirls, Debbie Vickers and Sue Knight, who join the surfing scene at the Sydney beach of Cronulla. The women go to the beach to admire the boys surfing, becoming 'surfer chicks', their status and sense of identity secured through their affiliation with a group of male surfers.

There is a stark contrast between the men and women. The women lie on the beach sunbathing while the men pump and carve along the waves. In this rigid opposition, the women are portrayed as passive whilst the men are often in action, riding the surf. These activities, sun soaking and surfing, conform to gendered spaces. The shore is for women, the sea is for men. The men police their territory. When Vickers asks one of the surfers, Strach, if she can borrow his board to try the sport he refuses. She is also told by her friends that 'girls don't surf!' The connection between the sea and masculine authority is reinforced by the pictures of sailing ships in the headmaster's office at the local school. Wave riding and riding the high seas are manly pursuits. The only appropriate exercise for the young women is jazz ballet, classes of which are provided by their school.

Vickers and Knight eventually tire of the asymmetrical relations of the surf scene in which women are treated as servants and sex objects. Garry's death appears to prompt a change in their outlook. After his overdose, the group conduct a ceremony on the beach in his honour. A pyre is lit and Garry's board is then launched into the sea in imitation of a ship burial. Vickers places the ring Garry gave her on the tree branch that has been punched into the board as a kind of makeshift sail. Her action appears to symbolise a giving up on the hedonistic surfing lifestyle Garry embodied. The two girls, however, do not abandon surfing. They purchase a board and head to the beach where they are greeted by a holler of 'G'day Gidget', in reference to the fictional television character of that name. Some of the surfers they used to hang out with are more abusive. One screams 'You chicks are bent, fucking bent!' Vickers, however, is soon able to pop-up on the board and ride a wave. She provides an alternative spectacle for those on the beach to the usual sight of men practising the sport and meets with some appreciative looks from both sexes.

The narrative arc of *Puberty Blues* resolves on a positive note with Vickers and Knight forging their own path rather than following in the wake of the male surfers. There is, however, a negative undertow to the film that weakens its feminist potential. Fear of the feminine is, in fact, indicated when Vickers paints her nails immediately after getting her period. The red polish stands in for menstrual fluid which cannot be shown. The scene makes the connection between the lacquer and menstruation explicit. It confirms why the painted nails of Millie Farley in *Hard, Fast and Beautiful* received such emphasis. The polish acts as a metonym for women's corporeal mutability and reproductive potential and, by extension, motherhood. The menstrual as corporeal symbol of the maternal is rendered unrepresentable, substituted by the red lacquer, foreclosed. The film does not show the period because of cultural taboos which render it impossible to do so. These taboos, however, are motivated by the same logic that governs the cinematography of the film, which is largely hard-edged, phallocentric.

There are moments in which disturbances in the field of vision are registered in *Puberty Blues*, such as heat hazes or rain trickling down window panes, yet these are token, acting to reaffirm the sharp contours of the majority of the imagery, the aged grain of the film-stock notwithstanding. The rain in *Puberty Blues* is also a signifier of emotional turmoil. When Vickers is filmed through rain soaked glass her upset at the vacuous existence of the male surfers is being communicated. Water in the key sequence in which this occurs is burdened with emotional content. The downpour in *Puberty Blues* performs a similar function to that of a heavy shower that features in *Woman Basketball Player No. 5*. In the Chinese film, Lin is shown looking out of a window at rain falling during a scene depicting how loveless her marriage to her cousin is. The rain here signals her distress. She married the cousin because she was tricked into believing Tian had abandoned her yet she still loves her former beau. Rain in both these sequences acts to figure feeling. It falls within the film narrative rather than communicating anything subjacent to it.

In her essay 'The Red Cow Effect', Ettinger examines the psychic significance of the ritual sacrifice of the red heifer detailed in the *Tanakh* (the canon of the Hebrew bible). The rite, which involves mixing the ashes of the sacrificed animal with spring water and them sprinkling it on defiled individuals, can counteract corpse impurity. Ettinger suggests that this water, which is called *nida*-water, is officially used to detach defilement from purity. The word *nida*, however, has its etymological roots in terms for moving, shifting, sprinkling and dispersing. The word therefore indexes meanings that 'designate liquefied, flexible states'.[48] *Nida*-water therefore commonly referred to menstrual blood in Hebrew scripture. Ettinger sets out to 'open up towards the femininity of the Red Cow engraved in the Hebrew signifiers while working-through to shift its symbolic value, to expose and draw out from its ever-there signifiers a matrixial *she-law* and gaze, which indexes *jouissance* and establishes desire that evades the control of the phallic Law and Gaze'.[49] The ritual incorporates an aspect that resists the castration paradigm, a metramorphic dimension, enabling matrixial effects to infiltrate the Symbolic. It provides a means by which to mitigate the archaic trauma generated by exiting the Real. The film *Point Break* assumes a comparable role to this ritual in that it also expresses a metramorphosis. It provides an opening through which 'something of trauma's radical otherness may be intimated and hence encountered aesthetically and affectively'.[50] This aperture, closely associated with the cinematography and soundtrack of the film, is not bound to the film's narrative.

Seeing Beyond the Narrative

In *Point Break*, a binary opposition is established between the FBI and the Ex-Presidents, between the forces of law and order and criminal elements.[51] This opposition, as already discussed, is implicitly established during the opening credits of the film which cut continually between Bodhi and Utah, leisure and work, agile serenity and athletic violence. Shortly after this sequence, the FBI is introduced as an organisation comprised in significant part of data analysts. In the words of its local Director, Harp, the organisation catches criminals through 'good database analysis'. Data is given information. It is unitary. Databases comprises of units of known facts. The FBI database is shown in action when Utah seeks information on Tyler, pulling up her criminal record and other aspects of her personal history including the loss of her parents. This fact is digested unfeelingly by the agent who uses the information as a means by which to gain Tyler's confidence. The traumatic aspect of this experience, of her loss, is not contained in the information Utah sees on screen.

Serres suggests that a preoccupation with data has led humanity to lose its senses. We are now addicted to data, 'not data that comes from the world, or language, but encoded data'.[52] The Information Age forms a period in which the world has been coded and gridded, placed at a distance. Bodhi stands in contrast to this alienation from physical surroundings. *Bodhi* in Buddhism is associated with understanding *dharma*, the state of nature. Through his moniker, Bodhi is therefore constructed as having insight into dependent origination, the Buddhist idea that nothing is singular, everything is linked. This places him at odds with a data culture that seeks to divide the world into discrete, independent units of information. When Utah first sees Bodhi surfing, Tyler advises him that he is referred to as the Bodhi Zephyr, a light wind. He embodies the natural world rather than represents it. In this initial encounter between Utah and Bodhi, the music that accompanies the surfer as he rides waves occasionally includes a sound like a didgeridoo, aligning him with indigenous Australia. It is an indigenous identity that is figured as primitive. Tyler refers to him in the scene as 'a modern savage'. His savagery is exemplified by his close connection with water, his feel for it. It is a primitivism that renders him resistant to data culture. Despite their best efforts at database analysis, the FBI has been unable to catch the Ex-Presidents.[53] Bodhi and his group are able to live below the radar, off-the-grid.

The FBI, a law enforcement agency, becomes associated with the Symbolic, the legal-linguistic structure of psychic life, and, by extension, the Father. Their desire for data, requiring a partitioning of the world into units of information, aligns them with the castration paradigm. The link between the figure of the Father and the FBI is additionally foregrounded by the surname of Angelo Pappas. Pappas means priest in Greek but also connotes papa, the old fashioned term for father. Pappas, bearing the Name-of-the-Father, enforces the law, prohibiting particular forms of behaviour. That he symbolises the phallus is made clear early in the film when Alvarez, a detective, remarks, 'Pappas – what a hard-on!' Within a Lacanian framework, desire is antithetical to the Law. In this sense, desire is seemingly incarnated through the figure of Bodhi who forms an alternative, aberrant father figure for Utah. Bodhi, however, also frequently assumes the status of symbolic phallus, with his gang reliant upon him for their sense of identity. At this level, both Bodhi and Pappas form caricatures of psychic figures, illustration of processes. This is in

7.5 *Point Break* (1991): Bodhi's big gun

keeping with Bigelow's earlier film *Blue Steel* in which she makes the phallic part of the narrative, thereby exposing it and its operations.[54]

Through drawing attention to the phallic, Bigelow is able to disrupt its smooth operation. Like in *Blue Steel*, in which a Smith & Wesson revolver forms a central character, guns form an obvious way in which phallicism, phallic logic, is foregrounded. The gun as a phallic indicator is referenced repeatedly. In the run up to the scene of the first bank robbery, the criminals loudly load a variety of guns. In the second skydiving sequence, Bodhi has a large revolver with him that he leaves in the plane when he jumps (7.5). Utah grabs the abandoned weapon and leaps out after him. He must in turn give up this weapon, this phallic symbol, to pull Bodhi's parachute cord. The theme of giving up on guns and, more importantly, what they symbolise links *Point Break* to *Blue Steel*. The phallic, if taken as the sole logic of subjectivity, forecloses reconciliation with the Real, bars any possibility of working through the trauma of separation from it and the accompanying anxiety and violence. It is not, however, through her narrative engagement with the phallic that Bigelow contests the hegemony of the phallus. She achieves resistance to phallic dominance predominantly through her cinematography. This acts as a kind of noise disrupting the smooth flow of visual information, discrete objects.

The FBI is also associated with suppressing noise. The importance of information, and of its clear transmission, is indicated during a conversation in which Harp asks: 'Special Agent Utah – Are you receiving my signal?' Utah responds, 'Zero distortion, sir!' The means of transmission of this

7.6 *Point Break* (1991): Tyler the garconne

signal are, however, shown to be a source of irritation and, on occasion, to fail. Surveillance technology is associated with pain as is indicated by Pappas's remark to an FBI associate who is attaching a listening device to his torso in preparation for a raid on some drug dealing surfers: 'Watch it – you're going to tear my skin!' Later, during this raid, Utah tries to radio his colleagues and warn them that the surfers are heavily armed yet he cannot make himself heard over the sound of a lawn mower's motor in the neighbouring garden. This interference, or noise, as will be examined, also manifests itself in relation to *Point Break*'s status, as a whole, as signal.

Bigelow, however, does not set up noise and signal as oppositions. The film consistently refuses oppositional logic. This is made most obvious through Tyler. Her character echoes that of Megan Turner in *Blue Steel* whose surname her forename resembles. Tyler also physically bears some similarities to the police officer in that she eschews long hair, at times appearing androgynous (7.6). Her given name is one that is used for both genders reinforcing her sexual ambiguity. The name Tyler refers in England to the doorkeeper of a public house, to a person who occupies the threshold, suggesting a liminal status. Tyler also surfs with the men, transgressing into a masculine gendered space in a comparable way to Turner joining the police. There are aspects of the surf group's behaviour that Tyler rejects or is not privy to. She is not a member of the Ex-Presidents. She also withdraws from a discussion of big wave riding suggesting that it is for 'macho assholes with a death wish' and complaining that there is 'too much testosterone here'. She cannot, however, be easily contrasted with the men. Tyler is one of them yet apart from them, resisting easy positioning. Tyler's ability to withstand falling into either of two oppositional terms, namely masculinity and femininity, stands for a broader refusal of oppositions at the level of the film as a whole.

Filming with Flare

Opposition requires difference. Ettinger, however, resists differential logic, associated as it is with the cut, castration, separation. She acknowledges difference but by degree rather than by way of distinction. To explain this conception, she uses the idea of the swerve which she links to Merleau-Ponty's idea of *écart* or kept distance. Ettinger suggests that 'the swerve is a measure of difference in the field of affectivity that is analogous up to a point to Merleau-Ponty's *écart* in the field of sensibility'.[55] For Merleau-Ponty, being is something which the subject has a tentative hold on. Because of its dynamism, its being through times and therefore its being always deferred, there can never be coincidence between the I that thinks of itself, has a sense of itself, and the itself that is that I. Additionally, *écart* is explained in relation to differentiation. Consciousness as being in language keeps a part of what it is to be at a distance, differs from it: 'to be conscious = to have a figure on the ground – one cannot go back any further'.[56] The figure obscures the ground, keeps it at a remove. The subject is always linguistically and temporally kept at a distance from fully knowing its being.

The swerve comprises tentative comprehension like the *écart*. It is, however, dissimilar in that it is transgressive. It does not keep distance. It is rather 'a process of differentiating in borderspacing and borderlinking, of inscriptive exchange between/with-in several matrixial entities'.[57] The swerve 'dissolves the individual borderlines so that they become thresholds'.[58] This phenomenon can best be described as registered fluctuations of affect. The matrixial involves the energetic exchange of affects, varying, differing, in intensities. The regular dialogue with Merleau-Ponty in Ettinger's thinking (of which the reference to *écart* forms an instance) points towards how a reconciliation of phenomenology and psychoanalysis might take place. For Ettinger, however, there is no ontologically prior body that forms the ground for psychic life. In the corpo-Real psychic and physical co-emerge, rather than either I or body preceding each other, grounding each other.

The affective encounters of the matrixial cannot be represented. Representation requires practices of coding, it involves discrete forms. The matrixial, as a pre-linguistic, hence missed, experience of linkage rather than separation cannot be accounted for by such forms. It is instead alluded to at a sub-narrative level. In *Blue Steel*, colour and gesture form two means by which the matrixial impresses on the subject, insinuates into awareness, without being inscribed in the narrative. Colour performs a comparable role in *Point Break* in the sequences featuring the first bank to be robbed. As well as the quality of light in these scenes, which is from a broad source, soft and spread out, taking the edges of things, there is also a blue filter evident at some points. This chromatically links *Point Break* with *Blue Steel* in which similar filters are used to soften definition. Blue is, of course, also a colour associated with the sea. *Blue Crush*, for example, connotes the percussive violence of the ocean through its title but also references something pressed out of shape by colour, a privileging of colour over form. *The Big Blue* (Dir. Luc Besson, France, 1988), a film about free diving, suggests the immensity of the ocean through its title, the sea is an enormous expanse of colour, aquamarine. *The Big Blue*, through the sense of boundlessness it fosters, evokes the oceanic. The oceanic, as feeling, is the sense of oneness with the external world that so perturbed Freud, as Theweleit explains, 'for him the whole oceanic business is somehow under water, dark and threatening'.[59]

Colour is not, however, the primary means by which the matrixial exerts itself on consciousness. Shortly after Tyler rescues Utah from his first, failed, attempt at surfing, she is shown riding waves. Flare and water gets on the lens during the sequence. This disturbing of the image by sun and sea is reminiscent of the footage of surfing in the opening credits. It reinforces that the activity of surfing is associated with visual disturbance, produces optical noise. Additionally, the combing waves crash and churn, generating acoustic noise. The surf sequences therefore register as disturbances in the sonic and visual fields. The distinct contours associated with the castration paradigm, hard-edged images and cut-glass phonics, sharp sounds, are forsaken. Flaring can be exploited to reinforce the authenticity of footage. In *Point Break*, however, its presence, along with sea spray, also functions to give the physical world to the viewer. It encourages proximity with natural phenomena. More than this, the flare and the saltwater droplets impede easy vision. This means that the viewer, like Utah and Pappas at different times in the film, is deprived of clear sightedness, their vision is interrupted. They are forced to see noise.

This noise, unformed, uninformative, yet energetic, signals the closeness of forms of communication beyond signification. There is a strong sense in *Point Break* of something just beyond, behind, beneath the surface of the image, of the film as a film separating one space from another, one psychic register from another. This register also compels through the use of gesture. There are repetitive physical actions in the film, the hand that caresses the sea as a surfer threads the pipe, the waxing of the board, fleeting, yet cumulatively insistent, pressing, that provide means by which the beyond of the castration paradigm insinuates itself into perception.[60] These touching moments comprise an aesthetic dimension to subjectivity, a pleasure in actions, motions, textures, that point towards a matrixial sensibility.

The Last Wave

The recurring waves in *Point Break*, the surf, form the most powerful means by which the matrixial comes to resonate with the viewer. Pollock has written that the matrixial 'surfs beneath/beside the phallic'.[61] The waves, by way of their repeated appearances, their fascinating convolutions, transmit energy from the disavowed matrixial dimension to subjectivity. This dimension cannot access the Symbolic (which operates through the cut of differences) as it is characterised by connection, linkage. The night surfing sequence discussed earlier ends with Tyler and Utah alone in the calm sea. Utah struggles to articulate what riding the waves was like: 'I can't describe what I'm feeling.' Tyler, however, quiets him remarking 'You don't have to!' She releases the agent from the need to analyse and inform, to pull feeling into language, into the Symbolic. Her comment indicates that there are other forms of communication, other ways of being, that are available. The scene cuts to a shot from beneath the surfers, looking upwards at them. A camera has been positioned below the waves, suggesting there is something operative below the action film's surface tension.

Tyler's silencing of Utah is echoed towards the end of the film when the agent prevents her declaring her love. On the surface this may seem to manifest his desire to control her voice and have the last word in their final scene together. A closer reading, however, reveals that Utah has learnt the lesson Tyler was giving by removing his need to describe, to put an experience of connection with the world into words. She showed him that signification works against linkage. Utah is now appreciative of the existence of felt as well as worded connection. There is, however, more going on here than crude symbolisations of the potential for affective relations. The silence in the narrative gestures towards the need to attend elsewhere, to become open to a different logic to the one of phallic hegemony that the film overtly signals and deconstructs. This logic, the matrixial, operates on a supplementary affective level that tinges the narrative, curls around its edges, as is evident in the final scene of *Point Break*, which, through the presence of rain and surf, mirrors its opening.

The conclusion to the film possesses strong intertextual elements which contribute to its significance. It draws on scenes from *Big Wednesday* and *Dirty Harry* (Dir. Don Siegel, USA, 1971) for inspiration. In *Big Wednesday*, the character of Bear foresees Big Wednesday in 1962, suggesting that one day 'there'll be a swell so big and strong that it'll wipe clean everything that went before it'. He adds that on that day surfers will have an opportunity to distinguish themselves and 'draw the line'. Bodhi's prophecy of the Fifty Year Storm, which comes to fruition in the final sequence, set at Bells Beach, Australia, replicates Bear's prescience. Both films conclude with big waves.[62]

At the end of *Point Break*, Utah also throws his FBI badge into the sea. This mirrors the denouement of *Dirty Harry*, a film that Bigelow is also in dialogue with in *Blue Steel*. *Dirty Harry* centres upon an unreconstructed male police officer with vigilante tendencies, Harry Callahan, who is in pursuit of a deranged serial killer, Charles 'Scorpio' Davis in Los Angeles. The film ends with Scorpio taking a boy who is fishing in a water-filled quarry pit hostage. Laughing, he threatens to kill the child unless Harry drops his gun. The detective refuses to give up his weapon, shooting the murderer in the shoulder forcing him to let go of his own gun and the boy. Scorpio endeavours to retrieve his pistol, cackling again as Harry shoots once more, this time fatally, sending the killer flying into the pit. The laughter is cut-short, replaced by the sound of lapping water, waves. The detective re-holsters his gun and then throws his detective's shield into the pond, turns and walks away.

In this finale, Harry divests himself of the badge, the symbol of formal justice, but not the gun, the putative deliverer of material justice.[63] It therefore reaffirms a particular vision, one that is 'explicitly phallic in its identification of man with gun'.⁶⁴ Harry's decision to retain his firearm, his metal dick, despite discarding his detective's shield, demonstrates that his faith in the phallus remains intact. Utah, however, does not carry a gun in his final encounter with Bodhi. He has already renounced the values which accompany exclusive adherence to the castration paradigm, suppression of the matrixial, even if he only becomes aware of this belatedly. After a fist fight with Bodhi in the swash, Utah proclaims: 'You've got to go down. It's got to be that way.' Ultimately, however, he refuses to perpetuate the cycle of violence associated with anxiety towards the feminine.

Karen E. Tatum has suggested that within patriarchy Woman is socially constructed as a 'terrain of terror', a figure of abjection, with her abject 'nature' used 'to justify physical violence against her'.⁶⁵ The tendency in contemporary Western culture is to expel, sometimes by physical force, what is labelled as abject. In *Point Break*, however, rather than destroying Bodhi, Utah lets him go. Utah, as an agent of the FBI, stands for phallocentrism in the film. Bodhi, however, through his close connection to waves figures the matrixial, that which is beyond figuration. The end of the film posits reconciliation between these two paradigms through the crush and rumble of waves coupled with a steady barrage of rain. Through these combined natural elements, worlds presented as separate in the opening sequence (through cross-cutting) are now conjoined. The cut of difference is rejected.

The storm that forms the backdrop to this coming together, however, also impresses upon the viewer the presence of what a figure such as Bodhi, a signifier, can only point towards. The massive waves form an amplification of forces, affective intensities, which have been present throughout the film. The scene vibrates with affect. It fosters an aesthetic wit(h)nessing and therefore provides a passageway to relief from the oppression of signification, separation. There is a release from oppositional imperatives. In this context, it is important to note that the sea should not be seen to stand for fluidity. The waves in *Point Break* are not fluids in the way Luce Irigaray conceives of them. In her essay 'The "Mechanics" of Fluids', Irigaray does discuss waves, particularly acoustic ones, yet these are conceived of as oppositional to solids. She suggests that 'if every psychic economy is organized around the phallus (or Phallus), we may ask what this primacy owes to a teleology of reabsorption of fluid in a solidified

7.7 *Point Break* (1991): The force of the sea

form'.⁶⁶ The phallic is the ideal and the fluid is the repressed other which acts as its guarantor. This logic remains phallic in its oppositionality.

Waves in *Point Break*, however, generate metramorphosis, enabling the matrixial to resonate in the cinematic encounter. They are not things to be contrasted with other things, not figures, discrete forms. Ettinger has described a metramorphosis as that which 'composes/traces home and habituation in one and the same psychic move, aglitter with their specific affect and trembling with it'.⁶⁷ The terminology here, luminous and tremulous, could be used to describe the sea, quivering and sparkling. Christine Buci-Glucksmann has described Ettinger's art practice in similar terms, referring to it as one of 'undulatory abstraction' due to its superimposed layers, the colours that implicate, rolling into each other. She suggests that 'an undulation is like the waves of the sea, which go out and come back in, always the same and always different, with their mottling and their infinite colour-effects'.⁶⁸ Films that represent the sea, that feature it or other bodies of water as a central character, harness similar visual effects, communicate similar differences in repetition.

The massive whitecaps which Bodhi paddles, disappears within, form the final appearance of a set of waves that has travelled through the film as a whole (7.7). These waves register, rather than represent, affective exchanges. The recurring sound of the waves, their roar and hiss, institutes interference within the castration paradigm, signalling, through noise, the presence of another subjacent paradigm. This occurs in *Big Wednesday* as well when the steady rumble of the waves in the last surf sequence sounds like a blow-torch, suggesting cold sea giving off heat. The waves provide access to traces, which are engraved as affected events in the viewer, the listener, at a sub-symbolic level. These traces are registered as impressions, intensities, as feelings, but not recognised as signs. They form an intuitive communication. Ettinger calls this co-poiesis, an experience in which the 'matrixial memory of the event, paradoxically both unforgettable and in/of oblivion – a memory carrying a load no linear story can convey – is transmitted and cross-inscribed'.[69]

The waves as memories of connectivity, of borderlinking, of the energetic exchanges of intrauterine severality, deliver their communications to the viewer through a pressure that builds cumulatively throughout the film. This communication is not achieved through figuration. To see the waves as metaphors for the matrixial is to misunderstand their operation. Metaphors carry, waves, however, do not function like this. Sea waves do not transport water from one place to another, they travel through water. Such waves are not packets, not discrete units of substance, but intensities. In *Point Break*, Bigelow encourages the emergence of these intensities through a film aesthetic that takes the edge off phallic hegemony. Through her cinematography and soundscape, she produces work which refuses to privilege the phallic, opening a space through which the matrixial can simultaneously be registered. This provides the possibility for processing the traumatic effects that accompany the entry into language, and alleviating anxiety over the feminine and the violence that accompanies it. *Point Break* therefore forms a genuine feminine sports film in ways that many of the others discussed in this book do not and cannot. Their form is too complicit with phallocentrism even if their narratives are profoundly anti-patriarchal.

8

Conclusion: Raging Whippet

Strata of Sexism

Drew Barrymore's directorial debut, *Whip It* (Dir. Drew Barrymore, USA, 2009), adapted from the novel *Derby Girl* by Shauna Cross forms a typical expression of "Girl Power" with its young hero, 17 year old Bliss Cavendar. Girl Power is characterised by assertiveness, athleticism, independent thinking and youthfulness.[1] It is an age-specific brand of feminism, reserved for teenage and early twenty-something's, popularised by the pop group The Spice Girls.[2] *Whip It* traces Bliss's efforts to escape her oppressive mother Brooke, who wishes to mould both her daughters into successful beauty pageant competitors, and become a successful roller derby player. Bliss and her family live in the small (fictional) town of Bodeen in Texas. The roller derby league is based in the nearby city of Austin.[3] This city is the spiritual home of all-women's flat track roller derby as the first twenty-first century-league was founded there in 2003.[4]

The film, as a coming of age parable, provides an outwardly emancipatory message for its young female target audience. Bliss follows her own desires rather than permitting her mother to live out her dreams through her. She embraces roller derby as a form of physical feminism, an athletic challenge to patriarchal authority. The sport provides her with the confidence to slough off an uncaring (and potentially unfaithful) boyfriend, the indie musician Oliver. Bliss perfects an emotional and physical toughness that the film celebrates as empowering. *Whip It*, however, manifests contradictions. There is undoubtedly a strong liberatory message at work in the film yet as a physical feminist manifesto it still leaves much to be desired. The tensions in the film, conflicting messages, which will be examined, are common in contemporary, mainstream sports films featuring female athletes. *Whip It* is therefore symptomatic. It exhibits many of the difficulties that accompany efforts to break with traditional stereotypes of gender roles and of sexuality. Reactionary ideas about gender are embedded in a medium such as film in multiple ways. As this analysis will demonstrate, a film that contests conservative ideas on one level is reactionary on another. *Whip It* therefore echoes issues discussed in relation to films featured in earlier chapters.

Feminist Movement

The sport of roller derby, which forms the means of Bliss's liberation, is a contact sport involving two teams of five players wearing roller-skates. It is played on an oval shaped track. A 'bout' of roller derby comprises of two 30 minute periods. In each team four players are 'blockers', who operate as a group, and one is a 'jammer'. The blockers form packs with the jammers skating behind them. The jammers are skaters who try to race through the pack and lap players from the opposing team. The blockers seek to prevent the jammer from the rival team from achieving this aim and also to help their own jammer by blocking their opposite numbers.

Roller derby originated in the United States and its history can be traced back to the mid-1930s. A major revival in the sport has occurred in the last decade. It is now an extremely popular all-female amateur sport in the United States and elsewhere. There are male roller derby leagues but these are less prevalent. Bliss therefore chooses a sport culturally coded as feminine as the means by which to excel as a sportswoman. Roller derby is, however, different from other 'feminine' sports such as gymnastics, ice skating and synchronised swimming in that it involves collisions. Collision sports feature forceful, purposeful impacts between players. Other collision sports include American football, ice hockey and rugby. These sports are traditionally regarded as bastions of male sporting prowess. Roller derby's 'feminine' status is therefore questionable.

The physical violence involved in blocking in roller derby is ably captured in *Whip It*. Jennifer Carlson has argued that in actual roller derby the aggressive environment facilitates gender critique.[5] She regards the hard-hitting femininity embodied by players as contrasting with a restrictive 'emphasised femininity' that posits woman as 'physically inferior to men, weak, docile, concerned with their appearance, and attentive to enhancing their heterosexual desirability'.[6] Carlson reads roller derby players as engaging in hyperbolic citations of feminine norms. She also suggests that skaters merge aspects of 'emphasized femininity (such as sexual availability evidenced by mini-skirts) with elements antithetical to this femininity (such as the valuation of large bodies and aggression)' as a means to 'expose the contingency of emphasised femininity as a coherent system of gender norms'.[7]

Nancy J. Finlay is more cautious towards roller derby as a site of resistance to patriarchy.[8] She states that among the players, 'the gender relations negotiated between femininities and with masculinities form a complex matrix of acquiescence, adaptation and resistance'.[9] Finlay views the "derby girl" as embodying an alternative femininity. It is a femininity that displays the pride in toughness and aggression associated with hegemonic masculinity yet mixed with an intentionally feminised image: 'the quintessential posturing of the derby girl juxtaposes caricatured expressions of physical strength with teasing exposure of cleavage and clothes that mock conventional feminine modesty but also serve as markers of femininity'.[10]

Carlson and Finlay are therefore in agreement that aggression in actual roller derby forms only one aspect of what renders the sport a productive site of opposition to patriarchal ideology. This reality is reflected in *Whip It*. Bliss, for instance, fuses conventionally feminine and masculine attributes in her skating persona Babe Ruthless. The name draws attention to the amalgam of attributes alluded to by Finlay: Bliss as jammer is easy on the eye, a 'babe', yet also pitiless.[11] It is less her character, however, than those of her teammates, such as Bloody Holly and Maggie Mayhem, and her main rival, Iron Maven, who exhibit the potent combination of brawn and raunchiness that comprises the gender subversive potential of roller derby players.[12]

The aggression Bliss learns from roller derby is one that bleeds from the track into her everyday life. In this, her coming of age forms the antithesis to that of Diana in *Girlfight*. As discussed in Chapter 2, boxing teaches Diana to channel her aggression, resisting high-school provocations, refusing to respond to taunts and teasing with violence. Bliss, however, mirrors her teammate Smashley Simpson in failing to restrict her violent behaviour to bouts. Bliss and Smashley are both shown attacking people outside the context of their sport. Smashley assaults her boyfriend at an after-bout party. Bliss takes revenge on her former childhood friend Corbi for a high school prank by pushing her off a stairwell. She also slaps her lover Oliver because she feels he has behaved badly. These acts of violence are not signs of empowerment. Instead, they betray anger management issues making *Whip It* a 'coming of rage' film in contrast to *Girlfight* where Diana's transition to adulthood is coupled with learning to control violent behaviour.

Bliss and her best friend Pash both possess names associated with heightened emotions. To experience bliss is to be delighted or joyous. A passion is an overpowering feeling. Both women are portrayed as unable to control their emotions. Pash, for example, grabs her manager at work and kisses him 'passionately'. Bliss takes pleasure in inflicting pain as is evident in her look of delight after barging Corbi to the ground. There is therefore a risk the film reinstalls stereotypes of women as overly emotional. In Bliss's case there is also the added danger that, because she is unable to recognise the difference between the derby track and her everyday life, she mistakes being violent in general for being liberated. Her brutal treatment of Corbi, in particular, is not a behaviour that can be read as in any way expressive of physical feminism.

Rollerplay

Bliss's attack on Corbi is provoked by finding what appear to be two naked, embracing Barbies suspended by string in her school locker (8.1). This practical joke is homophobic, a spiteful comment on the close relationship enjoyed by Bliss and Pash. Lesbianism is here employed as stigma, as a means to injure. The two idealised female bodies in their bound embrace are also, however, used against their maker Mattel's intention. Corbi, the cheerleader whose name sounds similar to Barbie, uses the dolls not as toys but, instead, to fashion a sexual insult. The connection of Barbie with sex is something the company has sought hard to police and prevent. Mattel lost a legal battle against a shop selling fetish-wear which was named 'Barbie's Shop' in reference to its Canadian owner Barbara Anderson-Walley. The company argued the shop-name infringed the Barbie trademark yet it is likely the case was also motivated by what Barbie's business was selling. That Mattel felt their brand name was being tainted by its association with alternative lifestyles is lent credence by the maker also bringing legal action against doll maker Susanne Pitt for

8.1 *Whip It* (2009): Barbies in bondage

manufacturing a leather clad "Dungeon Doll" which had the head of "Superstar Barbie".

In *Whip It*, as the dolls show, non-heteronormative sexuality is gestured towards yet not fully embraced. There are also possible lesbian undercurrents in the interactions between Eva Destruction and Rosa Sparks in the hot-tub after one of the bouts. Additionally, sadomasochism is referenced. In one bout, for example, when Bliss has zipped past the opposing team thanks to using the momentum of a teammate, the compere, 'Hot Tub' Johnny Rocket, shouts 'You've been whipped!' and makes the sound of a lash and a gesture as if cracking a whip. Here the roller-derby players are figured as dominatrices. This reinforces the close connection between violence and eroticism fostered by the sport.

Sport, as an art of suffering, has been linked with consensual SM (sadomasochism) by Andrea Beckmann.[13] Collision and contact sports, like some SM activities, involve consenting to physical attack.[14] The potential sexual aspect to roller derby's physical aggression is indicated by Smashley's grappling with her boyfriend. Bliss is advised by Bloody Holly that the boyfriend enjoys being aggressed. If this pleasure in the infliction of pain also exists on the track, as Johnny intimates, then this would render it a theatre for the staging of lesbian SM encounters.

As a performance of roller derby, *Whip It* encourages reading the sport as a kind of sexual roleplay. Roleplay involves acting out roles with erotic intent, either as foreplay or the main event. It usually includes a power differential so play involving doctors and nurses, police officers and prisoners, and teachers and students, is common. This aspect of SM, focussed on power as much as, if not more than, pain, is referred to as D/s or dominance and submission.[15] If roller derby is framed as a form of roleplay then it is transformed into erotic spectacle. Some of the teams in *Whip It*, the Holy Rollers, the Hurl Scouts, the Flight Attendants, parody Catholic high school schoolgirls, girl scouts and air hostesses respectively, fit straightforwardly within role play dynamics.[16] The teams masquerading as schoolgirls and scouts are also engaging in obvious ageplay, a specific sub-category of role play, acting as if they are younger than they are.[17]

The identities of these sides all occupy the submissive pole of the D/s opposition. In this sense, D/s does not ostensibly map smoothly onto roller derby. There is no girl-scout leader, headmistress or pilot present to assume the position of dominance. It is through the final result of the game that the ultimate status of the two competing teams within the dynamic is established. Competitive sport, with its winners and losers, therefore forms an unusual kind of roleplay in which D/s positions are assumed retrospectively rather than agreed in advance. Roller derby, through its costuming, draws attention to the D/s structure that underpins all comparable sports, all competitive sports.

The sport at once revels in, and resists, being role play. The costumes in roller derby, including those in *Whip It* (designed by Catherine Marie Thomas), disrupt any easy reading of the players as figures of submissiveness. The documentary *Brutal Beauty: Tales of the Rose City Rollers* (Dir. Chip Mabry, USA, 2010) powerfully captures the gender incongruities of roller derby apparel. The thickset 'brutal beauties' display more flesh than the svelte skaters who form their counterparts in *Whip It*. The clothing in the fiction film is therefore tame by comparison. The high school and scout uniforms worn in *Whip It* would usually signal a lack of power and imply subservience. In roller derby, however, these uniforms are coupled with a suit of armour: a helmet, and elbow and knee pads. The figure of the skater therefore transmits mixed messages, wearing the attire of both mistress and servant, resisting easy interpretation. The players embody the figure of the 'switch'.[18] They are capable of assuming either dominant or submissive roles. Their potential to act out either position is only realised at the end of each bout. The game is therefore one of exquisite tension. *Whip It* showcases the way sport and sex are symbiotic in contemporary society. SM is not mere motif in roller derby. The sport does more than merely cite a SM vocabulary through its costumes and narratives. It performs D/s. Like *Pumping Iron II*, with its celebration of the developing phenomenon of muscle worship or *Fast Girls* with its lust for Lycra, *Whip It* demonstrates how sport is bound up with 'deviant' sexuality.

The pleasure the women take in their bruises is informative in this context. Bloody and Smashley are shown admiring each other's bruising at a post-bout party. Bruises on women in films often act to index violence in the home. They are concealed beneath clothing or behind sunglasses (see *Internal Affairs* (Dir Mike Figgis, USA, 1990)). In *Whip It*, by contrast, bruising indicates participation in a bout.[19] Each bruise forms a source of pride, signalling a player's commitment, their willingness to endure pain and injury for their team. The scene at the party demonstrates that the bruises possess an aesthetic dimension. These haematomas, purple, yellow, green, are admired for colour and size. Bloody and Smashley respectively hitch up and pull down their shorts, to appreciate bruising on a buttock and hip. They are watched by two youths, one wide-eyed, one grinning lasciviously.

The bruises also serve as reminders of the day's bout. Their status as a mnemonic technology is exploited. Marcel Swiboda has explored pain as a technique of memory.[20] In this context, the bruise, as the painful trace of physical encounter, becomes a means of recollection. It calls a previous event to mind. In SM, marks are similarly celebrated for their beauty and as memorials to the endurance of pain. In the context of SM, Staci Newmahr reads the bruise as preserving and affirming the corporal suffering a body has undergone, acting as a kind of corporeal guarantee.[21] The bruises in *Whip It*, in fact, form comparable attestations to pleasure in pain cementing the crossover between roller derby and some forms of sexual physical disciplining.

Raging Whippet

The SM component to roller derby is given creditable acknowledgment in *Whip It*. The film conspires, however, to articulate a conservative message about femininity which is bound up with its D/s content. This message is articulated through costume, dialogue and *mise-en-scène*. These three aspects of the film each, at different times, contribute to weakening its feminist credentials. As with many of the films discussed in earlier chapters, an outwardly emancipatory narrative is structurally undermined. *Whip It* is a homophone for whippet: a breed of sports dog that is descended from greyhounds yet lacks their stature. Whippets are often used as racing dogs. Whippet racing is popular in Delaware, Illinois and Indiana. Race meets are also held regularly in Texas where Bodeen is located. The film's title, *Whip It*, therefore invites viewing the skaters as equivalent to dogs racing around a track. It perpetuates the longstanding linkage of women and animals, an association usually detrimental to both.[22] This connection is not solely signalled by the title. It is a recurring theme.

The equation of women with animals by men is made explicit in *Whip It* when Colby, the boyfriend of Corbi, visits the Oink Joint, the fast food restaurant where Bliss and Pash wait tables. Colby orders the restaurant's signature dish, the 'squealer', instructing Bliss: 'You bring me a squealer, and I don't mean Corbi.' Here he compares the sounds his girlfriend makes during sex to the high-pitched cry of a pig. The comparison also serves to link female vocalisation with sharpness, shrillness and nonsense. Later, Bliss also embraces animal sounds, pulling a puppy dog face and whimpering in Pash's car. Her association with dogs will be cemented in a scene in which she is shown admiring herself in her roller-derby costume. There is a large soft-toy dog standing adjacent to the mirror. Both the dog and the mirror can be read as ways of reflecting who Bliss is.

Clothing in the film also reinforces the linking of woman and animal. Bliss and Pash, for example, must wear aprons with pig faces at the Oink Joint. They are made to dress up as swine. For her first trip to a roller-derby match, Bliss wears a top which has zebra heads embroidered on it. She wears this top again later in the film after moving out of the house of her parents. Maggie Mayhem is also shown at one point sporting a yellow tee-shirt with a tiger emblazoned on it. Several of the women possess tattoos of creatures that affirm their animalism.

Seemingly contradicting this reading, some men are linked to animality. Leo, the Hurl Scouts coach, is also shown wearing a tee-shirt with lions on it. This top forms a visual reference to his name. It also aligns him, as a wearer of big cats, with Maggie. Leo, however, is contaminated with femininity because he coaches a woman's team. His masculinity is visibly undermined by the knee brace he is forced to wear. He is symbolically castrated, lacking. Birdman (Carlo Alban), the manager of the Oink Joint, is similarly compromised through his proximity to women. His avian name, like Leo's, is taken from the animal kingdom. In Birdman's case, his ethnicity may also be a factor as he is a Latino. His name reflects his lack of access to the privileges that accompany white Anglo-Saxon masculinity in Bodeen. Bliss's father Earl, the 'henpecked' husband, is also advised by his eldest daughter to 'crawl back under [his] turtle shell'. He is also figured as animal. His inability to stand up to his wife renders him unmanly. Earl, however, will redeem himself as father figure towards the end of *Whip It*, reassuming his position within 'mankind' by challenging his wife's wishes for Bliss's future.

Linking sportsmen with animals in film is, of course, a regular occurrence. Rocky possesses the 'eye of the tiger' and Robert De Niro as Jake LaMotta is a 'raging bull'. The 'animality' of the two boxers, however, operates to negate the artistry of their endeavours. They become brutes rather than human beings. In the ring their 'natural' aggression is permitted free rein. The connection of athletes of either sex with animals therefore implicitly figures them as feminine. In *Kansas City Bomber* (Dir. Jerrold Freeman, USA, 1972), about the trials, tribulations, and triumphs of roller derby player and single mother K.C. Carr, Horrible Hank Hopkins is figured as a pig by his fellow players and, at one point, in a scene in a bar, is subject to oinking noises. Sportsmen referred to in such terms are fantasised as returning to a state of nature. Sport in this conception is not a part of culture. It returns the athlete and, by extension, their audience, to the body. The body is, as Judith Butler points out, often posited as preceding representation, as outside culture, rather than an effect of it.[23] The body is imagined as base nature. In patriarchal culture, nature is frequently fantasised as parallel with woman.[24] Sport as a physical pursuit, as bodily, therefore carries feminine associations although these are usually disavowed.

Whip It, through its foregrounding of the animal-woman connection draws attention to animal-male athlete equivalences. The film foregrounds how sport, as a mainstay of hegemonic masculinity, is often founded on a forsworn feminine: the body. The body, with or without penis, as body, is antithetical to mind. It occupies the negative pole of the binary opposition, forming the bottom to culture's top in the innate roleplay of binary oppositions within logocentrism. Sport, as Raewynn Connell has compellingly argued, is often used as a tool to maintain unequal social relations of gender. Connell suggests that 'men's greater sporting prowess has become a theme of backlash against feminism' that 'serves as symbolic proof of men's superiority and right to rule'.²⁵ The film, however, signals the trace of the feminine at the core of this physical 'proof', its central flaw.

Despite this positive interrogation of the animal-sport matrix, however, *Whip It* ultimately affirms a repressive vision of women. It is the master of ceremonies, Johnny, who anchors the meaning ascribed to derby through his running commentaries. Johnny regards derby as erotic spectacle. At one point, he delights in a catfight that breaks out on the track.²⁶ His mimicking whip-cracking is his most telling action. This not only draws attention to roller derby as an expression of SM interests, it also cements the woman-animal connection. In cracking his invisible whip towards the track, Johnny transforms into lion tamer. The bout becomes a circus performance with the women figured as trained animals. They are engaging in animal-play, a subcategory of sexual role play in which participants perform as creatures such as ponies or puppies. In the bout they act out their taming by Johnny. His words bring them to heel, undermining their emancipatory efforts. Johnny states during one bout: 'by day these girls are your favourite waitresses, nurses, teachers'. This draws attention to the temporariness, if not illusoriness, of women's liberation on the track. Their achievements are not carried into everyday life where they continue to work in poor paying service industry jobs and in traditional roles in caring professions. Johnny's voiceover, his commentary, seeks to jam the liberatory message embodied by these female athletes, transforming derby into a menagerie.

The Athletic Object

Despite the reactionary roles played by costume, dialogue and *mise-en-scène*, however, *Whip It* still embodies a powerful emancipatory message. The location of this radical feminist dimension is present primarily in its cinematography during the bouts that are portrayed. Jennifer Barker has explored the movie camera as muscle in *The Tactile Eye*. She argues that 'the physical movement of the camera is the closest approximation of muscular movement of the human body'.²⁷ In *Whip It*, the camera, tracking acts of jamming and blocking, following the action from up close and on high, forms another athlete skating alongside the players. Given roller derby in the film is an all-women sport this participant invites identification as female. It could be argued that the camera in *Whip It* is, at times, a sportswoman. The 'muscular embrace' it pulls the audience into is that of the female athlete.[28]

The expansive movements of the camera mirror the extensive gestures of the athletes. Roller derby provides an opportunity for women to explore their gestural potential. This is indicated in the name of Bliss's team, the Hurl Scouts. To link back to Chapter 1, the Scouts do not throw like girls, they hurl. To hurl means to throw with force, to be gesturally uninhibited. Like the films discussed in Chapter 3, *Whip It* therefore challenges patriarchy through its visible utterances, its gestures. These utterances are articulated both by the athletes on screen and the camera that follows and parallels them. Barker suggests that films foster 'muscular empathy' through characters and camerawork.[29] Aspects of her remarks about empathising with the camera's physique could easily be applied to *Whip It*'s derby sequences:

> When the film swivels suddenly with a whip pan, or moves slowly with a long take or a tracking shot, or stretches itself out in widescreen to take in a vast landscape, we feel those movements in our muscles because our bodies have made similar movements: we have whipped our heads from side to side, moved slowly and stealthily, and stretched out our bodies in ways that are distinctly human but inspired by attitudes like those that inspire the film's movements.[30]

Rapid movements are present in the camerawork and in the actions of the players during bouts. *Whip It* therefore provides a valuable space through which its audience can empathise with the athleticism of sportswomen.

The fast camerawork during the bouts also performs another valuable role. It works to resist the objectification of the bodies of the women despite Johnny's efforts to speak their sexiness, secure it. The concluding race in *Whip It* can be productively compared with the final race in *Fast Girls*. The camerawork during the relay race in *Fast Girls* is, at times, not rapid. It loiters, tarries. For Freud, tarrying was one of the symptoms of perversion. He suggests that sexual perversions can involve activities that '*linger* over the intermediate relations to the sexual object which should normally be traversed rapidly on the path towards the final sexual aim'.[31] In *Fast Girls*, the camera dawdles on the abdominals, chest, legs, and face of athletes as they sprint around the track. It divides the sportswomen into desirable parts, fetish objects. In keeping with the experiences of actual roller derby players, *Whip It*, by contrast, refuses to objectify.[32] This

8.2 *Whip It* (2009): Pigs might fly

also contrasts it with *Soul Surfer*, in which Alana's posing during a photo-shoot for a Rip Curl campaign, a scene included to construct a contrast between her idealised body and Bethany's perceived imperfection, asserts her enduring role as sex object as well as successful athlete.

Whip It is therefore a cinematographically liberating film, in terms of both gesture and shot choices. This positive dimension is, however, undercut by the film's persistent equation of femininity and animality, an association cemented in the closing shot of Bliss atop the Oink Joint seated on the back of a massive model pig, the sun in her face (8.2). The illuminating *mise-en-scène* reveals that 'pigs might fly' as far as female emancipation goes in Bodeen. *Whip It*'s mixed messages make it comparable to most of the films discussed in earlier chapters. It reflects the ongoing struggles over women's liberation, a struggle in which the figure of the female athlete has a vital part to play through challenging the frailty myth that was, for a long time, defining.

Like many of the films already discussed, *Whip It* also enhances our understanding of ways in which sport can be conceptualised as more than a competitive physical activity. The film again foregrounds how sport contributes to extending and enhancing the visibility of sexual practices that exceed the heteronormative penis–vagina coital model. It also portrays the aesthetic dimension to sport explored in depth in Chapter 1 and Chapter 7. This aspect appears in the fluid pleasures of the camerawork tracing the actions of the derby players. It is also indicated by a brief verbal exchange between the Iron and Bliss. Iron compliments Bliss on a vault she performs to avoid colliding with some players prone on the track:

'Nice jump!' Here the artistry of the athletic feat is positively appraised. The handling of the camerawork used for the bouts in *Whip It*, through its energetic, yet precise, motions, contains a comparable artistry. In the strong hands of director Drew Barrymore and cinematographer Robert Yeoman, the camera becomes a means of demonstrating how aesthetics can comprise a powerful means of championing a progressive sexual politics. *Whip It* shows how aesthetics in sports film about female athletes can contest the frailty myth and contribute to sexual emancipation.

Notes

Introduction

1. Aaron Baker, *Contesting Identities: Sports in American Film* (Urbana: University of Illinois Press, 2006), p. 50.
2. Dayna B. Daniels, 'You throw like a girl: sport and misogyny on the silver screen', *Film & History* 35/1 (2005), pp. 29–38; p. 29.
3. In a significant recent study, Katharina Lindner engages in a qualitative analysis of films featuring female and male athletes. She concludes that films starring sportswomen generally reinforce heteronormativity although some depictions of female athletes are potentially subversive. See Lindner, 'Bodies in Action: Female Athleticism on the Cinema Screen', *Feminist Media Studies* 11/3 (2011), pp. 321–45.
4. Jayne Caudwell, '*Girlfight* and *Bend it Like Beckham*: Screening Women, Sport, and Sexuality', *Journal of Lesbian Studies* 13/3 (2009), pp. 255–71; p. 256.
5. Deborah Tudor, *Hollywood's Vision of Team Sports: Heroes, Race, and Gender* (New York: Garland Publishing, 1997).
6. Seán Crosson, *Sport and Film* (London: Routledge, 2013); Aaron Baker and Todd Edward Boyd (eds), *Out of Bounds: Sports, Media and the Politics of Identity* (Bloomington: Indiana University Press, 1997); C. Richard King and David J. Leonard (eds), *Visual Economies of/in Motion: Sport and Film* (Frankfurt: Peter Lang, 2006); Ron Briley, Michael K. Schoenecke and Deborah A. Carmichael (eds), *All-Stars and Movie Stars: Sports in Film and History* (Lexington: University Press of Kentucky, 2008); Emma Poulton and Martin Roderick (eds), *Sport in Films* (Abingdon: Routledge, 2008) and Zachary Ingle and David M. Sutera (eds), *Gender and Genre in Sports Documentaries: Critical Essays* (Lanham: Scarecrow Press, 2012).

7   Tudor, *Hollywood's Vision of Team Sports*, p. 80.
8   Crosson, *Sport and Film*, p. 123.
9   For a useful summary of Gramsci's idea of hegemony see Sue Golding, *Gramsci's Democratic Theory: Contributions to a Post-Liberal Democracy* (Toronto: University of Toronto Press, 1992), pp. 106–10.
10 Griselda Pollock, *Vision and Difference: Femininity, Feminism and the Histories of Art* (London: Routledge, 1988), p. 85.
11 Pollock, *Vision and Difference*, p. 7.
12 Baker, *Contesting Identities*, p. 89.
13 Tudor, *Hollywood's Vision of Team Sports*, p. 82.
14 Lucy Bolton, *Film and Female Consciousness: Irigaray, Cinema and Thinking Women* (New York: Palgrave, 2011), p. 10.
15 Bolton, *Film and Female Consciousness*, p. 10.
16 Thoughtful approaches to the study of film inspired by Deleuze include Felicity Coleman's *Deleuze and Cinema* (Oxford: Berg, 2011), Patricia Pisters's *The Matrix of Visual Culture: Working with Deleuze in Film Theory* (Stanford: Stanford University Press, 2003) and Alison Young's *The Scene of Violence: Cinema, Crime, Affect* (Abingdon: Routledge, 2010).
17 See, for instance, Caroline Bainbridge's *A Feminine Cinematics: Luce Irigaray, Women and Film* (New York: Palgrave, 2008), Bolton's *Film and Female Consciousness*, Catherine Constable's *Thinking in Images: Film Theory, Feminist Philosophy and Marlene Dietrich* (London: BFI, 2005) and Liz Watkins's 'Light, colour and sound in cinema', *Paragraph* 25/3 (2002), pp. 118–28.
18 Bolton, *Film and Female Consciousness*, p. 174.
19 Bainbridge, *A Feminine Cinematics*, p. 12.
20 Bainbridge, *A Feminine Cinematics*, p. 14.
21 The difference in tenor between Bainbridge and Watkins is made particularly clear when their respective essays in the special issue of *Paragraph* on Irigaray's work are read in tandem. See Bainbridge, 'Feminine enunciation in women's cinema', *Paragraph* 25/3 (2002), pp. 129–41 and Watkins's 'Light, colour and sound in cinema'. The contrast between Bolton's reading of *In the Cut* (Dir. Jane Campion, USA, 2003) in *Film and Female Consciousness* and Watkins's in 'The (Dis)Articulation of Colour: Cinematography, Femininity and Desire in Jane Campion's *In the Cut*', in Wendy Everett (ed.), *Questions of Colour in Cinema: From Paintbrush to Pixel* (Oxford: Peter Lang, 2007), pp. 197–216 is also revealing. Watkins has developed her thinking in relation to colour further in her book *Film Theories and Philosophies of Colour: The Residual Image* (London: Routledge, 2015), in press.

22 Watkins, 'Light, colour and sound in Cinema', p. 128.
23 Griselda Pollock, *Encounters in the Virtual Feminist Museum* (London: Routledge, 2007), p. 222.
24 Griselda Pollock, 'A matrixial installation: artworking in the freudian space of memory and migration', in Catherine de Zegher and Griselda Pollock (eds), *Art as Compassion* (Brussels: ASA Publishers, 2011), pp. 191–241; p. 237.
25 Griselda Pollock, 'A very long engagement: singularity and difference in the critical writing of Eva Hesse' in Griselda Pollock and Vanessa Corby (eds), *Encountering Eva Hesse* (Munich: Prestel, 2006), pp. 23–55; p. 53.
26 Rosalind Galt, *Pretty: Film and the Decorative Image* (New York: Columbia University Press, 2011), p. 66.
27 T.J. Clark, *Image of the People: Gustave Courbet and the 1848 Revolution* (Berkeley: University of California Press, 1973), p. 13.
28 Amy Campbell, 'Women, sport, and film class', *Women's Studies Quarterly* 33:1/2 (2005), pp. 210–23; p. 211.
29 Theodor W. Adorno, *The Culture Industry: Selected Essays on Mass Culture* (London: Routledge, 1991), p. 77.
30 Ibid.
31 Adorno, *The Culture Industry*, p. 78.
32 See, for example, the discussion of docile bodies in relation to the school bell. Michel Foucault, *Discipline and Punish: The Birth of the Prison* (London: Penguin, 1991), p. 150.
33 Louis Althusser, 'Ideology and the ideological state apparatus', in *Lenin and Philosophy and Other Essays* (New York: Monthly Review Press, 2001), pp. 85–126, p. 118.
34 Ibid. My emphasis.
35 John Mowitt, *Percussion: Drumming, Beating, Striking* (Durham: Duke University Press, 2002), p. 56.
36 Judith Butler, *Bodies that Matter: On the Discursive Limits of 'Sex'* (New York: Routledge, 1993), p. 122.
37 Judith Butler, 'Athletic genders: hyperbolic instance and/or the overcoming of sexual binarism', *Stanford Humanities Review* 6/2 (1998), pp. 103–11.
38 Lawrence Taylor & Steven Oberman, *Drunk Driving Defense*, 6th Edition (New York: Aspen Publishers, 2006), p. 244.
39 See Adele Pavlidis and Simone Fullagar, 'Narrating the multiplicity of "Derby Grrrl": exploring intersectionality and the dynamics of affect in roller derby', *Leisure Sciences* 35 (2013), pp. 422–37.

Chapter 1 The Ascent of Woman

1. Michel Serres, *The Natural Contract* (Ann Arbor: University of Michigan Press, 1995), p. 49.
2. Sally Ann Ness, 'Bouldering in Yosemite: emergent signs of place and landscape', *American Anthropologist* 113/1 (2011), pp. 71–87; p. 77.
3. Ibid.
4. Dianne Chisholm, 'Climbing like a girl: an exemplary adventure in feminist phenomenology', *Hypatia* 23/1 (2008), pp. 9–40; p. 18.
5. Iris Marion Young, 'Throwing like a girl', in *On Female Body Experience* (Oxford: Oxford University Press, 2005), pp. 27–45.
6. Sara Ahmed, *Queer Phenomenology: Orientations, Objects, Others* (Durham: Duke University Press, 2006), p. 56.
7. Young, 'Throwing like a girl', p. 32.
8. Young, 'Throwing like a girl', p. 33.
9. For an extended discussion of the relationship of immanence and transcendence to the lived body see M.C. Dillon, *Merleau-Ponty's Ontology*, 2nd Edition (Evanston: Northwestern University Press, 1998).
10. Young, 'Throwing like a girl', p. 36.
11. Young, 'Throwing like a girl', pp. 36–7.
12. Young, 'Throwing like a girl', p. 39.
13. Chisholm, 'Climbing like a girl', p. 11.
14. Chisholm, 'Climbing like a girl', p. 20.
15. Chisholm, 'Climbing like a girl', p. 22.
16. Hill discusses the merits of style over brute strength in climbing in Chris Noble's *Women Who Dare: North America's Most Inspiring Women Climbers* (Guilford: Falcon Guides, 2013), p. 133.
17. Victoria Robinson, *Everyday Masculinities and Extreme Sport: Male Identity and Rock Climbing* (Oxford: Berg, 2008), pp. 138–41.
18. Chisholm, 'Climbing like a girl', p. 33.
19. Lynn Hill, *Climbing Free: My Life in the Vertical World* (London: Harper Collins, 2002), p. 44.
20. Chisholm, 'Climbing like a girl', p. 31.
21. Peter Livesey, 'I feel rock', in Ken Wilson (ed.), *The Games Climbers Play* (London: Diadem, 1978), pp. 74–82; p. 76.
22. Luce Irigaray, *This Sex Which is Not One* (Ithaca: Cornell University Press, 1985), p. 171.
23. Livesey, 'I feel rock', p. 75.

24 Chisholm, 'Climbing like a girl', p. 31.
25 Livesey, 'I feel rock', p. 80.
26 Chisholm, 'Climbing like a girl', p. 31.
27 Ness, 'Bouldering in Yosemite', p. 76.
28 Ibid.
29 Ibid.
30 Ness, 'Bouldering in Yosemite', p. 81.
31 Ness, 'Bouldering in Yosemite', p. 82.
32 Ibid.
33 Ibid.
34 Michel Serres, *The Five Senses: A Philosophy of Mingled Bodies* (London: Continuum, 2008), p. 93.
35 Michel Serres, *The Five Senses*, p. 154.
36 Hill, *Climbing Free*, p. 175.
37 Hill, *Climbing Free*, p. 268.
38 Steven Connor, 'Michel Serres's *Les Cinq Sens*', in Niran Abbas (ed.), Mapping Michel Serres (Ann Arbor: University of Michigan Press, 2005), pp. 153–69; p. 165.
39 Maurice Merleau-Ponty, *The Visible and the Invisible* (Evanston: Northwestern University Press, 1968), p. 125.
40 Serres, *The Five Senses*, p. 133.
41 Michel Serres, *Conversations on Science, Culture and Time: Michel Serres with Bruno Latour* (Ann Arbor: University of Michigan Press, 1995), p. 132.
42 Serres, *The Five Senses*, p. 114.
43 Hill, *Climbing Free*, p. 44.
44 Serres, *The Five Senses*, p. 114.
45 Serres, *The Five Senses*, p. 231.
46 Serres, *The Five Senses*, p. 330.
47 Serres, *The Natural Contract*, p. 106.
48 See Ian Heywood, 'Climbing monsters: excess and restraint in contemporary rock climbing', *Leisure Studies* 24/4 (2006), pp. 455–67.
49 Hill, *Climbing Free*, p. 143.
50 Heywood, 'Climbing monsters', p. 458.
51 Hill, *Climbing Free*, p. 183.
52 Hill, *Climbing Free*, p. 229.
53 Ibid.
54 Hill, *Climbing Free*, p. 258.
55 Hill, *Climbing Free*, p. 44.

56 Hill, *Climbing Free*, p. 228.
57 Hill, *Climbing Free*, p. 160.
58 Serres, *The Natural Contract*, p. 33.
59 Serres, *The Natural Contract*, p. 17.
60 See Nicholas Chare, 'Writing perceptions: the matter of words and the Rollright Stones', *Art History* 34/2 (2011), pp. 244–67.
61 Serres, *The Natural Contract*, p. 104.
62 Ibid.
63 Serres, *The Natural Contract*, p. 38.
64 Serres, *The Natural Contract*, p. 90.
65 Serres, *The Natural Contract*, p. 38.
66 Teresa de Lauretis, *Alice Doesn't: Feminism, Semiotics, Cinema* (Bloomington: Indiana University Press, 1984), p. 186.
67 Serres, *The Five Senses*, p. 120.
68 Hill, *Climbing Free*, p. 270.
69 Serres, *The Natural Contract*, p. 124.

Chapter 2 Sexing the Canvas

1 Leah Hager Cohen, *Without Apology: Girls, Women and the Desire to Fight* (London: Weidenfeld & Nicolson, 2005), pp. 153–54.
2 Mary Ann Doane, *The Desire to Desire: The Woman's Film of the 1940s* (Bloomington: Indiana University Press, 1987), p. 95.
3 Griselda Pollock, *Vision and Difference: Femininity, Feminism and the Histories of Art* (London: Routledge, 1988), p. 62.
4 Pollock, *Vision and Difference*, p. 63.
5 Ibid.
6 Pollock, *Vision and Difference*, p. 66.
7 Ibid.
8 Vivian Sobchack, *The Address of the Eye: A Phenomenology of Film Experience* (Princeton: Princeton University Press, 1992), p. 148.
9 Sobchack, *The Address of the Eye*, p. 144.
10 Pollock, *Vision and Difference*, p. 89.
11 Sobchack, *The Address of the Eye*, p. 144.
12 Tudor, *Hollywood's Vision of Team Sports*, pp. 85–92.
13 Shelley G. MacDonald, *Observations on Boxing: A Psychoanalytic Study* (Dagenham: University of East London Press, 2000), p. 6.
14 MacDonald, *Observations on Boxing*, p. 12.

15 For a discussion of the pervasive myth of women's frailty in Western culture see Colette Dowling, *The Frailty Myth: Redefining the Physical Potential of Women and Girls* (New York: Random House, 2001).
16 Martha McCaughey, *Real Knockouts: the Physical Feminism of Women's Self-Defense* (New York: New York University Press, 1997), p. 90.
17 McCaughey, *Real Knockouts*, p. 201.
18 McCaughey, *Real Knockouts*, p. 10.
19 McCaughey, *Real Knockouts*, p. 11.
20 Elizabeth Grosz, *Volatile Bodies: Towards a Corporeal Feminism* (Bloomington: Indiana University Press, 1994), p. 142.
21 Jillian M. Báez, 'Towards a *Latinidad Feminista*: the multiplicities of Latinidad and feminism in contemporary cinema', *Popular Communication* 5/2 (2007), pp. 109–28, p. 117.
22 Young, 'Throwing like a girl', p. 42.
23 Doane, *The Desire to Desire*, p. 78.
24 Young, 'Throwing like a girl', p. 45.
25 Leslie Heywood & Shari L. Dworkin, *Built to Win: the Female Athlete as Cultural Icon* (Minneapolis: University of Minnesota Press, 1993), p. 121.
26 Ibid.
27 In an instance of potentially subversive role reversal in *Knockout*, during a fight between Tanya 'Terminator' Tessaro and Christy McKee for the WFBA Lightweight Championship, the number cards are held up by a man with a bare torso.
28 María Teresa Márquez, 'No longer counted out: fighting isn't what it used to be', in Delilah Montoya (ed.), *Women Boxers: the New Warriors* (Houston: Arte Público Press, 2006), pp. 9–17; p. 12.
29 Carlo Rotella, *Good With their Hands: Boxers, Bluesmen, and Other Characters from the Rust Belt* (Berkeley: University of California Press, 2002), p. 16.
30 MacDonald, *Observations on Boxing*, p. 2.
31 Allen Guttmann, *The Erotic in Sports* (New York: Columbia University Press, 1996), p. 71.
32 Katharina Lindner, 'Fighting for subjectivity: articulations of physicality in *Girlfight*', *Journal of International Women's Studies* 10/3 (2009), pp. 4–17; p. 10.
33 Laura Mulvey, 'Visual pleasure and narrative cinema', in *Visual and Other Pleasures* (Basingstoke: Macmillan, 1989), pp. 14–26, p. 19.
34 Young, 'Throwing like a girl', p. 44.
35 Rozsika Parker and Griselda Pollock, *Old Mistresses: Women, Art and Ideology* (London: Pandora, 1981), p. 124.

36 Báez, 'Towards a *Latinidad Feminista*', p. 118.
37 Young, 'Throwing like a girl', p. 45.
38 Young, 'Throwing like a girl', p. 44.
39 Anne Karpf, *The Human Voice: How This Extraordinary Instrument Reveals Essential Clues About Who We Are* (New York: Bloomsbury, 2006), p. 175
40 Karpf, *The Human Voice*, p. 27.
41 Ibid.
42 Karpf, *The Human Voice*, p. 163.
43 Don Ihde, *Listening and Voice; Phenomenologies of Sound*, 2nd Edition (New York: State University of New York Press, 2007), p. 190.
44 Ibid.
45 Ibid.
46 Gloria Steinem, 'Introduction', in Amy Handy & Steven Korté (eds), *Wonder Woman* (New York: Abbeville Press, 1995), pp. 5–19.
47 This theme also features multiple times in the baseball film *A League of their Own*. In one scene the coach of the Rockford Peaches, Jimmy Dugan, screams abuse at the right fielder Evelyn Gardner, reducing her to tears. He will later be shown restraining himself from bellowing at her again, having learnt the error of his acoustic ways.
48 Sarah E. Ullman, 'Social reactions, coping strategies, and self-blame attributions in adjustment to sexual assault', *Psychology of Women Quarterly* 20 (1996), pp. 505–26; p. 512.
49 See Katrina Vickerman and Gayla Margolin, 'Rape treatment outcome research: empirical findings and the state of the literature', *Clinical Psychology Review* 29/5 (2009), pp. 431–48; p. 438.
50 Wendy S. David, Tracy L. Simpson and Ann J. Cotton, 'Taking charge: a pilot curriculum of self-defence and personal safety training for female veterans with PTSD because of military sexual trauma', *Journal of Interpersonal Violence* 21/4 (2006), pp. 555–65.
51 Maud Lavin, *Push Comes to Shove: New Images of Aggressive Women* (Cambridge, MASS: MIT Press, 2010), p. 250.
52 Jayne Caudwell, '*Girlfight* and *Bend it Like Beckham*: screening women, sport, and sexuality', *Journal of Lesbian Studies* 13/3 (2009), pp. 255–71; p. 260.
53 E. M. Forster, *Aspects of the Novel* (London: Edward Arnold, 1974), p. 47.
54 Ibid.
55 Forster, *Aspects of the Novel*, p. 48.

56 Virginia Woolf, *A Room of One's Own & Three Guineas* (London: Penguin, 1993), pp. 60–1.
57 Woolf, *A Room of One's Own*, p. 61.
58 Forster, *Aspects of the Novel*, p. 52.
59 Forster, *Aspects of the Novel*, p. 53.
60 Woolf, *A Room of One's Own*, p. 26.
61 Forster, *Aspects of the Novel*, p. 53.
62 Jane Austen, *Northanger Abbey* (Boston: Little, Brown & Co, 1903), p. 8.
63 Ibid.
64 Young, 'Throwing like a girl', p. 44.
65 Woolf, *A Room of One's Own*, p. 63.
66 Ibid.
67 Woolf, *A Room of One's Own*, p. 38.
68 Mary Ann Doane, 'The close-up: scale and detail in cinema', *Differences: A Journal of Feminist Cultural Studies* 14/3 (2003), pp. 89–111, p. 91.
69 Doane, 'The close-up', p. 107.
70 Woolf, *A Room of One's Own*, pp. 5–7.
71 This editing technique is also employed, although in a slightly different way, in *Knockout*.
72 Elaine Scarry, *The Body in Pain: The Making and Unmaking of the World* (Oxford: Oxford University Press, 1985), pp. 19–20.
73 Lynda Nead, 'Stilling the punch: boxing, violence and the photographic image', *Journal of Visual Culture* 10/3 (2011), pp. 305–23; p. 320.
74 Nead, 'Stilling the punch', p. 320.
75 Jacqueline Rose, 'Sexuality in the field of vision' in *Sexuality in the Field of Vision* (London: Verso, 1986), pp. 224–33; p. 232.
76 Mischa Merz, *Bruising: A Journey Through Gender* (Sydney: Picador, 2000), p. 55.
77 Laura Mulvey, 'Visual pleasure and narrative cinema', p. 26.
78 Caudwell has acknowledged Diana's emancipation but drawn attention to the cult of individualism accompanying it. She forcefully argues that *Girlfight* 'offers an idealistic version of agency and free choice; a version of agency that suits those driving a neo-liberal agenda'. Jayne Caudwell, '*Girlfight*: boxing women', *Sport in Society* 11:2/3 (2008), pp. 227–39; p. 236.
79 David Scott, *The Art and Aesthetics of Boxing* (Lincoln: University of Nebraska Press, 2008), p. xxix.
80 Merz, *Bruising*, p. 15.

81 Rosalind Galt, *Pretty: Film and the Decorative Image* (New York: Columbia University Press, 2011), pp. 106–7.
82 Nicholas Chare, 'Sexing the canvas; calling on the medium', *Art History* 32/4 (2009), pp. 664–89.
83 MacDonald, Observations on boxing, p. 6.
84 Griselda Pollock, 'Killing men and dying women: a woman's touch in the cold zone of American painting in the 1950s', in Fred Orton and Griselda Pollock, *Avant-Gardes and Partisans Reviewed* (Manchester: Manchester University Press, 1996), pp. 219–94; p. 242.
85 Pollock, 'Killing men and dying women', p. 257.
86 Pollock, 'Killing men and dying women', p. 258.
87 Doane, 'The close-up', p. 91.

Chapter 3 Athletic Gestures

1 Adam Kendon, *Gesture: Visible Action as Utterance* (Cambridge: Cambridge University Press, 2004), p. 7.
2 Kendon, *Gesture*, p. 15.
3 Kendon, *Gesture*, p. 8.
4 Kendon, *Gesture*, p. 24.
5 Tudor, *Hollywood's Vision of Team Sports*, p. 95.
6 Giorgio Agamben, *Means Without End: Notes on Politics* (Minneapolis: University of Minnesota Press, 2000), p. 56.
7 Agamben, *Means Without End*, p. 55.
8 Agamben, *Means Without End*, p. 56.
9 Agamben, *Means Without End*, p. 58.
10 Ibid.
11 Agamben, *Means Without End*, p. 59.
12 Luce Irigaray, 'The gesture in psychoanalysis', in Teresa Brennan (ed.), *Between Feminism and Psychoanalysis* (London: Routledge, 1989), pp. 127–38; p. 134.
13 Irigaray, 'The gesture in psychoanalysis', p. 133.
14 Kendon, *Gesture*, p. 98.
15 Sigmund Freud, 'Beyond the pleasure principle', in *The Penguin Freud Library Volume 11: On Metapsychology* (London: Penguin, 1991), pp. 275–338; p. 284.
16 For a discussion of the insights the fort/da game afford into sport in general see Steven Connor, *A Philosophy of Sport* (London: Reaktion, 2011), pp. 137–8.
17 Freud, 'Beyond the Pleasure Principle', p. 285.

18 Irigaray, 'The gesture in psychoanalysis', p. 131.
19 Ibid.
20 Ibid.
21 Ibid.
22 Ibid.
23 Irigaray, 'The gesture in psychoanalysis', p. 132.
24 Ibid.
25 Ibid.
26 Irigaray, 'The gesture in psychoanalysis', p. 133.
27 Ibid.
28 Ibid.
29 Irigaray, 'The gesture in psychoanalysis', p. 134.
30 Agamben, *Means without End*, p. 58.
31 Griselda Pollock, 'Killing men and dying women', p. 253.
32 Young, 'Throwing like a girl', p. 43.
33 See Nancy Henley, 'Status and sex: some touching observations', *Bulletin of the Psychonomic Society* 2 (1972), pp. 91–3; B. Major, A. M. Schmidlin & L. Williams, 'Gender patterns in social touch: the impact of setting and age', *Journal of Personality and Social Psychology* 58/4 (1990), pp. 634–43.
34 Young, 'Throwing like a girl', p. 45.
35 There is, however, currently no conclusive research that shows a link between the menstrual cycle and poor athletic performance. The scene therefore shows how women can, themselves, perpetuate myths about performance failures. See Constance Lebrun, 'Effect of the different phases of the menstrual cycle and oral contraceptives on athletic performance', *Sports Medicine* 16/6 (1993), pp. 400–30.
36 The nationality of the foreign team is made apparent when one of the sailors shouts in English.
37 For a discussion of this documentary see Yingchi Chu, *Chinese Documentaries: From Dogma to Polyphony* (Abingdon: Routledge, 2007), p. 72. Chu focuses on how beds are used in the film to contrast peasants and landlords yet a strong distinction is also forged at the level of clothing.
38 David Efron, *Gesture, Race and Culture* (Paris: Mouton, 1972), p. 90.
39 For a discussion of touch in relation to sports coaching in films see my article 'Handling pressures', which includes analyses of films about basketball and soccer including *The Heart of the Game* (Dir. Ward Serrill, USA, 2005), *Her Best Move* (Dir. Norm Hunter, USA, 2009), *She's the Man* (Dir. Andy Fickman, USA, 2006), and *The Winning Season* (Dir. James C. Strouse, USA, 2009). Nicholas Chare,

'Handling pressures: analysing touch in american films about youth sport', *Sport, Education and Society* 18/5 (2013), pp. 663–77.
40. See M. W. Kraus, C. Huang and D. Keltner, 'Tactile communication, cooperation, and performance: an ethological study of the NBA', *Emotion* 10/5 (2010), pp. 745–49.
41. Tiffany Field, *Touch* (Cambridge, Mass: MIT Press, 2001), p. 19.
42. Ibid.
43. Rebecca Schneider, *Performing Remains: Art and War in Times of Theatrical Reenactment* (Abingdon: Routledge, 2011), p. 35.
44. Erin Manning, *Politics of Touch: Sense, Movement, Sovereignty* (Minneapolis: University of Minnesota Press, 2007), p. 127.

Chapter 4 Venus in Spikes

1. Susan Sontag, 'Fascinating fascism', in *Under the Sign of Saturn* (London: Penguin, 2009), p. 93.
2. See Susan Tegel, 'Leni Riefenstahl: art and politics', *Quarterly Review of Film and Video* 23/3 (2006), pp. 185–200.
3. Sontag, 'Fascinating fascism', p. 90. For a consideration of Céline's relationship to Nazism see my book *Auschwitz and Afterimages: Abjection, Witnessing and Representation* (London: I.B.Tauris, 2011), pp. 11–44.
4. Sontag, 'Fascinating fascism', p. 91.
5. Ibid.
6. Adorno, *The Culture Industry*, p. 118.
7. Adorno, *The Culture Industry*, p. 120.
8. Adorno, *The Culture Industry*, p. 121.
9. Adorno, *The Culture Industry*, p. 122.
10. Sontag, 'Fascinating fascism', p. 92.
11. Michael Mackenzie, 'From Athens to Berlin: The 1936 Olympics and Leni Riefenstahl's *Olympia*', *Critical Inquiry* 29/2 (2003), pp. 302–36; p. 316.
12. Ibid.
13. Leni Riefenstahl, *The Last of the Nuba* (London: Collins, 1976); Leni Riefenstahl, *The People of Kau* (London: Collins, 1976).
14. Sontag, 'Fascinating fascism', p. 90.
15. Yvonne Tasker, *Spectacular Bodies: Gender, Genre and Action Cinema* (London: Routledge, 1993), p. 50.
16. Mackenzie, 'From Athens to Berlin', p. 335.
17. Ibid.

18 bell hooks, 'The feminazi mystique', *Transition* 73 (1997), pp. 156–62; p. 162.
19 Riefenstahl, *The People of Kau*, p. 223.
20 Riefenstahl, *The People of Kau*, p. 10.
21 Riefenstahl, *The People of Kau*, p. 11.
22 Ibid.
23 Riefenstahl, *The People of Kau*, p. 224.
24 Ibid.
25 Riefenstahl, *The People of Kau*, p. 10.
26 Riefenstahl, *The Last of the Nuba*, p. 18.
27 Sigmund Freud, 'Fetishism', in *The Penguin Freud Library Volume 7: On Sexuality* (London: Penguin, 1991), pp. 351–7; p. 351.
28 Ibid.
29 Laura Mulvey, *Fetishism and Curiosity* (Bloomington: Indiana University Press, 1996), p. 6.
30 Brigitte Peucker, 'The fascist choreography: Riefenstahl's tableaux', *Modernism/Modernity* 11/2 (2004), pp. 279–97; p. 286.
31 For a discussion of the locations used in this sequence see Peucker, 'The fascist Choreography', p. 286; Bonita Rhoads, 'Sontag's captions: writing the body from Riefenstahl to S&M', *Women's Studies: An Interdisciplinary Journal* 37/8 (2008), pp. 942–70; p. 958.
32 Cooper C. Graham, '*Olympia* in America, 1938: Leni Riefenstahl, Hollywood, and the Kristallnacht', *Historical Journal of Film, Radio and Television* 13/4 (1993), pp. 433–50; p. 440.
33 María Graciela Rodríguez, 'Behind Leni's outlook: a perspective on the film *Olympia*', *International Review for the Sociology of Sport* 38/1 (2003), pp. 109–16; p. 110.
34 Klaus Theweleit, *Male Fantasies Volume 1: Women, Floods, Bodies, History* (Cambridge: Polity, 1987), pp. 283–4.
35 Rodríguez, 'Behind Leni's outlook', p. 110.
36 Theweleit, *Male Fantasies Volume 1*, p. 429.
37 Allen Guttmann, *The Erotic in Sports* (New York: Columbia University Press, 1996), p. 113.
38 Guttmann, *The Erotic in Sports*, p. 118.
39 Guttmann, *The Erotic in Sports*, p. 119.
40 Joy McKenzie, *The Best in Sportswear Design* (London: Batsford, 1997), p. 7.
41 Sarah E. Braddock, 'High-performance fabrics', in Maria O'Mahony and Sarah E. Braddock, *Sportstech: Revolutionary Fabrics, Fashion, and Design* (London: Thames & Hudson, 2002), p. 56.

42   McKenzie, *The Best in Sportswear Design*, p. 9.

43   Judith Halberstam, *In a Queer Time and Place: Transgender Bodies, Subcultural Lives* (New York: New York University Press, 2005), pp. 18–9.

44   Freud, 'Fetishism', p. 355.

45   Kaori O' Connor, *Lycra: How a Fiber Shaped America* (New York: Routledge, 2011).

46   Close-fitting sports clothing is also central to the Japanese phenomenon of buruma, a sexual fetish for snug athletics bloomers.

47   Michel Serres, *The Natural Contract*, p. 106.

48   The phenomenon of the feminine apologetic is discussed in more detail in Chapter 5.

49   Lycra has historically been culturally coded as feminine as is evident from the climber Ron Kauk's assertion that 'John Wayne never wore Lycra'. Kauk favoured climbing in jeans over the Lycra tights sported by other male climbers at the time because he regarded spandex as 'girly'. Today, however, Lycra is regarded as a unisex material in sport. Kauk is quoted in Hill, *Climbing Free*, p. 202.

50   Mulvey, *Fetishism and Curiosity*, p. 5.

51   Ibid.

52   Ibid.

53   Mulvey, *Fetishism and Curiosity*, pp. 7–8.

54   Thomas Elsaesser, 'Leni Riefenstahl: the body beautiful, art cinema and fascist aesthetics', in Pam Cook and Philip Dodd (eds), *Women and Film: A Sight and Sound Reader* (Philadelphia: Temple University Press, 1993), pp. 186–97; p. 197.

55   Sontag, 'Fascinating fascism', p. 91.

56   Ibid.

57   Sontag, 'Fascinating fascism', p. 92.

58   Sontag, 'Fascinating fascism', p. 93.

59   Elsaesser, 'Leni Riefenstahl', p. 188.

60   Rosalind Galt, *Pretty: Film and the Decorative Image* (New York: Columbia University Press, 2011), p. 11.

61   Ibid., p. 43.

62   Riefenstahl, *The Last of the Nuba*, p. 20.

Chapter 5 Muscle Pictures

1   Douglas Sadao Aoki, 'Posing the subject: sex, illumination, and *Pumping Iron II: The Women*', *Cinema Journal* 38/4 (1999), pp. 24–44; p. 26.

2   Jocelyn Robson and Beverly Zalcock, 'Looking at *Pumping Iron II: The Women*', in Tamsin Wilton (ed.), *Immortal Invisible: Lesbians and the Moving Image* (London: Routledge, 1995), pp. 182–92.
3   Alan Mansfield and Barbara McGinn, 'Pumping irony: the muscular and the feminine', in Sue Scott and David Morgan (eds), *Body Matters* (London: Falmer Press, 1993), p. 56.
4   Cindy Patton, 'Rock hard: judging the female physique', *Sport and Social Issues* 25/2 (2001), pp. 118–40; p. 128.
5   Nathalie Gassel, 'My muscles, myself: selected autobiographical writings', in Joanna Frueh, Laurie Fierstein and Judith Stein (eds) *Picturing the Modern Amazon* (New York: Rizzoli, 2000), pp. 117–19.
6   Juan Jiménez Salcedo, 'Nathalie Gassel y la escritura andrógina, *Asparkía* 19 (2008), pp. 89–103; p. 90.
7   Jan Baetens, 'Nathalie Gassel: le corps et la pensée, le muscle et l 'écriture', *L'Esprit Créateur* 44/3 (2004), pp. 5–12. See also Adrienne Angelo, 'Philosophy in the Weight Room: Nathalie Gassel and the Crisis of Self-Representation', *Australian Journal of French Studies* 51/1 (2014), pp. 75–87.
8   Jan Baetens, 'Nathalie Gassel', p. 8.
9   Salcedo, 'Nathalie Gassel y la escritura andrógina', pp. 99–100.
10 Baetens, 'Nathalie Gassel', p. 12.
11 Joanna Frueh, *Monster Beauty: Building the Body of Love* (Berkeley: University of California Press, 2001), p. 81.
12 All translations are my own unless otherwise stated. Gassel, *Construction d'un corps pornographique*, p. 61.
13 Mansfield & McGinn, 'Pumping irony', p. 64.
14 Maria R. Lowe, *Women of Steel: Female Bodybuilders and the Struggle for Self-Definition* (New York: New York University Press, 1998), p. 115.
15 Ibid.
16 Eve Kosofsky Sedgwick, 'Gosh Boy George, you must be awfully secure in your masculinity', in Maurice Berger, Brian Wallis and Simon Watson (eds), *Constructing Masculinity* (New York: Routledge, 1995), pp. 11–20.
17 Cynthia Lewis, 'Sporting Adam's rib: the culture of women bodybuilders in America', *The Massachusetts Review* 45/4 (2004/2005), pp. 604–31; p. 630.
18 Nathalie Gassel, *Éros androgyne* (Paris: L'Acanthe, 2000), p. 27.
19 Nathalie Gassel, *Musculatures* (Paris: Le Cercle, 2001), p. 13.
20 Gassel, *Musculatures*, p. 14.
21 Alphonso Lingis, *Foreign Bodies* (New York: Routledge, 1994), p. 37.

22 Judith Halberstam, *Female Masculinity* (Durham: Duke University Press, 1998), p. 15.
23 Halberstam, *Female Masculinity*, p. 234.
24 Gassel, *Construction d'un corps pornographique*, p. 31.
25 Gassel, *Musculatures*, p. 92.
26 Salcedo, 'Nathalie Gassel y la escritura andrógina', p. 99.
27 Elizabeth Grosz, *Volatile Bodies: Towards a Corporeal Feminism* (Bloomington: Indiana University Press, 1994), p. 156.
28 Salcedo, 'Nathalie Gassel y la escritura andrógina', p. 91.
29 The word Gassel uses for sing here, 'chant', also carries the connotation of edge, of delineation. Gassel, *Construction d'un corps pornographique*, p. 17.
30 Gassel, *Construction d'un corps pornographique*, p. 51.
31 Acker, 'Against ordinary language', p. 21.
32 Peter Schwenger, *Fantasm and Fiction: On Textual Envisioning* (Stanford: Stanford University Press, 1999), p. 70.
33 Baetens, 'Nathalie Gassel', p. 9.
34 Baetens, 'Nathalie Gassel', p. 12.
35 Gassel, *Éros androgyne*, p. 58.
36 Gassel, *Musculatures*, p. 11. The word 'bleu' that is translated as bruise here also means to blue and therefore carries the additional connotation of ink contusing the paper.
37 For a useful overview of the musculature of the hand see B. John Melloni, *Melloni's Illustrated Dictionary of the Musculoskeletal System* (New York: Parthenon, 1988).
38 Gassel, *Éros androgyne*, p. 68.
39 Gassel, *Construction d'un corps pornographique*, p. 21.
40 Patton, 'Rock hard', p. 128.
41 Michelle Bridges, *Crunch Time: Lose Weight Fast and Keep it Off* (Camberwell: Viking, 2009), p. 69.
42 Claudia Schippert, 'Can muscles be queer? reconsidering the transgressive hyper-built body', *Journal of Gender Studies* 16:2 (2007), pp. 155–71; p. 165.
43 See Patton, 'Hegemony and orgasm – or the instability of heterosexual pornography', *Screen* 30:1/2 (1989), pp. 100–13.
44 Chris Holmlund, *Impossible Bodies: Femininity and Masculinity at the Movies* (London: Routledge, 2002), p. 28.
45 The erotic appeal of buttocks is, of course, age old. Patricia Rubin, for instance, traces visual fascination for firm posteriors through the history of art in her admirable article 'Art history from the bottom up', *Art History* 36/2 (2013), pp. 280–309. Gym defined glutes are, however, a much more recent erotic

phenomenon. Their appeal is bound up with the broader erotic potential of the workouts required to achieve them.

46 Holmlund, *Impossible Bodies*, p. 28.
47 Muscle and female desire in the context of lesbian sexuality is discussed by Louise Allen. Allen explores how lesbian fans of Martina Navratilova are aroused by her strong hands, arms and legs. Her fans fragment her, fantasising about her in muscular parts. These parts, however, index strength of character and lesbian identity as well as forming loci of sexual attraction. See Allen, *The Lesbian Idol: Martina, kd and the Consumption of Lesbian Masculinity* (London: Cassell, 1997), pp. 70–2.
48 I explore the phenomenon of the sexual desire for female muscle in contemporary life in my essay 'Getting Hard' which also provides an overview of existing literature on the topic. See Nicholas Chare, 'Getting hard: female bodybuilders and muscle worship', in Adam Locks and Niall Richardson (eds), *Critical Readings in Bodybuilding* (New York: Routledge, 2012), pp. 199–214. See also Tanya Bunsell, *Strong and Hard Women: An Ethnography of Female Bodybuilding* (London: Routledge, 2013), pp. 74–85 and Nicholas Chare, 'Literary Veins: Women's bodybuilding, muscle worship and abject performance', *Performance Research* 19/1 (2014), pp. 91–101.
49 For an extended discussion of synaesthesia as it relates to visual perception see my book *After Francis Bacon: Synaesthesia and Sex in Paint* (Farnham: Ashgate, 2012).
50 I am grateful to Dominic Williams for drawing my attention to this film's fetishisation of skin.
51 Gassel, *Éros androgyne*, p. 33.
52 Gassel, *Éros androgyne*, p. 47; p. 52.
53 Patton, 'Hegemony and orgasm – or the instability of heterosexual pornography', p. 105.
54 Marcia Ian, 'The primitive subject of female bodybuilding: transgression and other postmodern myths', *Differences* 12:3 (2001), pp. 69–100; p. 75.
55 Gassel, *Musculatures*, p. 108.
56 Gassel, *Musculatures*, p. 38.
57 R. W. Duff and L.K. Hong, 'Self-images of women bodybuilders', *Sociology of Sport Journal* 1/4 (1984), pp. 374–80; p. 378.
58 Holmlund, *Impossible Bodies*, p. 23.
59 Patton, 'Hegemony and orgasm – or the instability of heterosexual pornography', p. 108.
60 Ian, 'The primitive subject of female bodybuilding', p. 81.
61 Jacqueline E. Brady, 'Pumping iron with resistance: Carla Dunlap's victorious body', in Michael Bennett and Vanessa D. Dickerson, *Recovering the Female*

Body: Self-Representations by African American Women (New Brunswick: Rutgers University Press, 2001), pp. 253–78; p. 268.
62. Brady, 'Pumping iron with resistance', p. 265.
63. Holmlund, *Impossible Bodies*, p. 26.
64. Catherine Hakim outlines the concept of erotic capital in her book *Honey Money: The Power of Erotic Capital* (London: Allen Lane, 2011).

Chapter 6 Shaping the Self

1. E. Ann Kaplan, 'Trauma and aging: Marlene Dietrich, Melanie Klein, and Marguerite Duras', in *Figuring Age: Women, Bodies, Generations*, ed. Kathleen Woodward (Bloomington: Indiana University Press, 1999), pp. 171–94; p. 182.
2. Martina Navratilova, *Shape your Self: An Inspirational Guide to Achieving your Personal Best* (London: Time Warner, 2006), p. 72.
3. For a discussion of the relationship between ageing and muscle see Gunnar Grimby and Bengt Saltin, 'The ageing muscle', *Clinical Physiology* 3/3 (1983), pp. 209–18.
4. Kevin Morgan et al, 'Customary physical activity, psychological well-being and successful ageing', *Ageing and Society* 11 (1991), pp. 399–415.
5. Young, 'Throwing like a girl', p. 44.
6. Susan Brownmiller, *Femininity* (New York: Simon & Schuster, 1984), p. 166.
7. Susan K. Cahn, *Coming on Strong: Gender and Sexuality in Twentieth-Century Women's Sport* (Cambridge, Mass: Harvard University Press, 1995), p. 50.
8. Gilda Zwerman, *Martina Navratilova* (New York: Chelsea House, 1995), p. 67.
9. Toby Miller, *Sportsex* (Philadelphia: Temple University Press, 2001), p. 112.
10. Martina Navratilova, *Being Myself* (London: Collins, 1985), p. 246.
11. Young, 'Throwing Like a Girl', p. 40.
12. Martina Navratilova, *Tennis My Way* (New York: Charles Scribner's Sons, 1983), p. 143.
13. Navratilova, *Tennis My Way*, p. 126.
14. Zwerman, *Martina Navratilova*, p. 67.
15. Johnette Howard, *The Rivals: Chris Evert versus Martina Navratilova* (London: Yellow Jersey Press, 2005), p. 84.
16. Navratilova, *Being Myself*, p. 203.
17. Ibid., p. 206.
18. Miller, *Sportsex*, p. 106.
19. Gina Daddario, *Women's Sport and Spectacle: Gendered Television Coverage and the Olympic Games* (Westport: Praeger, 1998), p. 26.

20 Miller, *Sportsex*, p. 113.
21 Miller, *Sportsex*, p. 114.
22 Ibid.
23 Ibid.
24 Miller, *Sportsex*, p. 104.
25 Ibid.
26 Ibid.
27 Sheila Jeffreys, 'Transgender activism', *Journal of Lesbian Studies* 1/3–4 (1997), pp. 55–74; p. 57.
28 Navratilova, *Shape your Self*, p. xii.
29 Manning, *Politics of Touch*, p. 126.
30 Ibid.
31 Manning, *Politics of Touch*, p. 52.
32 Judith Halberstam, *In a Queer Time and Place: Transgender Bodies, Subcultural Lives* (New York: New York University Press, 2005), pp. 88–9.
33 Transgender subjectivity does not require sex reassignment surgery. In this sense, *Second Serve* is not an accommodating vision of transgender. For a thoughtful discussion of the debate around transgender and surgery see Gayle Salomon, *Assuming a Body: Transgender and Rhetorics of Materiality* (New York: Columbia University Press, 2010), pp. 84–8.
34 Jayne Caudwell, '[Transgender] Young men: gendered subjectivities and the physically active body', *Sport, Education and Society*, iFirst (2012), pp. 1–17, p. 7.
35 Parinya Charoenpahl is now retired from competition and works as a trainer.
36 Jeffreys, 'Transgender activism', p. 71. See also Jeffreys's most recent book, *Gender Hurts: A Feminist Analysis of the Politics of Transgenderism* (London: Routledge, 2014). Janice Raymond criticises Richards as part of an early broader attack on transgender in *Transsexual Empire* (London: The Women's Press, 1980), p. 102; p. 184.
37 Judith Butler, 'Athletic genders: hyperbolic instance and/or the overcoming of sexual binarism' *Stanford Humanities Review* 6/2 (1998), pp. 103–11, p. 108.
38 Butler, 'Athletic genders', p. 104.
39 Butler, 'Athletic genders', p. 104.
40 Butler, 'Athletic genders', p. 105.
41 Roland Barthes, 'The death of the author' in *Image Music Text*, trans. Stephen Heath (London: Fontana, 1977), pp. 142–8; p. 146.
42 Jacques Derrida, *Of Grammatology*, trans. Gayatri Spivak (Baltimore: Johns Hopkins, 1976), p. 73.
43 Butler, 'Athletic genders', p. 105.

44 Butler, 'Athletic genders', p. 108.
45 Butler, 'Athletic genders', p. 108.
46 Bruno Rigauer, *Sport and Work*, trans. Allen Guttmann (New York: Columbia University Press, 1981), p. 41.
47 See Mandy Merck, *In your Face: 9 Sexual Studies* (New York: New York University Press, 2000), pp. 52–70.
48 Wendy Dozoretz, 'The mother's lost voice in *Hard, Fast and Beautiful*', *Wide Angle* 6/3 (1984), pp. 50–7; p. 54.
49 Merck, *In Your Face*, p. 69. Wendy Dozoretz also points out that Florence's voice is frequently usurped by her mother. See Dozoretz, 'The mother's lost voice in *Hard, Fast and Beautiful*', p. 52.
50 Butler, 'Athletic genders', p. 109.
51 Butler, 'Athletic genders', p. 110.
52 Johnette Howard, *The Rivals*, p. 5.
53 Pat Griffin, *Strong Women, Deep Closets: Lesbians and Homophobia in Sport* (Champaign: Human Kinetics, 1998), 54. For further discussion of media constructions of the two players see Nancy E. Spencer, '"America's sweetheart" and "Czech-Mate": a discursive analysis of the Evert-Navratilova rivalry', *Journal of Sport and Social Issues* 27/1 (2003), pp. 18–37.
54 Cahn, *Coming on Strong*, p. 266.
55 Zwerman, *Martina Navratilova*, p. 15.
56 For a discussion of the feminine apologetic see Lowe, *Women of Steel*, pp. 121–2.
57 Zwerman, *Martina Navratilova*, p. 131. For an analysis of Navratilova's negotiations with her media image through time see Leila Armstrong, 'Mainstreaming Martina: lesbian visibility in the '90s', *Canadian Women's Studies* 16/2 (1996), pp. 10–14.
58 Butler, 'Athletic genders', p. 111.
59 Butler, 'Athletic genders', p. 109.
60 Judith Butler, *Undoing Gender* (New York: Routledge, 2004), p. 27.
61 Halberstam, *Female Masculinity*, p. 15. Louise Allen also draws attention to ways in which Navratilova's body can be read as that of a masculine woman thereby disrupting 'the heterosexual equation of masculinity with men'. Allen, *The Lesbian Idol*, p. 145.
62 Susan Sontag, *Regarding the Pain of Others* (London: Hamish Hamilton, 2003), p. 110.
63 Howard, *The Rivals*, p. 55.
64 Adrian Rifkin, 'Dancing years, or writing as a way out', in Dana Arnold (ed.), *Art History: Contemporary Perspectives on Method* (Oxford: Wiley-Blackwell, 2010), pp. 150–6; pp. 150–64.

65 Maurice Merleau-Ponty, 'Cézanne's doubt', in Galen A. Johnson (ed.), *The Merleau-Ponty Aesthetics Reader: Philosophy and Painting* (Evanston: Northwestern University Press, 1993), p. 67.
66 Jennifer M. Barker, *The Tactile Eye: Touch and the Cinematic Experience* (Berkeley: University of California Press, 2009), p. 73.

Chapter 7 Surfing Aesthetics

1 Tony Butt, Paul Russell and Rick Grigg, *Surf Science: An Introduction to Waves for Surfing* (Honolulu: University of Hawaii Press, 2002), p. 41.
2 The name Johnny Utah connotes Johnny Unitas the legendary American football player popularly known as 'the golden arm' for his throwing skills.
3 Gaston Bachelard, *L'Eau et les Rêves: Essai sur l'imagination de la matière* (Paris: Le Livre de Poche, 2011), p. 133.
4 Bracha Ettinger, *The Matrixial Borderspace* (Minneapolis: University of Minnesota Press, 2006), p. 161.
5 Ettinger, *The Matrixial Borderspace*, p. 52.
6 Ettinger, *The Matrixial Borderspace*, p. 183.
7 Julia Kristeva, *Powers of Horror: An Essay on Abjection* (New York: Columbia University Press, 1982).
8 Judith Butler, 'Disturbance and dispersal in the visual field', in Catherine de Zegher and Griselda Pollock (eds), *Art as Compassion* (Brussels: ASA Publishers, 2011), pp. 149–65; p. 164.
9 Ettinger, *The Matrixial Borderspace*, p. 66.
10 Ibid.
11 Ettinger, *The Matrixial Borderspace*, p. 187.
12 Ettinger, *The Matrixial Borderspace*, pp. 140–1.
13 Griselda Pollock, *Encounters in the Virtual Feminist Museum: Time, Space and the Archive* (London: Routledge, 2007), p. 225.
14 Ettinger, *The Matrixial Borderspace*, pp. 64–5.
15 Ettinger, *The Matrixial Borderspace*, p. 181.
16 Ettinger, *The Matrixial Borderspace*, p. 64.
17 See McCaughey, *Real Knockouts*, pp. 177–211.
18 I am grateful to Griselda Pollock for drawing my attention to the subtle re-inscription of patriarchal values through the voice of Charlie in relation to the first film *Charlie's Angels* (Dir. McG, USA, 2000).
19 The death of Madison is, of course, also the death of any challenge to the heteronormative worldview of the angels. The bad angel has demonstrated lesbian

tendencies. When the extra-textual factor of Demi Moore's age is taken into account, a woman over the age of 30 who has aspired to join the cult of youth could also be seen to be being punished here. She should have stayed retired as physical feminism and Hollywood acting is a young woman's preserve.

20   Jacqueline Rose, 'Sexuality in the field of vision', in *Sexuality in the Field of Vision* (London: Verso, 1986), pp. 224–33; p. 227.
21   Ettinger, *The Matrixial Borderspace*, p. 126.
22   Ettinger, *The Matrixial Borderspace*, p. 65.
23   Ettinger, *The Matrixial Borderspace*, p. 157.
24   Jacques Lacan, *The Ethics of Psychoanalysis, 1959–1960: The Seminar of Jacques Lacan VII*, trans. Dennis Porter (London: Routledge, 1999), p. 55.
25   Lacan, *The Ethics of Psychoanalysis, 1959–1960*, p. 54.
26   Lacan, *The Ethics of Psychoanalysis, 1959–1960*, p. 67; p. 70.
27   Lacan, *The Ethics of Psychoanalysis, 1959–1960*, p. 55.
28   Ettinger, *The Matrixial Borderspace*, p. 158.
29   Ettinger, *The Matrixial Borderspace*, p. 151.
30   Ibid.
31   Ettinger, *The Matrixial Borderspace*, p. 153.
32   Ettinger, *The Matrixial Borderspace*, p. 159.
33   Ibid.
34   Merleau-Ponty, 'Cézanne's doubt', p. 69.
35   Merleau-Ponty, 'Cézanne's doubt,' p. 70.
36   André Leroi-Gourhan, *Gesture and Speech*, trans. Anna Bostock Berger (Cambridge, Mass: MIT Press, 1993) p. 195.
37   Rosi Huhn, 'The folly of reason', in Catherine de Zegher and Griselda Pollock (eds), *Art as Compassion* (Brussels: ASA Publishers, 2011), pp. 43–55; p. 52.
38   Milena Marinkova, *Michael Ondaatje: Haptic Aesthetics and Micropolitical Writing* (New York: Continuum, 2011), p. 9.
39   Ibid.
40   See Laura U. Marks, *The Skin of Film: Intercultural Cinema: Embodiment and the Senses* (Durham: Duke University Press, 1999).
41   Ettinger, *The Matrixial Borderspace*, p. 176.
42   In *Soul Surfer*, Hamilton encounters a child rendered withdrawn and numb after surviving the 2004 Indian Ocean tsunami.
43   Jacques Lacan, *The Four Fundamental Concepts of Psychoanalysis*, trans. Alan Sheridan (London: Penguin, 1991), p. 55.
44   Griselda Pollock, 'Art as transport station of trauma? haunting objects in the works of Bracha Ettinger, Sarah Kofman and Chantal Akerman', in Nicholas Chare

and Dominic Williams (eds), *Representing Auschwitz: At the Margins of Testimony* (Houndmills: Palgrave Macmillan, 2013), pp. 194–221; p. 206.

45 Butler, 'Disturbance and dispersal in the visual field', p. 162.
46 Ibid.
47 Pollock, *Encounters in the Virtual Feminist Museum*, p. 107.
48 Bracha Ettinger, 'The red cow effect: the metramorphosis of hallowing the hollow and hollowing the hallow', in Juliet Steyn (ed.), *Act 2: Beautiful Translations* (London: Pluto Press, 1996), pp. 82–119; p. 88.
49 Ettinger, 'The red cow effect', p. 90.
50 Pollock, 'Art as transport station of trauma?', p. 206.
51 Sean Redmond examines this opposition at length in his insightful essay on masculinity in *Point Break*, 'All that is male melts into air'. See Redmond, 'All that is male melts into air: Bigelow on the edge of *Point Break*', in Deborah Jermyn and Sean Redmond (eds), *The Cinema of Kathryn Bigelow: Hollywood Transgressor* (London: Wallflower Press, 2003), pp. 106–124.
52 Serres, *The Five Senses*, p. 104.
53 The informatics failure of the FBI enables Utah to engage in anachronistic undercover work. He is tasked with generating field data rather than the forensic data privileged by Harp.
54 For a discussion of *Blue Steel* in relation to Ettinger, see my essay 'Encountering *Blue Steel*: changing tempers in cinema', in Griselda Pollock (ed.), *Visual Politics of Psychoanalysis: Art and the Image in Post-Traumatic Cultures* (London: I.B.Tauris, 2013), pp. 190–207.
55 Ettinger, *The Matrixial Borderspace*, p. 182.
56 Maurice Merleau-Ponty, *The Visible and the Invisible* (Evanston: Northwestern University Press, 1968), p. 191.
57 Ettinger, *The Matrixial Borderspace*, p. 182.
58 Ibid.
59 Theweleit, *Male Fantasies*, p. 253.
60 I provide a discussion of comparable phenomena in *Alien* (Dir. Ridley Scott, USA, 1979) in *After Francis Bacon*, pp. 131–76.
61 Griselda Pollock, 'Introduction: femininity: aporia or sexual difference?', in Ettinger, *The Matrixial Borderspace*, pp. 1–38; p. 6.
62 The sequence is actually filmed at a beach in Ecola State Park, Oregon.
63 For an extended discussion of these differing conceptions of justice see Stewart Asquith, 'Justice, retribution, and children', in John Muncie, Gordon Hughes and Eugene McLaughlin (eds), *Youth Justice: Critical Readings* (London: Sage, 2002), pp. 275–83.

64 Drucilla Cornell, *Clint Eastwood and Issues of American Masculinity* (New York: Fordham University Press, 2009), p. 1.

65 Karen E. Tatum, *Explaining the Depiction of Violence Against Women in Victorian Literature* (Lewiston: Edwin Mellen Press, 2005), p. 43.

66 Irigaray, *This Sex Which is Not One*, p. 110.

67 Ettinger, *The Matrixial Borderspace*, p. 160.

68 Christine Buci-Glucksmann, 'Eurydice's becoming-world' in Catherine de Zegher and Griselda Pollock (eds), *Art as Compassion* (Brussels: ASA Publishers, 2011), pp. 69–88; p. 81.

69 Ettinger, *The Matrixial Borderspace*, p. 145.

Chapter 8 Conclusion

1 Shauna Cross, *Derby Girl* (New York: Henry Holt, 2007). The phenomenon is explored at length by Susan Hopkins in *Girl Heroes: The New Force in Popular Culture* (London: Pluto Press, 2002).

2 One member of the Spice Girls was, of course, known as 'Sporty Spice' emphasising the physical dimension to this 'brand' of emancipation.

3 There are now over 1,190 roller derby leagues in existence. See Ellen Parnavelas, *The Roller Derby Athlete* (London: Bloomsbury, 2012), p. 11.

4 Adele Pavlidis has examined how the revival of roller derby in Austin is intimately linked to the strong Riot Grrrl movement there. Bliss's punk credentials are, however, minimal, restricted to dyeing her hair blue early in the film. Her fashion aesthetic aligns her closer to indie. See Pavlidis, 'From Riot Grrrls to roller derby? Exploring the relations between gender, music and punk', *Leisure Studies* 31/2 (2012), pp. 165–76.

5 Jennifer Carlson, 'The female signifiant in all-women's roller derby', *Sociology of Sport Journal* 27/4 (2010), pp. 428–40.

6 Carlson, 'The female signifiant in all-women's roller derby', p. 429.

7 Carlson, 'The female signifiant in all-women's roller derby', pp. 437–8.

8 Nancy J. Finlay, 'Skating femininity: gender maneuvering in women's roller derby', *Journal of Contemporary Ethnography* 39/4 (2010), pp. 359–87.

9 Finlay, 'Skating femininity,' p. 383.

10 Finlay, 'Skating femininity,' p. 372.

11 The name, of course, also connotes Babe Ruth, the legendary baseball outfielder and pitcher for the New York Yankees. Babe Ruth, born in Pigtown in Baltimore, derived his nickname from his rookie status at the Baltimore Orioles. Babe Ruthless is similarly a rookie. Drawing on the moniker of a celebrated baseball player,

however, also draws attention to her being 'less Ruth', unable to be Ruth as women's baseball is viewed as a lesser sport to the men's game. Babe Ruthless cannot excel on the baseball pitch so she must shine on the track in an all-female sport.

12 Bliss's restrained sexual suggestiveness may be an indirect product of the plot. She is masquerading as a 22 year old in order to compete in derby yet is actually 17.
13 Andrea Beckmann, *The Social Construction of Sexuality and Perversion: Deconstructing Sadomasochism* (Houndmills: Palgrave Macmillan, 2009), p. 60.
14 Ibid, pp. 78–9.
15 Newmahr, *Playing on the Edge*, p. 69.
16 A cursory web search of 'sexy' costumes for women revealed that high school schoolgirl, girl-scout, and air hostess are commonplace.
17 One of the Holy Rollers, Iron Maven, reveals she is 36. Bliss, at 17, could act as a Girl Scout Ambassador (16–18 years of age) so is the only member of the Hurl Scouts not acting outside her age.
18 For a discussion of switching see Danielle Lindemann, *Dominatrix: Gender, Eroticism, and Control in the Dungeon* (Chicago: University of Chicago Press, 2012), p. 31.
19 Gloria Anzaldúa draws attention to the bruise as a marker of aggressed femininity in *Borderlands/La Frontera*. Anzaldúa, *Borderlands/La Frontera*, 3rd Edition (San Francisco: Aunt Luke Books, 2007), p. 45.
20 Marcel Swiboda, 'Life and thought in the rushes: mnemotechnics and orthographic temporal objects in the philosophy of Bernard Stiegler', *New Formations* 77 (2012), pp. 111–26; p. 113.
21 Newmahr, *Playing on the Edge*, p. 73.
22 See, for example, Lori Gruen, 'Dismantling oppression: an analysis of the connection between women and animals', in Greta Gaard (ed.) *Ecofeminism: Women, Animals, Nature* (Philadelphia: Temple University Press, 1993), pp. 60–90.
23 Judith Butler, *Bodies that Matter*, p. 30.
24 Rozsika Parker and Griselda Pollock, *Old Mistresses: Women, Art and Ideology* (London: Pandora, 1981), p. 121.
25 R.W. Connell, *Masculinities*, 2nd edition (Cambridge: Polity, 2005), p. 54.
26 These are a regular feature in *Kansas City Bomber*. The film is bookended by five lap catfights between K.C. and derby rivals Big Bertha Bogliani and Jackie Burdette respectively.
27 Jennifer M. Barker, *The Tactile Eye: Touch and the Cinematic Experience* (Berkeley: University of California Press, 2009), p. 110.
28 Barker, *The Tactile Eye*, p. 123.

29 Barker, *The Tactile Eye*, p. 73.
30 Barker, *The Tactile Eye*, p. 75.
31 Freud's emphasis. Sigmund Freud, 'Three essays on the theory of sexuality (1905)' in *The Penguin Freud Library Volume 7: On Sexuality* (London: Penguin, 1991), pp. 33–169; p. 62.
32 In their study of roller derby and body image, Andrea Eklund and Barbara Masberg reveal that players have reported they perceive their bodies as tools of the derby trade rather than as 'an object for display'. See Eklund & Masberg, 'Participation in roller derby, the influence on body image', *Clothing and Textiles Research Journal* 32/1 (2014), pp. 49–64; p. 55.

Bibliography

Adorno, Theodor W., *The Culture Industry: Selected Essays on Mass Culture* (London: Routledge, 1991).

Agamben, Giorgio, *Means without End: Notes on Politics*, trans. Vincenzo Binetti and Cesare Casarino (Minneapolis: University of Minnesota Press, 2000).

Ahmed, Sara, *Queer Phenomenology: Orientations, Objects, Others* (Durham: Duke University Press, 2006).

Allen, Louise, *The Lesbian Idol: Martina, kd and the consumption of lesbian masculinity* (London: Cassell, 1997).

Althusser, Louis, 'Ideology and the ideological state apparatus', in *Lenin and Philosophy and Other Essays* (New York: Monthly Review Press, 2001), pp. 85–126.

Angelo, Adrienne, 'Philosophy in the weight Room: Nathalie Gassel and the crisis of self-representation', *Australian Journal of French Studies* 51/1 (2014), pp. 75–87.

Anzaldúa, Gloria, *Borderlands / La Frontera*, 3rd Edition (San Francisco: Aunt Luke Books, 2007).

Aoki, Douglas Sadao, 'Posing the subject: sex, illumination, and *Pumping Iron II: The Women*', *Cinema Journal* 38/4 (1999), pp. 24–44.

Armstrong, Leila, 'Mainstreaming Martina: lesbian visibility in the '90s', *Canadian Women's Studies* 16/2 (1996), pp. 10–14.

Asquith, Stewart, 'Justice, retribution, and children', in John Muncie, Gordon Hughes and Eugene McLaughlin (eds), *Youth Justice: Critical Readings* (London: Sage, 2002), pp. 275–83.

Austen, Jane, *Northanger Abbey* (Boston: Little, Brown & Co, 1903).

Bachelard, Gaston, *L'Eau et les Rêves: Essai sur l'imagination de la matière* (Paris: Le Livre de Poche, 2011).

Baetens, Jan, 'Nathalie Gassel: le corps et la pensée, le muscle et l 'écriture', *L'Esprit Créateur* 44/3 (2004), pp. 5–12.

Báez, Jillian M. 'Towards a *Latinidad Feminista*: the multiplicities of latinidad and feminism in contemporary cinema', *Popular Communication* 5/2 (2007), pp. 109–28.

Bainbridge, Caroline, 'Feminine enunciation in women's cinema', *Paragraph* 25/3 (2002), pp. 129–41.

―――― *A Feminine Cinematics: Luce Irigaray, Women and Film* (New York: Palgrave, 2008).

Baker, Aaron, *Contesting Identities: Sports in American Film* (Urbana: University of Illinois Press, 2006).

Baker, Aaron and Todd Edward Boyd (eds), *Out of Bounds: Sports, Media and the Politics of Identity* (Bloomington: Indiana University Press, 1997).

Barker, Jennifer M., *The Tactile Eye: Touch and the Cinematic Experience* (Berkeley: University of California Press, 2009).

Barthes, Roland, 'The death of the author', in *Image Music Text*, trans. Stephen Heath (London: Fontana, 1977), pp. 142–8.

Beckmann, Andrea, *The Social Construction of Sexuality and Perversion: Deconstructing Sadomasochism* (Houndmills: Palgrave Macmillan, 2009).

Bolton, Lucy, *Film and Female Consciousness: Irigaray, Cinema and Thinking Women* (New York: Palgrave, 2011).

Braddock, Sarah E., 'High-performance fabrics', in Maria O' Mahony and Sarah E. Braddock (eds), *Sportstech: Revolutionary Fabrics, Fashion, and Design* (London: Thames & Hudson, 2002), pp. 38–84.

Brady, Jacqueline E., 'Pumping iron with resistance: Carla Dunlap's victorious body', in Michael Bennett and Vanessa D. Dickerson (eds), *Recovering the Female Body: Self-Representations by African American Women* (New Brunswick: Rutgers University Press, 2001), pp. 253–78.

Bridges, Michelle, *Crunch Time: Lose Weight Fast and Keep it Off* (Camberwell: Viking, 2009).

Briley, Ron and Michael K. Schoenecke and Deborah A. Carmichael (eds), *All-Stars and Movie Stars: Sports in Film and History* (Lexington: University Press of Kentucky, 2008).

Brownmiller, Susan, *Femininity* (New York: Simon & Schuster, 1984).

Buci-Glucksmann, Christine, 'Eurydice's becoming-world', in Catherine de Zegher and Griselda Pollock (eds), *Art as Compassion* (Brussels: ASA Publishers, 2011), pp. 69–88.

Bunsell, Tanya, *Strong and Hard Women: An Ethnography of Female Bodybuilding* (London: Routledge, 2013).

Butler, Judith, *Bodies that Matter: On the Discursive Limits of 'Sex'* (New York: Routledge, 1993).

_____ 'Athletic genders: hyperbolic instance and/or the overcoming of sexual binarism', *Stanford Humanities Review* 6/2 (1998), pp. 103–11.

_____ 'Disturbance and dispersal in the visual field', in Catherine de Zegher and Griselda Pollock (eds), *Art as Compassion* (Brussels: ASA Publishers, 2011), pp. 149–65.

Butt, Tony, and Paul Russell and Rick Grigg, *Surf Science: An Introduction to Waves for Surfing* (Honolulu: University of Hawaii Press, 2002).

Cahn, Susan K., *Coming on Strong: Gender and Sexuality in Twentieth-Century Women's Sport* (Cambridge, Mass: Harvard University Press, 1995).

Campbell, Amy, 'Women, sport, and film class', *Women's Studies Quarterly* 33:1/2 (2005), pp. 210–23.

Carlson, Jennifer, 'The female signifiant in all-women's roller derby', *Sociology of Sport Journal* 27/4 (2010), pp. 428–40.

Caudwell, Jayne, '*Girlfight*: boxing women', *Sport in Society* 11:2/3 (2008), pp. 227–39.

_____ '*Girlfight* and *Bend it Like Beckham*: screening women, sport, and sexuality', *Journal of Lesbian Studies* 13/3 (2009), pp. 255–71.

_____ '[Transgender] Young men: gendered subjectivities and the physically active body', *Sport, Education and Society*, iFirst (2012), pp. 1–17.

Chare, Nicholas, 'Sexing the canvas; calling on the medium', *Art History* 32/4 (2009), pp. 664–89.

_____ *Auschwitz and Afterimages: Abjection, Witnessing and Representation* (London: I.B.Tauris, 2011).

_____ 'Writing perceptions: the matter of words and the Rollright Stones', *Art History* 34/2 (2011), pp. 244–67.

_____ *After Francis Bacon: Synaesthesia and Sex in Paint* (Farnham: Ashgate, 2012).

_____ 'Getting hard: female bodybuilders and muscle worship', in Adam Locks and Niall Richardson (eds), *Critical Readings in Bodybuilding* (New York: Routledge, 2012), pp. 199–214.

_____ 'Encountering *Blue Steel*: changing tempers in cinema', in Griselda Pollock (ed.), *Visual Politics of Psychoanalysis: Art and the Image in Post-Traumatic Cultures* (London: I.B.Tauris, 2013), pp. 190–207.

_____ 'Handling pressures: analysing touch in American films about youth sport', *Sport, Education and Society* 18/5 (2013), pp. 663–77.

_____ 'Literary Veins: Women's bodybuilding, muscle worship and abject performance', *Performance Research* 19/1 (2014), pp. 91–101.

Chisholm, Dianne, 'Climbing like a girl: an exemplary adventure in feminist phenomenology', *Hypatia* 23/1 (2008), pp. 9–40.

Chu, Yingchi, *Chinese Documentaries: From Dogma to Polyphony* (Abingdon: Routledge, 2007).

Clark, T.J. *Image of the People: Gustave Courbet and the 1848 Revolution* (Berkeley: University of California Press, 1973).

Cohen, Leah Hager, *Without Apology: Girls, Women and the Desire to Fight* (London: Weidenfeld & Nicolson, 2005).

Coleman, Felicity, *Deleuze and Cinema* (Oxford: Berg, 2011).

Connell, R.W., *Masculinities*, 2nd edition (Cambridge: Polity, 2005).

Connor, Steven, 'Michel Serres's *Les Cinq Sens*', in Niran Abbas (ed.), *Mapping Michel Serres* (Ann Arbor: University of Michigan Press, 2005), pp. 153–69.

―――― *A Philosophy of Sport* (London: Reaktion, 2011).

Constable, Catherine, *Thinking in Images: Film Theory, Feminist Philosophy and Marlene Dietrich* (London: BFI, 2005).

Cornell, Drucilla, *Clint Eastwood and Issues of American Masculinity* (New York: Fordham University Press, 2009).

Cross, Shauna, *Derby Girl* (New York: Henry Holt, 2007).

Crosson, Seán, *Sport and Film* (London: Routledge, 2013).

Daddario, Gina, *Women's Sport and Spectacle: Gendered Television Coverage and the Olympic Games* (Westport: Praeger, 1998).

Daniels, Dayna B., 'You throw like a girl: sport and misogyny on the silver screen', *Film & History* 35/1 (2005), pp. 29–38.

David, Wendy S., and Tracy L. Simpson & Ann J. Cotton, 'Taking charge: a pilot curriculum of self-defence and personal safety training for female veterans with PTSD because of military sexual trauma', *Journal of Interpersonal Violence* 21/4 (2006), pp. 555–65.

De Lauretis, Teresa, *Alice Doesn't: Feminism, Semiotics, Cinema* (Bloomington: Indiana University Press, 1984).

Derrida, Jacques, *Of Grammatology*, trans. Gayatri Spivak (Baltimore: Johns Hopkins, 1976).

Dillon, M. C., *Merleau-Ponty's Ontology*, 2nd Edition (Evanston: Northwestern University Press, 1998).

Doane, Mary Ann, *The Desire to Desire: The Woman's Film of the 1940s* (Bloomington: Indiana University Press, 1987).

―――― 'The close-up: scale and detail in cinema', *Differences: A Journal of Feminist Cultural Studies* 14/3 (2003), pp. 89–111.

Dowling, Colette, *The Frailty Myth: Redefining the Physical Potential of Women and Girls* (New York: Random House, 2001).

Dozoretz, Wendy, 'The mother's lost voice in *Hard, Fast and Beautiful*', *Wide Angle* 6/3 (1984), pp. 50–7.

Duff, R.W., and L.K. Hong, 'Self-images of women bodybuilders', *Sociology of Sport Journal* 1/4 (1984), pp. 374–80.

Efron, David, *Gesture, Race and Culture* (Paris: Mouton, 1972).

Eklund, Andrea, and Barbara Masberg, 'Participation in roller derby, the influence on body image,' *Clothing and Textiles Research Journal* 32/1 (2014), pp. 49–64.

Elsaesser, Thomas, 'Leni Riefenstahl: the body beautiful, art cinema and fascist aesthetics', in Pam Cook and Philip Dodd (eds), *Women and Film: A Sight and Sound Reader* (Philadelphia: Temple University Press, 1993), pp. 186–97.

Ettinger, Bracha, 'The red cow effect: the metamorphosis of hallowing the hollow and hollowing the hallow', in Juliet Steyn (ed.), *Act 2: Beautiful Translations* (London: Pluto Press, 1996), pp. 82–119.

—— *The Matrixial Borderspace* (Minneapolis: University of Minnesota Press, 2006).

Field, Tiffany, *Touch* (Cambridge, Mass: MIT Press, 2001).

Finlay, Nancy J., 'Skating femininity: gender maneuvering in women's roller derby', *Journal of Contemporary Ethnography* 39/4 (2010), pp. 359–87.

Forster, E.M., *Aspects of the Novel* (London: Edward Arnold, 1974).

Foucault, Michel, *Discipline and Punish: The Birth of the Prison*, trans. Alan Sheridan (London: Penguin, 1991).

—— 'Fetishism', in *The Penguin Freud Library Volume 7: On Sexuality* (London: Penguin, 1991), pp. 351–357.

Freud, Sigmund, 'Three essays on the theory of sexuality (1905)', in *The Penguin Freud Library Volume 7: On Sexuality* (London: Penguin, 1991), pp. 33–169.

—— 'Beyond the pleasure principle', in *The Penguin Freud Library Volume 11: On Metapsychology* (London: Penguin, 1991), pp. 275–338.

Frueh, Joanna, *Monster Beauty: Building the Body of Love* (Berkeley: University of California Press, 2001).

Galt, Rosalind, *Pretty: Film and the Decorative Image* (New York: Columbia University Press, 2011).

Gassel, Nathalie, *Éros androgyne* (Paris: L'Acanthe, 2000).

—— '*My Muscles, Myself: Selected Autobiographical Writings*', in Joanna Frueh, Laurie Fierstein and Judith Stein (eds), *Picturing the Modern Amazon* (New York: Rizzoli, 2000), pp. 117–19.

—— *Musculatures* (Paris: Le Cercle, 2001).

—— *Construction d'un corps pornographique* (Bruxelles: Éditions cercle d'art, 2005).

Golding, Sue, *Gramsci's Democratic Theory: Contributions to a Post-Liberal Democracy* (Toronto: University of Toronto Press, 1992).

Graham, Cooper C., '*Olympia* in America, 1938: Leni Riefenstahl, Hollywood, and the Kristallnacht', *Historical Journal of Film, Radio and Television* 13/4 (1993), pp. 433–50.

Griffin, Pat, *Strong Women, Deep Closets: Lesbians and Homophobia in Sport* (Champaign: Human Kinetics, 1998).

Grimby, Gunnar, and Bengt Saltin, 'The ageing muscle', *Clinical Physiology* 3/3 (1983), pp. 209–18.

Grosz, Elizabeth, *Volatile Bodies: Towards a Corporeal Feminism* (Bloomington: Indiana University Press, 1994).

Gruen, Lori, 'Dismantling oppression: an analysis of the connection between women and animals', in Greta Gaard (ed.), *Ecofeminism: Women, Animals, Nature* (Philadelphia: Temple University Press, 1993), pp. 60–90.

Guttmann, Allen, *The Erotic in Sports* (New York: Columbia University Press, 1996).

Hakim, Catherine, *Honey Money: The Power of Erotic Capital* (London: Allen Lane, 2011).

Halberstam, Judith, *Female Masculinity* (Durham: Duke University Press, 1998).

––––––– *In a Queer Time and Place: Transgender Bodies, Subcultural Lives* (New York: New York University Press, 2005).

Henley, Nancy, 'Status and sex: some touching observations', *Bulletin of the Psychonomic Society* 2 (1972), pp. 91–3.

Heywood, Ian, 'Climbing monsters: excess and restraint in contemporary rock climbing', *Leisure Studies* 24/4 (2006), pp. 455–67.

Heywood, Leslie, and Shari L. Dworkin, *Built to Win: the Female Athlete as Cultural Icon* (Minneapolis: University of Minnesota Press, 1993).

Hill, Lynn, *Climbing Free: My Life in the Vertical World* (London: Harper Collins, 2002).

Holmlund, Chris, *Impossible Bodies: Femininity and Masculinity at the Movies* (London: Routledge, 2002).

hooks, bell, 'The feminazi mystique', *Transition* 73 (1997), pp. 156–62.

Hopkins, Susan, *Girl Heroes: The New Force in Popular Culture* (London: Pluto Press, 2002).

Howard, Johnette, *The Rivals: Chris Evert versus Martina Navratilova* (London: Yellow Jersey Press, 2005).

Huhn, Rosi, 'The folly of reason', in Catherine de Zegher and Griselda Pollock (eds), *Art as Compassion* (Brussels: ASA Publishers, 2011), pp. 43–55.

Ian, Marcia, 'The primitive subject of female bodybuilding: transgression and other postmodern myths', *Differences* 12/3 (2001), pp. 69–100.

Ihde, Don, *Listening and Voice; Phenomenologies of Sound*, 2nd Edition (New York: State University of New York Press, 2007).

Ingle, Zachary and David M. Sutera (eds), *Gender and Genre in Sports Documentaries: Critical Essays* (Lanham: Scarecrow Press, 2012).

Irigaray, Luce, *This Sex Which is Not One*, trans. Catherine Porter (Ithaca: Cornell University Press, 1985).

—— 'The gesture in psychoanalysis', trans. Elizabeth Guild, in Teresa Brennan (ed.), *Between Feminism and Psychoanalysis* (London: Routledge, 1989), pp. 127–38.

Jeffreys, Sheila, 'Transgender activism', *Journal of Lesbian Studies* 1:3–4 (1997), 55–74.

—— *Gender Hurts: A Feminist Analysis of the Politics of Transgenderism* (London: Routledge, 2014).

Kaplan, E. Ann, 'Trauma and aging: Marlene Dietrich, Melanie Klein, and Marguerite Duras', in Kathleen Woodward (ed.), *Figuring Age: Women, Bodies, Generations* (Bloomington: Indiana University Press, 1999), pp. 171–94.

Karpf, Anne, *The Human Voice: How This Extraordinary Instrument Reveals Essential Clues About Who We Are* (New York: Bloomsbury, 2006).

Kendon, Adam, *Gesture: Visible Action as Utterance* (Cambridge: Cambridge University Press, 2004).

King, C. Richard and David J. Leonard, (eds), *Visual Economies of/in Motion: Sport and Film* (Frankfurt: Peter Lang, 2006).

Kraus, M. W., and C. Huang and D. Keltner, 'Tactile communication, cooperation, and performance: an ethological study of the NBA', *Emotion* 10/5 (2010), pp. 745–9.

Kristeva, Julia, *Powers of Horror: An Essay on Abjection* (New York: Columbia University Press, 1982).

Lacan, Jacques, *The Four Fundamental Concepts of Psychoanalysis*, trans. Alan Sheridan (London: Penguin, 1991).

—— *The Ethics of Psychoanalysis, 1959–1960: The Seminar of Jacques Lacan VII*, trans. Dennis Porter (London: Routledge, 1999).

Lavin, Maud, *Push Comes to Shove: New Images of Aggressive Women* (Cambridge, MA: MIT Press, 2010).

Lebrun, Constance, 'Effect of the different phases of the menstrual cycle and oral contraceptives on athletic performance', *Sports Medicine* 16/6 (1993), pp. 400–30.

Leroi-Gourhan, André, *Gesture and Speech*, trans. Anna Bostock Berger (Cambridge, Mass: MIT Press, 1993).

Lewis, Cynthia, 'Sporting Adam's rib: the culture of women bodybuilders in America', *The Massachusetts Review* 45/4 (2004/2005), pp. 604–31.

Lindemann, Danielle, *Dominatrix: Gender, Eroticism, and Control in the Dungeon* (Chicago: University of Chicago Press, 2012).

Lindner, Katharina, 'Fighting for subjectivity: articulations of physicality in *Girlfight*', *Journal of International Women's Studies* 10/3 (2009), pp. 4–17.

—— 'Bodies in action: female athleticism on the cinema screen', *Feminist Media Studies* 11/3 (2011), pp. 321–45.

Lingis, Alphonso, *Foreign Bodies* (New York: Routledge, 1994).

Livesey, Peter, 'I feel rock', in Ken Wilson (ed.), *The Games Climbers Play* (London: Diadem, 1978), pp. 74–82.

Lowe, Maria R., *Women of Steel: Female Bodybuilders and the Struggle for Self-Definition* (New York: New York University Press, 1998).

MacDonald, Shelley G., *Observations on Boxing: A Psychoanalytic Study* (Dagenham: University of East London Press, 2000).

Mackenzie, Michael, 'From Athens to Berlin: The 1936 Olympics and Leni Riefenstahl's *Olympia*', *Critical Inquiry* 29/2 (2003), pp. 302–36.

Major, B. and A. M. Schmidlin and L. Williams, 'Gender patterns in social touch: the impact of setting and age', *Journal of Personality and Social Psychology* 58/4 (1990), pp. 634–43.

Manning, Erin, *Politics of Touch: Sense, Movement, Sovereignty* (Minneapolis: University of Minnesota Press, 2007).

Mansfield, Alan, and Barbara McGinn, 'Pumping irony: the muscular and the feminine', in Sue Scott and David Morgan (eds), *Body Matters* (London: Falmer Press, 1993), pp. 49–68.

Marinkova, Milena, *Michael Ondaatje: Haptic Aesthetics and Micropolitical Writing* (New York: Continuum, 2011).

Marks, Laura U., *The Skin of Film: Intercultural Cinema: Embodiment and the Senses* (Durham: Duke University Press, 1999).

Márquez, María Teresa, 'No longer counted out: fighting isn't what it used to be', in Delilah Montoya (ed.), *Women Boxers: the New Warriors* (Houston: Arte Público Press, 2006), pp. 9–17.

McCaughey, Martha, *Real Knockouts: the Physical Feminism of Women's Self-Defense* (New York: New York University Press, 1997).

McKenzie, Joy, *The Best in Sportswear Design* (London: Batsford, 1997).

Melloni, B. John, *Melloni's Illustrated Dictionary of the Musculoskeletal System* (New York: Parthenon, 1988).

Merck, Mandy, *In your Face: 9 Sexual Studies* (New York: New York University Press, 2000).

Merleau-Ponty, Maurice, *The Visible and the Invisible*, trans. Alphonso Lingis (Evanston: Northwestern University Press, 1968).

_____ 'Cézanne's doubt', in Galen A. Johnson (ed.), *The Merleau-Ponty Aesthetics Reader: Philosophy and Painting* (Evanston: Northwestern University Press, 1993), pp. 59–75.

Merz, Mischa, *Bruising: A Journey Through Gender* (Sydney: Picador, 2000).

Miller, Toby, *Sportsex* (Philadelphia: Temple University Press, 2001).

Morgan, Kevin, et al., 'Customary physical activity, psychological well-being and successful ageing', *Ageing and Society* 11 (1991), pp. 399–415.

Mowitt, John, *Percussion: Drumming, Beating, Striking* (Durham: Duke University Press, 2002).

Mulvey, Laura, 'Visual pleasure and narrative cinema', in *Visual and Other Pleasures* (Basingstoke: Macmillan, 1989), pp. 14–26.

_____ *Fetishism and Curiosity* (Bloomington: Indiana University Press, 1996).

Navratilova, Martina, *Tennis My Way* (New York: Charles Scribner's Sons, 1983).

_____ *Being Myself* (London: Collins, 1985).

_____ *Shape your Self: An Inspirational Guide to Achieving your Personal Best* (London: Time Warner, 2006).

Nead, Lynda, 'Stilling the punch: boxing, violence and the photographic image', *Journal of Visual Culture* 10/3 (2011), pp. 305–23.

Ness, Sally Anne, 'Bouldering in Yosemite: emergent signs of place and landscape', *American Anthropologist* 113/1 (2011), pp. 71–87.

Newmahr, Staci, *Playing on the Edge: Sadomasochism, Risk, and Intimacy* (Bloomington: Indiana University Press, 2011).

Noble, Chris, *Women Who Dare: North America's Inspiring Women Climbers* (Guildford: Falcon Guides, 2013).

O' Connor, Kaori, *Lycra: How a Fiber Shaped America* (New York: Routledge, 2011).

Parker, Rozsika, and Griselda Pollock, *Old Mistresses: Women, Art and Ideology* (London: Pandora, 1981).

Parnavelas, Ellen, *The Roller Derby Athlete* (London: Bloomsbury, 2012).

Patton, Cindy, 'Hegemony and orgasm – or the instability of heterosexual pornography', *Screen* 30:1/2 (1989), pp. 100–13.

_____ 'Rock hard: judging the female physique', *Sport and Social Issues* 25/2 (2001), pp. 118–40.

Pavlidis, Adele, 'From Riot Grrrls to roller derby? exploring the relations between gender, music and punk', *Leisure Studies* 31/2 (2012), pp. 165–76.

Pavlidis, Adele and Simone Fullagar, 'Narrating the multiplicity of "Derby Grrrl": exploring intersectionality and the dynamics of affect in roller derby', *Leisure Sciences* 35 (2013): 422–37.

Peucker, Brigitte, 'The fascist choreography: Riefenstahl's tableaux', *Modernism/Modernity* 11/2 (2004), pp. 279–97.

Piper, Heather, and Ian Stronach, *Don't Touch: The Educational Story of a Panic* (London: Routledge, 2008).

Pisters, Patricia, *The Matrix of Visual Culture: Working with Deleuze in Film Theory* (Stanford: Stanford University Press, 2003).

Pollock, Griselda, *Vision and Difference: Femininity, Feminism and the Histories of Art* (London: Routledge, 1988).

_____ 'Killing men and dying women: a woman's touch in the cold zone of American painting in the 1950s', in Fred Orton and Griselda Pollock, *Avant-Gardes and Partisans Reviewed* (Manchester: Manchester University Press, 1996), pp. 219–94.

_____ 'A very long engagement: singularity and difference in the critical writing of Eva Hesse', in Griselda Pollock and Vanessa Corby (eds), *Encountering Eva Hesse* (Munich: Prestel, 2006), pp. 23–55.

_____ *Encounters in the Virtual Feminist Museum* (London: Routledge, 2007).

_____ 'A matrixial installation: artworking in the freudian space of memory and migration', in Catherine de Zegher and Griselda Pollock (eds), *Art as Compassion* (Brussels: ASA Publishers, 2011), pp. 191–241.

_____ 'Art as transport station of trauma? haunting objects in the works of Bracha Ettinger, Sarah Kofman and Chantal Akerman', in Nicholas Chare and Dominic Williams (eds), *Representing Auschwitz: At the Margins of Testimony* (Houndmills: Palgrave Macmillan, 2013), pp. 194–221.

Poulton, Emma and Martin Roderick (eds), *Sport in Films* (Abingdon: Routledge, 2008).

Raymond, Janice, *Transsexual Empire* (London: The Women's Press, 1980).

Redmond, Sean, 'All that is male melts into air: Bigelow on the edge of *Point Break*', in Deborah Jermyn and Sean Redmond (eds), *The Cinema of Kathryn Bigelow: Hollywood Transgressor* (London: Wallflower Press, 2003), pp. 106–24.

Rhoads, Bonita, 'Sontag's captions: writing the body from Riefenstahl to S&M', *Women's Studies: An Interdisciplinary Journal* 37/8 (2008), pp. 942–70.

Riefenstahl, Leni, *The Last of the Nuba* (London: Collins, 1976).

_____ *The People of Kau* (London: Collins, 1976).

Rifkin, Adrian, 'Dancing years, or writing as a way out', in Dana Arnold (ed.), *Art History: Contemporary Perspectives on Method* (Oxford: Wiley-Blackwell, 2010), pp. 150–64.

Rigauer, Bruno, *Sport and Work*, trans. Allen Guttmann (New York: Columbia University Press, 1981).

Robinson, Victoria, *Everyday Masculinities and Extreme Sport: Male Identity and Rock Climbing* (Oxford: Berg, 2008).

Robson, Jocelyn, and Beverly Zalcock, 'Looking at *Pumping Iron II: The Women*', in Tamsin Wilton (ed.), *Immortal Invisible: Lesbians and the Moving Image* (London: Routledge, 1995), pp. 182–92.

Rodríguez, María Graciela, 'Behind Leni's outlook: a perspective on the film *Olympia*', *International Review for the Sociology of Sport* 38/1 (2003), pp. 109–16.

Rose, Jacqueline, 'Sexuality in the field of vision', in *Sexuality in the Field of Vision* (London: Verso, 1986), pp. 224–33.

Rotella, Carlo, *Good With their Hands: Boxers, Bluesmen, and Other Characters from the Rust Belt* (Berkeley: University of California Press, 2002).

Rowe, David, 'If you film it, will they come?: sports on film', *Journal of Sport and Social Issues* 22/4 (1998), pp. 350–9.

Rubin, Patricia, 'Art history from the bottom up', *Art History* 36/2 (2013), pp. 280–309.

Salcedo, Juan Jiménez, 'Nathalie Gassel y la escritura andrógina', *Asparkía* 19 (2008), pp. 89–103.

Salomon, Gayle, *Assuming a Body: Transgender and Rhetorics of Materiality* (New York: Columbia University Press, 2010).

Scarry, Elaine, *The Body in Pain: The Making and Unmaking of the World* (Oxford: Oxford University Press, 1985).

Schippert, Claudia, 'Can muscles be queer? reconsidering the transgressive hyper-built body', *Journal of Gender Studies* 16/2 (2007), pp. 155–71.

Schneider, Rebecca, *Performing Remains: Art and War in Times of Theatrical Reenactment* (Abingdon: Routledge, 2011).

Schwenger, Peter, *Fantasm and Fiction: On Textual Envisioning* (Stanford: Stanford University Press, 1999).

Scott, David, *The Art and Aesthetics of Boxing* (Lincoln: University of Nebraska Press, 2008).

Sedgwick, Eve Kosofsky, 'Gosh Boy George, you must be awfully secure in your masculinity', in Maurice Berger, Brian Wallis and Simon Watson (eds), *Constructing Masculinity* (New York: Routledge, 1995), pp. 11–20.

Serres, Michel, *Conversations on Science, Culture and Time: Michel Serres with Bruno Latour*, trans. Roxanne Lapidus, (Ann Arbor: University of Michigan Press, 1995).

―――― *The Natural Contract* (Ann Arbor: University of Michigan Press, 1995).

―――― *The Five Senses: A Philosophy of Mingled Bodies*, trans. Margaret Sankey and Peter Cowley (London: Continuum, 2008).

Sobchack, Vivian, *The Address of the Eye: A Phenomenology of Film Experience* (Princeton: Princeton University Press, 1992).

Sontag, Susan, *Regarding the Pain of Others* (London: Hamish Hamilton, 2003).

―――― 'Fascinating fascism', in *Under the Sign of Saturn* (London: Penguin, 2009), pp. 73–105.

Spencer, Nancy E., '"America's Sweetheart" and "Czech-Mate": a discursive analysis of the Evert-Navratilova rivalry', *Journal of Sport and Social Issues* 27/1 (2003), pp. 18–37.

Steinem, Gloria, 'Introduction', in Amy Handy and Steven Korté (eds), *Wonder Woman* (New York: Abbeville Press, 1995), pp. 5–19.

Swiboda, Marcel, 'Life and thought in the rushes: mnemotechnics and orthographic temporal objects in the philosophy of Bernard Stiegler', *New Formations* 77 (2012), pp. 111–26.

Tasker, Yvonne, *Spectacular Bodies: Gender, Genre and Action Cinema* (London: Routledge, 1993).

Tatum, Karen E., *Explaining the Depiction of Violence Against Women in Victorian Literature* (Lewiston: Edwin Mellen Press, 2005).

Taylor, Lawrence and Steven Oberman, *Drunk Driving Defense*, 6th Edition (New York: Aspen Publishers, 2006).

Tegel, Susan, 'Leni Riefenstahl: art and politics', *Quarterly Review of Film and Video* 23/3 (2006), pp. 185–200.

Theweleit, Klaus, *Male Fantasies Volume 1: Women, Floods, Bodies, History*, trans. Stephen Conway (Cambridge: Polity, 1987).

Tudor, Deborah, *Hollywood's Vision of Team Sports: Heroes, Race, and Gender* (New York: Garland Publishing, 1997).

Ullman, Sarah E., 'Social reactions, coping strategies, and self-blame attributions in adjustment to sexual assault', *Psychology of Women Quarterly* 20 (1996), pp. 505–26.

Vickerman, Katrina, and Gayla Margolin, 'Rape treatment outcome research: empirical findings and the state of the literature', *Clinical Psychology Review* 29/5 (2009), pp. 431–48.

Watkins, Elizabeth, *Film Theories and Philosophies of Colour: The Residual Image* (London: Routledge, 2015), in press.

Watkins, Liz, 'Light, colour and sound in cinema', *Paragraph* 25/3 (2002), pp. 118–28.

───── 'The (dis)articulation of colour: cinematography, femininity and desire in Jane Campion's *In the Cut*', in Wendy Everett (ed.), *Questions of Colour in Cinema: From Paintbrush to Pixel* (Oxford: Peter Lang, 2007), pp. 197–216.

Woolf, Virginia, *A Room of One's Own & Three Guineas* (London: Penguin, 1993).

Young, Alison, *The Scene of Violence: Cinema, Crime, Affect* (Abingdon: Routledge, 2010).

Young, Iris Marion, 'Throwing like a girl', in *On Female Body Experience* (Oxford: Oxford University Press, 2005), pp. 27–45.

Zwerman, Gilda, *Martina Navratilova* (New York: Chelsea House, 1995).

Filmography

50 Year Old Freshman (Dir. Deborah J. McDonald, USA, 2012)
2001: A Space Odyssey (Dir. Stanley Kubrick, USA, 1968)
Against the Ropes (Dir. Charles S Dutton, USA, 2004)
Alien (Dir. Ridley Scott, USA, 1979)
Apflickorna (Dir. Lisa Aschan, Sweden, 2011)
Au-delà des cimes (Dir. Rémy Tezier, France, 2008)
Beautiful Wave (Dir. David Mueller, USA, 2010)
Bend it Like Beckham (Dir. Gurinder Chadha, UK, 2002)
Big Blue, The (Dir. Luc Besson, France, 1988)
Big Wednesday (Dir. John Milius, USA, 1978)
Blades of Glory (Dirs. Will Speck & Josh Gordon, USA, 2007)
Blue Crush (Dir. John Stockwell, USA, 2002)
Blue Steel (Dir. Kathryn Bigelow, USA, 1989)
Boys Don't Cry (Dir. Kimberly Peirce, USA, 1999)
Bring it On (Dirs. Peyton Reed & Jim Rowley, USA, 2000)
Brutal Beauty: Tales of the Rose City Rollers (Dir. Chip Mabry, USA, 2010)
Chak De! India (Dir. Shimit Amin, India, 2007)
Champion Bodybuilder Valentina Chepiga: Still Climbing the Hill Over-40, Not Over It (Dir, Elliott Haimoff, USA, 2010)
Charlie's Angels (Dir. McG, USA, 2000)
Charlie's Angels 2: Full Throttle (Dir. McG, USA, 2003)
Cliffhanger (Dir. Renny Harlin, USA, 1993)
Crocodile Dundee (Dir. Peter Faiman, Australia, 1986)
Cruising (Dir. William Friedkin, USA, 1980)
Crying Game, The (Dir. Neil Jordan, UK, 1992)

Dirty Harry (Dir. Don Siegel, USA, 1971)
Fast Girls (Dir. Regan Hall, UK, 2012)
Flying (Dir. Paul Lynch, Canada, 1986)
Forever the Moment (Dir. Im Soon-rye, South Korea, 2008)
Four Weddings and a Funeral (Dir. Mike Newell, UK, 1994)
Girlfight (Dir. Karyn Kusama, USA, 2000)
Great Land Reform, The (China, 1953)
Gymnast, The (Dir. Ned Farr, USA, 2006)
Hard, Fast and Beautiful (Dir. Ida Lupino, USA, 1951)
Hard Grit (Dir. Richard Heap, UK, 1998)
Heart of the Game, The (Dir. Ward Serrill, USA, 2005)
Her Best Move (Dir. Norm Hunter, USA, 2009)
Highway Amazon (Dir. Ronnie Cramer, USA, 2001)
Hoosiers (Dir. David Anspaugh, USA, 1986)
In the Cut (Dir. Jane Campion, USA, 2003)
Internal Affairs (Dir Mike Figgis, USA, 1990)
Kansas City Bomber (Dir. Jerrold Freeman, USA, 1972)
Knockout (Dir. Lorenzo Doumani, USA 2003)
League of Their Own, A (Dir. Penny Marshall, USA, 1992)
Love and Basketball (Dir. Gina Prince-Bythewood, USA, 2000)
Million Dollar Baby (Dir. Clint Eastwood, USA, 2004)
Near Dark (Dir. Kathryn Bigelow, USA, 1987)
Olympia (Dir. Leni Riefenstahl, Germany, 1938)
Opponent, The (Dir. Eugene Jarecki, USA, 2000)
Pat and Mike (Dir. George Cukor, USA, 1952)
Perfect (Dir. James Bridges, USA, 1985)
Personal Best (Dir. Robert Towne, USA, 1982)
Piano, The (Dir. Jane Campion, New Zealand, 1993)
Point Break (Dir. Kathryn Bigelow, USA, 1991)
Predator 2 (Dir. Stephen Hopkins, USA, 1990)
Puberty Blues (Dir. Bruce Beresford, Australia, 1981)
Pumping Irene (Dir. C.C. Williams, USA, 1986)
Pumping Iron (Dirs. Robert Fiore and George Butler, USA, 1977)
Pumping Iron II: The Women (Dir. George Butler, USA, 1985)
Punch (Dir. Guy Bennett, Canada, 2003)
Quarterback Princess (Dir. Noel Black, USA, 1983)
Racing Against the Clock (Dir. Bill Haney, USA, 2004)
Renée (Dir. Eric Drath, USA, 2011)

Second Serve (Dir. Anthony Page, USA, 1986)
She's the Man (Dir. Andy Fickman, USA, 2006)
Sieg des Glaubens (Dir. Leni Riefenstahl, Germany, 1933)
Snowman's Pass (Dir. Rex Piano, Canada, 2004)
Soul Surfer (Dir. Sean McNamara, USA, 2011)
State of Mind, A (Dir. Daniel Gordon, UK, 2005)
Stick It (Dir. Jessica Bendinger, USA, 2006)
Swimsuit Issue, The (Dir. Måns Herngren, Sweden, 2008)
Talk to Her (Dir. Pedro Almodóvar, Spain, 2002)
Tightrope (Dir. Clint Eastwood, USA, 1984)
Triumph des Willens (Dir. Leni Riefenstahl, Germany, 1934)
Vertical Limit (Dir. Martin Campbell, USA, 2000)
When Billie Beat Bobby (Dir. Jane Anderson, USA, 2001)
Whip It (Dir. Drew Barrymore, USA, 2009)
Wimbledon (Dir. Richard Loncraine, UK, 2004)
Winning Season, The (Dir. James C. Strouse, USA, 2009)
Winning Team, The (Dir. Lewis Seiler, USA, 1952)
Woman Basketball Player No. 5 (Dir. Xie Jin, China, 1957)

Index

References in italics refer to illustrations

abject, 144, 159, 180
abjection, 180
Acker, Kathy, 116
acoustics, 4, 10, 38, 43, 51, 53–4, 82, 83, 127, 145, 147, 162, 165, 177, 180
Adorno, Theodor W, 8–9, 86–7
aesthetic, 7–8, 26–8, 29, 34, 36, 38, 65, 73–74, 101, 105, 106, 126, 154, 159, 161, 164, 169, 178, 180, 182, 189, 194
aesthetics, 8, 26, 34, 86, 88, 195
 fascist, 85, 86–8, 95, 103–7
affect, 25, 159–61, 164, 176, 180, 181
Against the Ropes, 41, 44
Agamben, Giorgio, 69–70, 73
ageing, 11–13, 131–5
ageism, 131
aggression, 43, 47–8, 50, 51, 53, 57, 60, 66, 79, 144, 153, 185, 187, 191
Ahmed, Sara, 19
alpinism, 23, 35
Althusser, Louis, 10–11
American football, 67, 73, 77–8, 184
androgynous, 113, 114, 175
androgyny eros, 97, 114, 124
animal, 128, 171, 190–2
animalism *see animality*
animality, 190–1, 194
animals, 190–2
antihero, 158
Apflickorna, 150
appearance, 11, 50, 89, 126, 135, 136, 139, 141, 149, 152, 185
athleticism, 11, 12, 13, 74, 99, 111, 117, 129, 132, 146, 147, 153, 154, 183, 193
athletics, 88, 97, 100, 150, 151

Au-delà des cimes, 5, 17, 23, 26, *27*, 35, 36, 37–8, *37*
Austen, Jane, 58–60

Bachelard, Gaston, 158
Baetens, Jan, 111, 112, 116
Bainbridge, Caroline, 6
Baker, Aaron, 1, 2, 3, 4
Barker, Jennifer, 154, 192, 193
Barrymore, Drew, 13, 183, 195
baseball, 44, 59, 75–6, 79
baseline, 142
 players, 136–7
basketball, 2, 4, 69, 73, 74, 79–80, 81, 82, 171
behaviour, gendered, 1, 67
Bend it Like Beckham, 3, 67, *68*, 150, *150*
Benn, Nigel, 57
Big Wednesday, 158, 168–9, 179, 181
Bigelow, Kathryn, 7, 157–8, 174–5, 179, 182
Blue Crush, 158, 167–8, 169, 170, 177
Blue Steel, 7, 174, 175, 177, 179
bodybuilding, 2, 109–30, *100*, *128*, *129*
Bolton, Lucy, 5, 6
borderlinking, 164, 176, 182
borderspace, 159, 160, 164, 169
 matrixial, 159, 164
Botwright, Vicky, 136
bouldering, 25, 27
Bowen, Lori, 110, 126, 129–30, *129*
boxing, 2, 4, 5, 41–57, 60–6, *62*, *64*, 81, 137, 167, 185
Boys Don't Cry, 44
Brady, Jacqueline E, 127–8
Bridges, Michelle, 118
bruises, 117, 189

239

Bueno, Maria, 154
bum *see* buttocks
butch, 152, 153
Butler, George, 109
Butler, Judith, 11, 146–7, 152–3, 159, 169, 191
buttocks, 4, 94, *95*, 98, 99, 113, 120, 121, 126, 189

camera, 5, 10, 28, 35, 43, 46–7, 49, 60–1, 63–4, 69, 82, 91, 92, 94, 96, 97–8, 99, 105, 107, 109, 118, 119, 119–123, 126, 140, 149, 154, 157, 166, 178, 192–5
camerawork, 4, 10, 32, 35, 38, 43, 49, 61, 98, 100, 117, 122–3, 126, 145, 193–5
close-up, 29, 46–7, 60–61, 63, 98, 109, 119, 122
lighting, 4, 121, 148
zoom, 35, 46, 61
canvas, 27, 41, 51, 61, 65–6, 91
Carlson, Jennifer, 184–5
castration, 65, 159, 176, 190
anxiety, 103, 133
paradigm, 161, 163, 167, 170, 172, 173, 177–81
catfight, 118, 192
Cézanne, Paul, 165
Chak De! India, 3, 74–5, 82, 83
characters
flat, 58, 59, 60, 168
round, 58–60
Charlie's Angels 2, 161–3, *162*, *163*
cheerleaders, 2, 5, 67, 186
cheerleading, 2
Cheng, Lydia, 109, 125
Chisholm, Dianne, 5, 15, 21–4, 26, 28, 39
chromatics, 7, 27, 51, 161, 177
cinematography, 4, 6, 10, 13, 29, 31, 35, 37, 38, 43, 46, 60, 61, 66, 105, 119, 126, 144, 161, 162, 163, 171, 172, 174, 182, 192
citation, 146
Clark, T J, 8
Cliffhanger, 17, 32–3, *33*, 36, 58
climbing, 2, 5, 7, 15–7, *16*, 21–40, 27, *32*, *33*, *39*, 45
free, 15, 22, 23, 27, 32, 34
gritstone, 5, 24, 29–31, 36
'Climbing like a Girl', 21
clothing, 19, 30, 80, 100–2, 136, 139, 151, 153, 188, 189, 190
costume, 13, 188, 189, 190, 192
see also Lycra
see also fabric
co-poiesis, 7, 182
coital, 3, 97, 111, 194
coitus, 118

colour, 6, 22, 30, 31, 41, 42, 51, 88, 96, 101–2, 150–151, 177, 181, 189
coming of age, 13, 168, 183, 185
Communism, 9, 10, 80, 82, 139
comportment, 19, 22, 77, 139, 148
acoustic, 51
bodily, 11, 45, 50–1, 65, 142
Connell, Raewynn, 191
Connor, Steven, 28
Connors, Jimmy, 138
contact sport, 81, 184, 187
corporeal activism, 155
cricket, 58, 59, 74, 75, 81
Crocodile Dundee, 121–2
cross-gender, 67, 78
Crosson, Seán, 2, 3, 4
Cruising, 121–2
culturally coded, 15, 22, 41, 70, 105, 113, 133, 184

D/s, 188–9
Date-Krumm, Kimiko, 132
De Beauvoir, Simone, 19
de Lauretis, Teresa, 37
deconstruction, 78, 113, 114, 146–7
definition, 23, 94, 95, 110, 124–5, 128, 177
Destivelle, Catherine, 5, 23, 26–7, 29, 36–8, 39, 40
Devers, Gail, 151
dialogue, 6, 10, 13, 55, 119, 150, 189, 192
Dirty Harry, 179
discipline, 104
Doane, Mary Ann, 46, 60
docile, 10, 185
dominance, 51, 53, 87, 119, 163, 174, 188
and submission *see* D/s
dualism, 62
Dunlap, Carla, 110, 125, 127–9
Durán, Roberto, 44

Eastwood, Clint, 42, 96
écart, 176
editing, 10, 31, 32, 37, 38, 61, 63, 66, 93, 105, 118, 119, 121, 145
Efron, David, 81, 83
emancipation, 58, 194, 195
emancipatory, 4, 13, 161–2, 183, 189, 192
emasculate, 149
empower, 13, 50, 52, 57, 161, 183
Éros androgyne, 114, 117, 122
ethic, 34
ethics, 40

Ettinger, Bracha, 5, 6–7, 159–61, 164–165, 167, 169, 171–72, 176, 181, 182
Eubank, Chris, 57
Evert, Chris, 137–9, 140, 152

fabric, 100–2
  see also Lycra
Fascism, 8, 85, 86–7, 88, 95, 103–7
fascist see Fascism
Fast Girls, 21, 85–6, 97–100, *99*, 102, 103, 189, 193
Female Masculinity, 113, 153
feminine
  apologetic, 101, 112, 151
  movement, 20, 137, 185
femininity, 3, 5, 6, 13, 19, 37, 42, 43, 45, 50, 62, 70, 93, 94, 106, 110–1, 113, 114, 124–125, 127, 132, 136, 139, 152, 153, 172, 176, 184, 185, 189, 190, 194
feminism, 13, 44, 183, 191
  physical, 43, 44–6, 47, 55, 161, 183, 186
fetish, 3, 4, 8, 62, 86, 91–2, 95–6, 100, 101, 103, 106, 113, 114, 121, 126, 150, 167, 186, 193
fetishism see fetish
field hockey see hockey
Field, Tiffany, 81, 82
fingernails see nails
fingerprints, 142, 143
fingertips, 36
Finlay, Nancy J, 185
flesh, 10, 11, 13, 17, 22, 36, 38, 45, 49, 57, 59, 70, 92, 94, 99, 103, 112, 113, 114, 115, 122, 123, 124, 132, 133, 142, 147, 188
Flying, 3, 4, 149
football, 2, 3, 67, 81
Forever the Moment, 3, 79, 81–2
Forster, E M, 58–9, 168
fort/da, 70–1, 73
Francis, Bev, 110–1, 113, 118, 127, *128*, 129, 153–4
Freud, Sigmund, 5, 7, 70–1, 72, 73, 91–2, 101, 177, 193

Galt, Rosalind, 8, 65, 105–6
Gassel, Nathalie, 111–2, 113–7, 118, 121, 122–3, 124, 126, 130, 152
gay, 119, 122, 140–1, 151
gaze, 3, 21, 49, 53, 59, 60, 61, 63, 134, 144, 167, 172
gendering, 15, 22, 41, 44, 54, 78, 114
gesture, 4, 7, 19, 57, 67–70, *68*, 72–83, 96, 117, 120, 122, 132, 138, 144, 145, 154, 169, 177, 178, 179, 187, 193, 194
  uninvited, 78, 79, 80
  waving, 82

gesture in psychoanalysis, the, 70, 74
Gidget, 170
Girlfight, 4, 42, 43, 44, 45, 46–8, 49, 50, 53–5, 56–8, 60, 61–2, *62*, 63–5, *64*, 66, 185–6
Girl Power, 161, 183
glare, 103, 106
gleam, 8, 90, 94, *95*, 103, 106
Graf, Steffi, 140
Grosz, Elizabeth, 114
gun, 163, 174, *174*, 179–80
  bolt gun, 32–3, *33*
Gunnell, Sally, 100
Guttmann, Allen, 95–7
gym, the, 4, 42, 44, 46, 50, 53, 56, 58, 60, 96, 109, 116, 117, 118, 120–1, 125, 126, 127, 139
Gymnast, The, 12–3, 132
gymnastics, 1, 3, 9–10, 12–3, 34, 73, 88, 104, 132, 150, 184

haematomas see bruises
Halberstam, Judith, 101, 113, 144, 153
Hamilton, Bethany, 165–6, 167
handball, 2, 79, 83
hands, 12, 23, 26, 28, 29, 37, 39, 52, 68, 73, 74, 75, 78, 79, 80, 81, 82, 97–8, 109, 117, 119, 120, 122, 123, 138, 139, 144, 150–1, 178, 195
handshake, 74, 78
Hard, Fast and Beautiful, 148–9, *149*, 151–2, 171
Hard Grit, 5, 17, 27, 28–30, 31–2, *32*, 38–9, *39*, 61
hearing, 51, 71, 82
hegemonic, 2, 7, 11, 13, 185, 191
hegemony, 3, 170, 174, 179, 182
hermaphrodite see hermaphroditic
hermaphroditic, 113, 123, 124, 126
heteronormative, 57, 121, 139, 194
  non-heteronormative, 187
heterosexual, 93, 94, 121, 136, 139, 162, 185
heterosexuality see heterosexual
Highway Amazon, 122
Hill, Lynn, 17, 22–3, 25, 26, 27, 28, 29, 30, 31, 34, 35–6, 39, 40
hockey, 2, 74–5, 81, 83
Holmlund, Chris, 120, 121, 126, 128
homoerotic see homoeroticism
homoeroticism, 48, 93, 94
homophobia, 140–1, 162
homosexual see gay
homosexuality, 140, 151
Hoosiers, 69

ice hockey, 184
ideology, 4, 8, 10, 23, 45, 132, 134

241

Ihde, Don, 52, 53
immanence, 20, 21
interpellation, 10–1, 13
intertextual, 179
intrauterine, 159, 161, 182
Irigaray, Luce, 6, 7, 24, 70, 71–2, 74, 78, 180

Jeffreys, Sheila, 142, 145
Jenneke, Michelle, 100
Joyner, Florence Griffiths, 150–1

Kansas City Bomber, 191
Karpf, Anne, 51, 66
Kendon, Adam, 68
kinaesthesia, 161
King, Billie Jean, 76–7, 77, 79, 136, 139, 140
Knockout, 44, 45
Kristeva, Julia, 159

Lacan, Jacques, 5, 65, 159, 160, 163, 164, 169, 173
language, 5, 6, 7, 11, 18, 23, 25–6, 28, 29–30, 31, 32, 34, 35, 36, 38, 39, 40, 61–2, 69, 72, 113, 116, 126, 143, 147, 160, 164, 165, 173, 176, 178, 182
  gendered, 25, 38
League of Their Own, A, 76, 79, 149
lens, 35, 47, 61, 62, 63, 64, 82, 91, 93, 157, 177
Leroi-Gourhan, André, 165
lesbian, 119, 121, 140, 150, 152, 153, 162, 186, 187
lesbianism *see* lesbian
lifestyle, alternative, 186
Lindner, Katharina, 49
Lingis, Alphonso, 113
Livesey, Peter, 23, 24–5
logic, differential, 178
logocentrism, 191
Lupino, Ida, 148
lustre, 91, 92
Lycra, 100–2, 189

MacDonald, Shelley, 44, 48, 65
make-up, 50, 112, 113, 153
manhandle, 56, 98
Manning, Erin, 83, 144
Marinkova, Milena, 166
Marks, Laura U, 167
martial arts, 45, 46, 55, 145
masculine *see* masculinity
masculinity, 3, 5, 15, 22, 24, 30, 33, 37, 41, 42, 43, 46, 48, 54, 58, 59, 62, 67, 70, 77, 78, 89, 96, 105, 112, 113–4, 119, 127, 132, 133, 153, 162, 170, 176, 185, 190–1

masturbation, simulation, 67, 70, 138
materiality, 30, 52, 63
maternal, 7, 30, 65, 66, 72, 158, 159, 160, 161, 164, 169, 171
  penis, 92, 103
matrixial, 7, 159–61, 164, 165, 167, 172, 176–9, 180, 181, 182
Mauresmo, Amélie, 141, 153
McCaughey, Martha, 45, 46, 55
McEnroe, John, 131, 138
McLish, Rachel, 110, 111, 118, 125, 127, 129
McNeill, David, 70
Merleau-Ponty, Maurice, 17–8, 19, 20, 21, 28, 154, 165, 176
Merck, Mandy, 148
Merz, Mischa, 63, 65
Miller, Toby, 136, 140
Million Dollar Baby, 42, 56
mirror, 8, 13, 18, 47, 49, 50, 52, 53, 67, 77, 98, 109, 121, 146, 151, 179, 185, 190, 193
mise-en-scène, 13, 92, 105, 189, 192, 194
Mixed Martial Arts (MMA), 44
(m)Other, 65, 66
m/Other, 159–60, 164, 167
Mother, 66, 160, 164, 169
motherhood, 37, 79, 171
Mother Nature, 15, 30
movement, freedom of, 17, 22, 56, 72
Mowitt, John, 10
Mulvey, Laura, 5, 49, 92, 103
muscle, 45, 49, 51, 59, 77, 96, 97, 99, 109, 111–129, *129*, 132, 133–4, 147, 165, 189, 192, 193
  erotica, 112, 126
  fantasies, 121, 122, 129
  hypermuscular, 111–4, 127
  worship, 3, 122, 189
musculature, 20, 165
music, 92, 100, 127–8, 173

nails, 109, 148–51, *149*, *150*, 171
  manicured, 109, 122, 149, 151
  painted, 149–50, 151, 171
Navratilova, Martina, 131–2, 133, 134–5, 136, 137, 138–9, 140–1, 142, 143, 146, 150, 152–5
Nead, Lynda, 62
Near Dark, 7
Ness, Sally Ann, 15, 25–6, 51
Newmahr, Staci, 189
Newton-John, Olivia, 139
noise, 9, 38, 52, 54, 127–128, 145, 157, 163, 174–5, 177–8, 181, 191
Nuba, the, 86, 88, 89–91, 106

objectification, 2, 3, 50, 51, 60, 72, 79, 86, 97, 134, 193
objectified *see* objectification
ocean, 157, 158–159, 162, 163, 164, 165–6, 168, 170, 177–8, 179, 180, 181–2
Olympia, 8, 86, 87–8, 89, 92–5, 95, 96, 102, 103, 104, 105–6
Olympics, 8, 67, 79, 82, 85, 86, 93, 105, 106
Opponent, The, 4, 48–9, 50, 52–3, 54–5, 56, 65, 66
Owens, Jesse, 93, 105

pain, 9, 23, 29, 38, 61, 86, 103, 118, 122, 144, 145, 175, 186, 187, 188, 189
Pat and Mike, 134, *135*
patriarchal, 1, 4, 37, 45, 57, 66, 79, 183
   culture, 3, 191
   ideology, 2, 4, 17, 89, 93, 142, 185
   logic, 46, 50
   society, 64, 79
   values, 13, 19, 49
patriarchy, 3, 4, 23, 45, 49, 50, 51, 53, 59, 63, 65, 180, 185, 193
Patton, Cindy, 110, 118, 119, 123, 126
Personal Best, 67, 70, 95–7, 100, 102, 103
perspiration *see* sweat
perversion, 193
phallic, 6, 16, 33, 39, 44, 89–90, 101, 103, 112, 149, 159, 160–1, 163, 166, 172, 173–4, 178, 179–81, 182
phallocentrism, 2, 6, 30, 161, 170, 180, 182
phallus *see* phallic
phenomenological *see* phenomenology
phenomenology, 5, 7, 17–20, 25, 42, 167, 176
photographs, 44, 62, 69, 74, 76, 86, 88–91, 103, 106, 118, 139, 146, 147–8, 151, 153–4, 155
photography *see* photographs
Piano, The, 122
Point Break, 7, 157–8, *158*, 159, 161, 166–7, 168, 169–70, 172–6, *174*, *175*, 177–9, 180, 181, *181*, 182
politics, sexual, 5, 30, 31, 45, 70, 99, 117, 141, 145, 161, 195
Pollock, Griselda, 3, 7, 41–3, 65, 74, 160, 169, 178
pornographic, 97, 111, 119, 121, 123
pornography *see* pornographic
Portugues, Gladys, 109, 125
post-coital, 4, 91
Post Traumatic Stress Disorder, 55, 167
power, 23, 35, 49, 65, 78, 79, 98, 119, 124, 128, 130, 132, 144, 166, 187, 188
Predator 2, 89
primitive (as trope), 89, 173

psychoanalysis, 5, 7, 65, 169, 176
PTSD *see* Post Traumatic Stress Disorder
Puberty Blues, 168, 170–1
Pumping Irene, 119, 126
Pumping Iron, 109, 112
Pumping Iron II: The Women, 109–11, *110*, 112, 113, 116, 117–21, *120*, 122, 123, 124, 125–30, *126*, *128*, *129*, 189

Quarterback Princess, 77–9, 80
queer, 24, 111

racism, 88
Real, 159, 160, 164, 169, 172, 174, 176
reel, 70–2, 73, 74
reel, film, 31
reflection, 49, 90, 92, 146
Renée, 141–2
Richards, Renée, 141–5, 153
Riefenstahl, Leni, 7, 8, 86, 88, 89–91, 92–4, 95, 96, 102, 103, 104–5, 106–7
Rifkin, Adrian, 154
Rigauer, Bruno, 148
roller derby, 13, 183–5, 187–9, 191, 192, 193
rugby, 81, 184

sadomasochism, 122, 187, 188–9, 192
sadomasochistic *see* sadomasochism
Salcedo, Juan Jiménez, 111, 114, 115
salophilia, 3, 96
Scarry, Elaine, 61
Schippert, Claudia, 119, 121
Schneider, Rebecca, 82
Schwarzenegger, Arnold, 109, 112
script, 60
sea *see* ocean
Second Serve, 143–5
Sedgwick, Eve Kosofsky, 112
self-defence, 45, 55, 161
Serres, Michel, 5, 26, 28, 29, 30, 34–5, 36, 38, 101, 173
sexism, 49, 75, 79, 97, 131, 168
sexist *see* sexism
sexual
   difference, 5, 6, 29, 30, 37, 42, 50, 160
   politics, 5, 30, 31, 45, 70, 99, 117, 141, 145, 161, 195
sexualised, 136, *138*
sexuality, 3, 24, 111, 120, 124, 140–1, 184, 187, 189
sinews, 10, 11, 19, 45, 132, 145
skin, 36, 42, 72, 82, 88, 90, 100, 101, 120, 121–2, 124, 175
SM *see* sadomasochism
smorgasbord, 100, 121

Snowman's Pass, 17, 27–8
Sobchack, Vivian, 42, 43
soccer *see* football
somatotype, 11
Sontag, Susan, 86, 87, 88, 92, 95, 103–104, 106, 154
Soul Surfer, 165–6, *166*, 167, 168, 169, 170, 194
sound, 4, 9, 10, 25, 29, 38, 38, 43, 51–4, 65, 69, 71, 82, 83, 102, 125, 128, 145, 151, 157, 159, 173, 175, 177, 179, 181, 186, 187, 190
   diegetic, 38, 157
soundscape, 38, 182
soundtrack, 10, 119, 120, 127, 145, 172
space
   acoustic, 53–4, 66
   gendered, 15, 20, 41–2, 43–44, 46, 48, 50, 54, 56, 58, 65, 170, 175
   intrauterine, 164
   masculine, 15, 44, 175
Spandex, 3, 100, 101
spectacle, 9, 49, 53, 60, 61–2, 63, 118, 129, 134, 147, 154, 167, 170, 188, 192
speech, 51, 68, 70, 72, 132, 162
State of Mind, A, 9, 10
stereotypes, 11, 12, 13, 45, 53, 134, 135, 142
   feminine, 142, 186
   gender, 1, 48, 83, 184
Stich, Michael, 131–2, 135, 136
Stick It, 1, 104
submission *see* D/s
surfing, 2, 7, 157–9, 162, 163, 165–6, 167–8, 170, 173, 175, 177–8, *181*, 181
sweat, 3, 4, 39, 49, 90, 91, 92, 94, 95–7, 100, 102, 103, 104, 106, 107, 115, 118, 142
Swiboda, Marcel, 189
swimming, 12, 75, 81, 94, 104, 166, 184
Symbolic, 159, 161, 164, 169, 172, 173, 178
synaesthesia, 22, 121

Tatum, Karen E, 180
tennis, 2, 11, 76–7, 81, 93, 131–43, *135*, 145, 148, 151, 152–4
   serve and volley, 136, 137, 142
Theweleit, Klaus, 93–4, 95, 177
Thing, the, 7, 159, 164, 167, 169
third-sex, 152
Throwing like a girl, 19, 79

Tightrope, 96
touch, 6, 22, 24, 26, 31, 51, 57, 76, 77, 77, 79, 80, 81–82, 83, 97, 98–9, *99*, 102, 120, 122, 144, 161, 165, *166*
trace, 7, 24, 36, 62, 65, 66, 69, 89, 96, 142, 147, 154, 161, 164, 181, 182, 189, 192
transcendence, 21–2
transgender, 143, 144–5
transsexual, 141, 142, 144, 145
transvestism, 144
trauma, 7, 16, 17, 54–5, 103, 145, 167–169, 172, 174, 182
Tregaro, Emma Green, 151
Tudor, Deborah, 2, 4, 43, 69

undecidable, 36, 78
US Open, 131, 137, 141

Vertical Limit, 15–7, *16*, 24
violence
   domestic, 46, 53, 60
   gestural, 79–80
vocalisations, 25, 51, 72, 190
voice, 6, 11, 25, 51–2, 53, 54, 82, 127, 129, 133, 141, 145, 149, 158, 162, 178
voiceover, 26, 149, 192
voyeuristic, 91, 100

water polo, 18, 68
Watkins, Liz, 6
waves, 93, 157, *158*, 159, 160, 163, 164, 165, 166, 167, 168, 169, 170, 177, 178, 179, 180–2
weightlifting *see* bodybuilding
When Billie Beat Bobby, 76–7, 77, 79, 132, 140
Whip It, 13, 117, 183–95, *187*, *194*
whippet, 190
Wimbledon, 131, 132, 133, 135, 137, 153, 154
Wimbledon, 132, 138, *138*, 140
wit(h)nessing, 164, 180
Woman Basketball Player No. 5, 73, 79–80, 82–3, 171
Wonder Woman, 52–3, 118
Woolf, Virginia, 59, 60–1

Young, Iris Marion, 5, 19–21, 22, 46, 47, 49, 50–1, 59, 60, 77, 79, 134, 137, 142

www.ingramcontent.com/pod-product-compliance
Lightning Source LLC
Chambersburg PA
CBHW062135300426
44115CB00012BA/1938